THE DEVELOPMENT OF SCHEDULED TRIBES IN MADHYA PRADESH

THE DEVELOPMENT OF SCHEDULED TRIBES IN MADHYA PRADESH

DIVYA SHRIVASTAVA

GYAN

GYAN PUBLISHING HOUSE

NEW DELHI-110002

Published from the grant provided by the Ministry of Tribal Affairs, Government of India

THE DEVELOPMENT OF SCHEDULED TRIBES IN MADHYA PRADESH

(Sociology)

ISBN : 81-212-0698-7

Published in 2000 in India by
Gyan Publishing House,
5, Ansari Road, Darya Ganj
New Delhi-110 002
Phone: 3282060, 3261060 Fax: 3285914
E-mail: gyanbook@del2.vsnl.net.in

Laser Typesetting at A.S. Printers, Delhi

Printed at Chawla Offset Printers, Delhi

Contents

Preface

According to 1991 census the total population of the country is 8385.84 lakh, out of which 677.58 lakh belong to Scheduled Tribes. There are 153.99 lakh Scheduled Tribes in Madhya Pradesh forming 23.27 per cent of the total population inhabiting predominantly 1.80 sq. km. areas, though, dispersed in the whole of the State.

These tribals occupy a very distinctive place in the mosaic of Indian society. Facing very tough living conditions they have managed since times immemorial to preserve their distinctive identity. They had a more or less self-sufficient social economy and remained cutoff from the main stream of society.

Prior to Independence the policy towards them was either of compassion or isolation. Foremost interest was shown by the missionaries basically with the interest in proselytization. The policy of isolation resulted in their exploitation by the Zamindars, landlords, moneylenders and contractors. This exploitation resulted in a number of movements against the oppressors especially the Britishers and stressed the need of freedom from exploitation of all sorts and a positive policy of economic progress.

After the Independence concrete steps were taken in the direction of the development of the tribal people. First and foremost was that the Constitution placed the responsibility for their welfare on the Government through the President and the Governor. New approach and strategy for the Tribal Development was started by both the State and Central Governments.

Among the earliest special programmes undertaken by the Government of India was the programme of establishing Special Multipurpose Tribal (SMPT) Blocks side by side with the general programme of Community Development. The SMPT Blocks were special programmes formulated in line with the provisions made in Articles 46 and 275 of the Constitution. It was based on the principle of giving particular attention to neglected tribal areas and population in the country. In Madhya Pradesh 10 SMPT Blocks were established under this scheme. Special emphasis was laid on schemes of Irrigation, Soil Conservation, Development of Communication, Health, Education, Village Industries, Co-operation and Housing.

As it was found that the tribal area and tribal population covered by SMPT was inadequate therefore, with a view to increasing the coverage of the area and population T.D. Blocks were formed on the recommendations of Dhebar Commission (1960). The Commission was setup with a view to reviewing tribal development after 10 years as provided in the Constitution.

The Commission suggested that the SMPT Blocks should be extended to wider tribal areas by carving out special TD Blocks. Under Tribal Development Blocks the area covered should be 150-200 sq. miles with 25000 population, out of which 55 per cent should be tribal.

The work of tribal development during the four plan periods was reviewed and it was found that the plans failed to a large extent to provide desirable gains to the tribal people. It was also found that the tribals would require protection and guidance to come on par with the general population at different points.

Keeping in view the above problems a shift in the Tribal Development policy was envisaged. During the formulation of the Fifth Plan a new strategy of Tribal Sub-Plan was evolved to solve the specific problems of the tribal areas. The emphasis was now on the solution of problems at the local level. The sub-plan laid stress on a suitable administrative structure and personnel policy to implement such programmes. It was a conscious effort to deal with the problems at the grass root level.

The first sub-plan was prepared within the framework of the Fifth Plan. It formulated schemes for the general problems of the tribal areas as well as specific problems in different pockets in sub-plan area. For this, areas of tribal concentration were identified and also such pockets which were inhabited by the Primitive Tribal Groups. This area was then divided into viable project areas. Detailed action plan for project area as well as for each identified Primitive Tribal Groups was prepared. Emphasis was laid on bridging developmental disparity between the general and tribal population by laying stress on agriculture, education, medical care, approach roads, employment opportunity, etc.

It has been about 20 years since the inception of Ist sub-plan strategy. It has been found that the results have not been in tandem with the investments made. As a remedial measure it has been suggested that the funds may be allocated directly to Integrated Tribal Development Projects. Another demand from the All India Tribal Forum and Adivasi Vikas Parishad has been to implement VI Schedule in the Tribal Sub-Plan area, on the line of the North-Eastern States.

Anthropological and sociological accounts of the tribal giving details of their traditional culture along with their specific problems as given by authors of repute inspired to know the legal measures-Constitutional provisions, developmental strategies-administrative, financial, etc. adopted and their impact on the tribals. The problems of the tribals as outlined in the famous book 'The Aboriginal Problem in the Central Provinces and Berar' by W.V. Grigron written in 1944 are still being faced by the tribals though a number of developmental measures to solve them have been taken up. In some respects, e.g. land alienation, availability of drinking water, loss of employment due to deforestation, displacement due to various projects, the situation has worsened. An account of these has been presented in this work with a hope to improving the situation by all those interested in the development of the tribal people. As the publication of the thesis in a book form took sometime, some crucial changes took place, in the meantime, important among them is the reorganization of the districts in the state and proposed reorganization of the Integrated Tribal Development Project (ITDPs) MADA pockets and the clusters. With a view to doing justice with the theme of the book the reorganized districts, together with the proposed reorganisation of the ITDPs, MADA pockets and clusters and the population figures, etc., zonewise have been given in Annexure No. IV.

Divya Shrivastava

Acknowledgements

In completing the thesis, help of National and State Archives, Government departments dealing with tribal development both State and Central and a number of non-governmental organizations (NGOS) was taken. I would particularly mention the name of Shri J.P. Vyas, Director of Tribal Area Development Planning and Smt. Kiran Vijay Singh, Director Tribal Research and Training Institute, Bhopal. Published and unpublished documents from the Directorate of Tribal Area Development Planning provided useful information about various plans and development works. The Tribal Research and Development Institute provided basic material about the tribals and photographs, quite useful into having a glimpse of the tribal people. It is difficult to name all the other officers and officials of these institutions who have readily helped in making the data available. However, I acknowledge my grateful thanks to all of them.

I am very much indebted to Prof. I.S. Chauhan, Vice-Chancellor Barkatullah University, Bhopal for his encouraging words and guidance in completing the thesis.

I am grateful to Dr. S. Soloman who provided his able guidance in completing this thesis.

My respectful regards are due to my father Dr. R.S. Shrivastava, Additional Director, Tribal Area Development Planning. Due to him an interest was created in my life encompassing every aspect and developmental process of the tribals. It was but natural, as since my childhood I have been hearing about S.T., T.A.D.P., T.S.P., S.C.A. fund allocations, etc. He is trained and committed to understanding a social phenomena and various social processes through inter-disciplinary approach. His understanding of the tribal people and long experience in the tribal field helped me in visualizing such a work and completing it, in spite of all the hazards which one has to face while working in the tribal areas.

Thanks are due to my mother too, who is an established writer in Hindi, recipient of the prestigious Bageshwari Award of Madhya Pradesh Hindi Sahitya Parishad, an activist in the field of girls' emancipation especially in spreading education and creating self-sufficiency among them. She has also a rare talent and art of making beautiful artifacts from the dried vegetation. She runs *Snehghar* a registered society not only for young girls but also for the aged women for helping them in all possible ways. In spite of all her preoccupations she encouraged and helped me in completing this work.

My husband, Rakesh Kumar Khare, a librarian helped me in getting access to different libraries and archives for books and materials. My daughter, Devyani, did not disturb me much, not at all, while at work. My special thanks are due to all of them.

I am grateful to the Ministry of Tribal Affairs the then Ministry of Social Justice and Empowerment, Government of India, which has provided a publication grant of Rs. 30,000 without which it would have been difficult to publish this book.

Divya Shrivastava

1

Introduction

Contemporary history in other countries is quite popular; in India it has yet to make a start. After independence, there have been many events but the process of development of the common people especially the scheduled tribes (ST), from 1952 through Five Year Plans is quite unique. The state of Madhya Pradesh has the largest scheduled tribes population and as such, a number of relief, protective and developmental measures have been taken up for them. My attention to the development of scheduled tribes was drawn and this topic was selected for my doctoral dissertation.

History is the record of the life of societies, of men, of the changes which the societies have gone through, of the ideas which have determined the actions of the societies and of the material conditions which have helped or hindered their development. Basically, history has been envisaged as the actions of kings, deeds done by them, empires won and lost and its effect on common people.

As per Freeman, "History is nothing but past politics and politics is nothing but present history." But as any serious student of history knows that this is a very narrow outlook towards history. Broadly, history gives us an idea about the growth of civilization, changes in national attitudes, development and decay of social organizations, religious beliefs and such other matter which constitute the stuff and substance of natural history.

It has rightly been said that the study of history would be meaningless without the appreciation of social significance. If history is to be useful to understand the present and to serve as a guide to the future, sociological interpretation of facts is absolutely necessary.

Conquerors of the world, kings, aggressors, establishers of kingdoms have been studied in history. It is clear that actors in history are all powerful people. Their rise and fall, life and death is what has made history.

However, at the end of the 18th century new ideas came in to the subject. It was asked where are the common people in historical research? Was it fruitful to read about the 'by-gone' days? If it had some utility then why not study the common people, that too in the present social context?

Periodization in history. The history of any country or region or of the world as a whole is generally divided into specific periods and sub-periods. This is done on the basis of some specific criteria. One criterion, which is common in traditional historical writings is to divide the history of a country in terms of dynasties that ruled over it. In this sense we have the history of India divided into the Mauryan, Gupta, Mughal periods, etc.

The division of history is also based on another criterion, for example, we have divisions based on the Renaissance, the Industrial Revolution, etc. But the criteria of division in this case are the development of certain aspects of cultural and economic lives rather than dynastic or political. Such divisions, unlike the divisions based on dynasties indicate broad periods and years, as developments in culture and economy cannot be traced back to any particular date, nor do they end on a specific date. To give an example from Indian history the period of the rise of Indian nationalism cannot be ascribed to any one particular event taking place on a particular date.

Another more important kind of division of history into periods or simply periodization is done on the basis of demarcation of stages in the development of society. In this kind of periodization each period denotes not only a broad chronology but a distinct form of society, economy, culture and political system and has a well-defined character of its own, distinguishable from other periods. The broadest commonly accepted periodization of history of most of the countries and of the world as a whole is division into ancient, medieval and modern periods. In Indian history the, ancient period ends at 1200 A.D. medieval period extends from 1200-1857 A.D. and modern 1857-1947 A.D.

Contemporary history

Until two or three decades ago, historians generally were reluctant to write about the period in which they lived. Many histories of the world written and taught in, 1950s, 1960s and even in the 1970s would stop with the year 1945. The history of the world after 1945 can be termed as contemporary history.

Even during the reign of Akbar, Abul Fazl wrote an exhaustive account of his policies, be it religious, political, economic, matters relating to art and architecture, relations with other states mainly Rajputs and welfare works undertaken by the state. This was written during the lifetime of Akbar. However, today his books—*Akbarnama* and *Ain-i-Akbari* work as guides for any serious student of the history of Akbar's reign.

Contemporary history means only the history of what is happening at the moment of writing or a record of events through which the historian has lived. According to one historian writing in the 1960's, "Our era has such a well-defined character that it is possible to speak of contemporary history in a specific sense, hence it is the crucial years from 1945 to the present day which can be regarded as specially the sphere of contemporary history.

Geoffrey Barraclough in his book, *An Introduction To Contemporary History*, has written, "One of the distinctive facts about contemporary history is that it is world history and that the forces shaping it cannot be understood unless we are prepared to adopt world-wide perspective." He considers the period designated by him as 'contemporary' to be different in quality and content, from what is known as modern history. According to him contemporary history has characteristics, which mark it off from the preceding period in much the same ways as what we call, 'Medieval history' is marked off from 'Modern history'. While no fixed dates can be given, contemporary history according to Barraclough, begins with the problems which are actual in the world today, first take visible shape.

Some characteristic features

Contemporary history is characterized by tremendous

changes in every aspect of social, economic and political life and in every area of human activity.

Limitations

(i) Non-availability of data—Many important official papers regarding the activities of the government are opened to the historians for study only after a lapse of 50 years (in case of some countries 30 years). Many people who are involved in the formulation of policies and in the activities of the government such as Prime Ministers, Ministers and high officials maintain diaries of their activities and notes or write their memoirs. These diaries and memoirs are generally not published in the lifetime of their authors. In the present context of our study the Scheduled Tribe (ST) wise figures for 1991, are not available so far but this difficulty could be overcome by taking into account the figures of the 1981 census. Similarly alternative sources can be found for unpublished material and confidential papers.

(ii) Personal bias—The writing of history is a valid and useful intellectual activity only if it is practised without bias. A historian who writes about the present is in a sense, a participant himself and is emotionally involved in the events and development that he is writing about. Therefore, it is said that his writing cannot be unbiased and objective. However, a trained student of contemporary history can overcome this difficulty and may keep his personal biases, prejudices and emotions away from analysing the various events of contemporary history.

(iii) Not knowing the end—A problem which arises while studying contemporary history is one of historical perspective or as one historian has put it, "Not knowing what happened in the end." The problem is notional rather than real. Every event has an end at a point of time and it can be analyzed in the same manner.

Contemporary History of Tribal Development

After independence many political, economic, social and cultural events have taken place but most important among them all is the developmental measures adopted for the common people. The community development, Five Year Plan programmes launched from the year 1952 are still a continuous process, the objective of which is to ensure all-round development of the people.

According to the 1991 Census the total population of the country is 8463.03 lakhs out of which 677.58 lakhs (8 per cent) belong to the scheduled tribes. In M.P., 153.99 lakhs ST, forming 23.27 per cent of the total population of the state, live. Thus, 22.73 per cent of the tribals of the country live in M.P. The tribal population predominantly inhabit 1.80 square kilometre area forming 40 per cent of the total geographic area of the state.

The development of the STs both by the Central and State Governments is a laudable responsibility conferred by the Constitution of India.

The author was born and brought up in M.P. So it is but natural that her attention should be drawn towards the problems and peculiar position of the largest segment of the population in MP i.e., the scheduled tribes. Away from the mainstream of the march of progress they are isolated in areas which lack basic amenities for a minimum standard of living. Tribals were unable to resist onslaught of foreign invasions, fight among local dynasties and took refuge in isolated pockets having good natural resources. Cut-off from the mainstream of society and subject to many prejudices which the society at large harboured towards them, the tribals were frozen in the ancient traditions and ways of living, oblivious of the hectic developmental activities going on in the society outside their environment.

Understanding their problems and recognising the need to bring them in the mainstream of society, the society at large has been trying to compensate the historical injustice done to them through developmental measures by governmental and voluntary agencies.

Even before Independence, the Britishers realized the peculiar problems of the tribals but did nothing constructive to solve them. However, certain voluntary organizations were functioning among them with a view to providing educational and health facilities. After independence, however, the problems faced by them have been identified and measures taken to solve them. The mood of a new and resurgent India was expressed in Article 46 of the Constitution, 'The state shall promote with special care the educational and economic interests of the weaker sections of the people and in particular of the scheduled castes and scheduled tribes and shall protect them from social injustices and all forms of exploitation.'

In line with the broad directions given by the Constitution, the government, both state and central, have adopted different measures to improve the condition of the scheduled tribes. All these measures are directed towards the following objectives:

(i) Introducing developmental schemes which help in bridging the gap between the general population and the tribals, and

(ii) Preparing them for adjustment with the changes taking place around them so that they are not misled.

The country in general and the Government of M.P. in particular, are committed to develop the tribals through Five Years Plans. In different five years plans different approaches have been adopted. In accordance with the approaches adopted, schemes have been prepared for the development of the tribal people. These approaches and developmental schemes based on them have been studied in a time frame—1947 to 1997 i.e. silver jubilee year of Independence and also end of the VIII plan. It will make a good history which will be quite useful for planners, administrators and general students of history. It will also enrich the discipline of history, especially contemporary history.

Methods of study

Before adopting the methods of study the subject matter of study has been analyzed. The process of tribal development has been divided into three different phases:

(i) British policy, welfare and relief measures before Independence (1833-1947),

(ii) Tribal development measures before adoption of tribal-sub-plan strategy (1947-74), and

(iii) Tribal sub-plan strategy and the progress made during the period between the Fifth to Eighth Plan (1975-97).

Though, the focus of study is the period between 1947-97, the British period from 1833-1947 has been studied with a view to knowing the tribal development measures before Independence. It will help in understanding the tribal problems and schemes to solve them in a better manner.

In accordance with the historical method, the record, both old, new and contemporary have been examined. The central and state governments publish a number of publications giving details of their policy for tribal development schemes, together with progress of developmental schemes. These publications, census reports, gazetteers, etc. are the backbone of the present study.

It will be difficult rather impossible, to do justice in the presentation of the subject matter of the present study in a proper perspective without taking recourse to sociological methods.

Sociology and history are very closely linked to each other. The primary interest of the sociologist is in finding the general laws of society while the historian aims at the reconstruction of historical sequence of events. Historians and sociologists have come closer now. Historians were concerned with dynasties, wars and revolutions but now the trend is in favour of social, economic and cultural history.

"Demographic characteristics" and "problems faced by them, i.e., the tribals" in Chapter-II would not have been possible to be presented in the manner required, had the participant-observation method so commonly applied by the sociologists and social anthropologists not been used. The tribal life and culture was observed closely through participant-observation by visiting some of their areas. Thus, looking to the subject matter of study, recourse to historical, statistical and participant-observation methods have been taken.

With a view to presenting the subject matter taken up for the present dissertation the contents have been divided into eight Chapters: Preface, gives the background of the study; Chapter I, i.e., Introduction outlines the objectives and methods of study, Chapter II, gives a vivid description of the scheduled tribes and the areas occupied by them together with the demographic features. With a view to understanding the present conditions of the tribes of M.P., Chapter III gives a description of the conditions of the tribes prior to Independence in central India. The new horizons provided by the Constitution of India for tribal development have been provided in chapter IV. The constitutional safeguards-reservation in services, various Acts and Rules, pertaining to the STs have also been described in this chapter.

In Chapter Vth, tribal development, strategy before and after Tribal Sub-Plan concept especially the Implementation Agency together with shift in priorities of programmes evolved during this period, have been discussed. The impact of development programmes has been discussed in two parts, i.e., Chapter VIth and VIIth. In Chapter VIth, the financial and in VIIth, physical achievements have been given. In Chapter VIIIth the conclusions and the highlights of the study have been given.

2

The Scheduled Tribes of M.P. Zonal Groupings, Demographic Characteristics, Problems as Faced by them

Historical Background

With a view or acquiring a deeper insight in the problems faced by the Tribals, it is necessary to make a study into different aspects of the history of tribals in India.

Ancient Period

There is much controversy regarding the aboriginality of the Indian tribes. A view prevails that the tribals are the pre-Aryan inhabitants of India. It is said that when the Aryans entered India they denoted the natives as 'Dasyus'. Present day tribes like Munda, Santhal, Gonds, etc., are said to be descendants of the 'Dasyus'. It was after the famous 'Battle of the ten kings' that the process of assimilation of the Aryans and the non-Aryans began in right earnest. The great epic *Ramayana* also contends that there were two groups of people which inhabited India, Aryans and the non-Aryans. Among the non-Aryans the important tribes were the Rakshasa, Vanaras, Nishadas, Gidharajas, Sabaras, Yakshas, Nagas, etc. Perhaps all the above mentioned tribes were identical with the 'Dasyus' mentioned in the 'Rig-Veda'. In the *Mahabharata*, the Munda is mentioned as one of the constituents of the 'Kaurava' army. Shalya the uncle of Pandavas was a non-Aryan and so was Susharma of Trigartha and Bhagadatta.

However, another view expressed by the historians is that the Austro-Asiatics were, contrary to the above view, not the natives of India but came from outside like the Aryans. It is considered that the Negritoes were the natives of India but they disappeared without leaving a trace and were followed by Proto-Austroloids who may be considered the true aborigines. They were followed by Austro-Asiatics.

Another view is that the pre-Dravidians were the original inhabitants of the country, then came the Proto-Austroloids, they were followed by the Mongoloids which included Nagas, Miris, Bodos, etc. of the North East Himalayan region. According to Guha's classification all the tribes of India can be classified into three types i.e., the Negritoes, the Proto-Austroloids and the Monogoloids. If these tribes are not aborigines of the exact area they now occupy, they are autochthones of India and to that extent they may be called the aborigines.[1]

Reference to the tribals in the period between 800-600 BC is very few. Continuous migration of the tribes took place in this period and it is difficult to pin-point their exact place of origin e.g., the 'Mundas' before settling in Chhotanagpur are believed to have inhabited Azamgarh. Bhils, which is a major tribes of central and western India have migrated from the north-west into Malwa.

Medieval Period. In the medieval period, the tribals were continuously harassed by the contemporary rulers. The Bhils of the western India were always attacked by the Muslims and Maratha invaders. There took a large scale conversion of the Bhils to Islam. The period between 1780-1800 saw numerous Bhil uprisings. The Gonds had ruled Garha near Jabalpur. In 1564, the Mughals captured Garha and the Gonds became a vassal of the Mughals. By 1780, Gond dynasty came to an end, when the Marathas defeated the last Gond ruler.

British Period. The British period is considered as the advent of modern period. With the entry of the missionaries into the tribal areas the administration started paying attention to their problems. The early period of the British administration was detrimental to the economic position of the tribes through ignorance and neglect of their rights and customs. The Britishers followed the policy of keeping the tribals aloof from the normal administration and isolate them from the rest of the countrymen. Due to this policy which proved to be detrimental to the welfare of the tribals, the Britishers had to face many tribal uprisings.

The Government of India Act 1919, continued the provision of administering the tribal areas separately from the rest of the province.

The governments' decision on the recommendation of the Simon Commission were embodied in the Government of India Act, 1935. Section 91 and 92 of the Act provided for the declaration of "Excluded Areas" and "Partially Excluded Areas".[2] Any Act of the federal or the provincial legislature would apply to these areas only on the direction of the Governor who was empowered to make such exceptions and modifications as considered necessary.

The British system of law and administration did nothing to bolster the tribals instead added much to damage the social structure of these tribes and weakend the authority of the social heads or Panchayats and the respect they formerly commanded. Although the public remained generally ignorant about the lot of the tribal people the ground was prepared for the new attitude and policies. A.V. Thakkar and some workers of the Servants of Indian Society did pioneering work among the tribes. Christian missionaries did much to ameliorate the conditions of the tribals, especially in Assam and Bihar. A few eminent British officials like Grigson and Hutton worked for their welfare for many years. Many all-India organizations like the 'Bharatiya Adimjati Sevak Sangh' were formed to improve the lot of the tribals.

So we see that the tribals have suffered since many centuries, injustice at the hands of the rulers as well as the common people. To protect themselves they isolated themselves further. It fell on the Government of Independent India to bring them into the mainstream of the society. For this it undertook a planned approach, but faced a problem as the population of the tribals in MP is huge, and they are scattered in a large area. Due to this the tribals face problems which are peculiar to the area which they inhabit. Hence, the government had to take steps which were in concurrence with their problems. To understand the tribal, we should first get familiar with the geographical conditions of the areas inhabited by them and their demographic characteristics.

There is no definition of Scheduled Caste and Scheduled Tribe in the Constitution. But the President is empowered to draw up a list in consultation with the Governor of each state, subject to revision by Parliament. The President has issued orders, in 1950 specifying the SC and ST in the different states in India, which have since been amended by Acts of Parliament.

Madhya Pradesh has the largest Scheduled Tribe population in the country. According to 1991 Census, the total population of the country is 8463.03 lakh (84.63 crores). The total population of the Scheduled Tribes in country is 677.58 lakhs (or 6.78 crores) (leaving Jammu and Kashmir) forming 8.00 per cent of the total population. The total population of M.P. according to the 1991 census is 661.81 lakhs (or 6.62 crores). The Scheduled Tribe population is 153.99 lakhs (or 1.54 crores) forming 23.27 per cent of the total population of state. Thus, 22.73 per cent tribals of the country live in M.P.

The percentage of tribal population in Orissa, Bihar, the two neighbouring states are 22.21 per cent and 7.66 per cent respectively.

There are 46 scheduled tribe communities in the state, divided into 161 sub-tribes.

It may be interesting to note that population of the Scheduled Tribes is least in the states viz., Goa 0.03 per cent, U.P. 0.21 per cent, Tamil Nadu 1.03 per cent and Kerala 1.10 per cent.

Madhya Pradesh comes at ninth place in relation to the proportion of the Scheduled Tribe population in the state. The other states having preponderance of Scheduled Tribe population are Mizoram (94.75 per cent), Lakshyadweep (93.15 per cent), Nagaland (87.70 per cent), Meghalaya (85.33 per cent). Dadara & Nagar Haveli 78.99 per cent, Arunachal Pradesh (63.66 per cent), Manipur (34.43 per cent) and Tripura (30.95 per cent). But population of STs is largest in M.P. as mentioned. Basic information about tribal sub-plan is provided as a benchmark for further studies in Annexure No. 1.

The spread of some of the important tribal groups and their population are as follows: As the tribewise figures of 1991 Census are not available still, the figures are based on 1981 Census.

Important Tribals of the State, their Population and Spread

(Census 1981) Figures in Lakhs

Sl. No.	*Name of the Tribes*	*Population*	*Percentage of the total ST population*	*Spread in the state*
1.	Gond	53.50	44.63	Whole state
2.	Bhil-Bhilala	25.06	20.90	Dhar, Jhabua, Ratlam, Khargone and Khandwa
3.	Kanwar	5.62	4.69	Raigarh, Bilaspur, Sarguja, Raipur, Durg, Rajnandgaon, Sahdol
4.	Saharia	2.62	2.19	Shivpuri, Morena, Gwalior, Guna, Vidisha, Rajgarh
5.	Baiga	2.49	2.08	Shahdol, Mandla, Sidhi, Balaghat, Rajnandgaon,
6.	Halba	2.36	1.97	Durg, Bastar, Rajnandgaon, Raipur and Balaghat
7.	Bharia	1.96	1.64	Jabalpur, Mandla, Raigarh, Shahdol, Bilaspur, Chhindwara, Panna
8.	Kol	1.24	1.04	Satna, Rewa, Shahdol and Sidhi
9.	Bhattra	1.17	0.98	Bastar
10.	Binjhwar	0.92	0.77	Balaghat, Bilaspur, Raipur
11.	Oraon	0.89	0.74	Sarguja, Raigarh
12.	Sonr	0.68	0.57	Chhattarpur, Panna, Tikamgarh, Sagar and Damoh
13.	Korku	0.67	0.56	Khandwa, Betul, Dewas, Hoshangabad
14.	Sawar	0.64	0.54	Bilaspur, Raigarh, Raipur,
15.	Agaria	0.56	0.47	Mandla, Sarguja, Sidhi, Shahdol
16.	Panika	0.53	0.43	Shahdol, Sidhi
17.	Sonr	0.49	0.41	Sagar, Chhattarpur, Panna Damoh, Tikamgarh
18.	Dhanwar	0.35	0.29	Bilaspur, Sarguja
19.	Pardhan	0.18	0.15	Seoni, Chhindwara, Balaghat, Betul
20.	Kamar	0.18	0.15	Raipur
21.	Korwa	0.16	0.4	Sarguja, Raigarh,
22.	Khairwar	0.15	0.13	Sarguja, Sidhi, Shahdol, Panna, Chhatarpur
	Total	119.87	100	

The Tribal Area of M.P. has been divided into following Five Zones viz. The western, the Central, the North-Eastern, the Eastern and Southern. The Zonal grouping along with the districts and the tribal population in each zone are given below:

(Census 1991)

District Name	*Total Population*	*Scheduled Tribe population*	*Percentage of ST popu. to total popu. of district*	*Percentage of ST to total popu. of ST in state*
1	*2*	*3*	*4*	*5*
(A) Western Zone				
1. Dhar	1367412	731272	53.48	4.75
2. Jhabua	1130405	968372	85.66	6.29
3. Khargone	1195723	398020	33.29	2.58
4. Badwani	832422	539690	64.83	3.50
5. Khandwa	1431662	383231	26.77	2.49
6. Ratlam	971888	226156	23.27	1.47
7. Indore	1835915	100913	5.50	0.65
8. Ujjain	1383086	29160	2.11	0.19
9. Mandsaur	1000510	29247	2.92	0.19
10. Neemuch	554698	45378	8.18	0.29
11. Shajapur	1133248	24452	2.37	0.16
12. Dewas	1033807	155493	15.04	1.01
13. Rajgarh	992764	32775	3.30	0.21
Total : Western Zone	14763540	3664159	24.82	23.79
(B) Central Zone				
1. Betul	1181501	443131	37.50	2.88
2. Chhindwara	1568702	540708	34.47	3.51
3. Seoni	1000831	369827	36.95	2.40
4. Mandla	721244	408433	56.63	2.65
5. Dindori	570019	377154	66.16	2.45
6. Balaghat	1365870	29865	21.86	1.94
7. Jabalpur	1768150	263458	14.90	1.71
8. Katni	881812	211008	23.93	1.37
9. Hoshangabad	903508	143384	15.87	0.93

1	2	3	4	5
10. Bhopal	1351479	41205	3.05	0.27
11. Raisen	876461	126254	14.40	0.82
12. Vidisha	970388	42689	4.40	0.28
13. Narsinghpur	785496	101368	12.90	0.66
14. Damoh	898125	111114	12.37	0.72
15. Sehore	841358	85643	10.18	0.56
16. Harda	363703	76654	21.07	0.50
Total : Center Zone	16048647	3640696	22.68	23.64
(C) Northern Zone				
1. Shahdol	1323054	612866	46.32	3.98
2. Umaria	420815	194898	46.31	1.26
3. Sidhi	1373434	418004	34.43	2.71
4. Rewa	1554987	193105	12.42	1.25
5. Sagar	1647736	138467	8.46	0.90
6. Satna	1465384	202412	13.81	1.31
7. Panna	687945	102520	14.90	0.66
8. Gwalior	1293567	40151	3.10	0.26
9. Datia	515360	7605	1.47	0.05
10. Morena	1279094	8578	0.67	0.05
11. Sheopur	431480	86638	20.08	0.56
12. Shivpuri	1132977	127762	11.28	0.83
13. Tikamgarh	940829	38850	4.13	0.25
14. Chhatarpur	1158076	43482	3.75	0.28
15. Bhind	1219000	3291	0.27	0.02
16. Guna	1310317	157426	12.01	1.02
Total : Northern Zone	17754055	2377055	13.38	15.44
(D) Eastern Zone				
1. Sarguja	1581872	897217	56.72	5.83
2. Korea	500758	220360	44.07	1.43
3. Raigarh	1065939	392385	36.81	2.55
4. Jashpur	656352	429092	65.37	2.79
5. Bilaspur	1694883	347216	20.48	2.25
6. Korba	825891	356222	43.13	2.31
7. Janjgir Champa	110200	135641	12.22	0.88
Total : Eastern Zone	7435895	2778133	37.36	18.04

1	2	3	4	5
(E) Southern Zone				
1. Bastar	1116896	742799	66.51	4.82
2. Kanker	532151	296584	55.73	1.92
3. Dantewada	622267	490505	78.82	3.18
4. Raipur	2562091	359749	14.04	2.34
5. Mahasamund	788251	220684	27.99	1.43
6. Dhamtari	557700	133594	23.95	0.87
7. Durg	2397134	298059	12.43	1.93
8. Rajnandgaon	1090747	294610	27.01	1.91
9. Kawardha	511746	102407	20.01	0.66
Total: Southern Zone	10179033	2938991	28.87	19.08
Grand Total	66181170	15399034	23.27	100.00

** However, the developmental units for the Tribal Sub-Plan are the ITDPs, MADA pockets and the clusters. Zonewise details of the total population, scheduled Tribes' population, no of the ITDPs, the MADA Pockets and the clusters are given in Annexure No. IV. As the tribals make their livelihood from the land, forests and natural resources available zonewise description of these as given in Annexure No. IV is as follows:

THE WESTERN ZONE

Population

This zone consists of Dhar, Jhabua, Khargone, Badwani, Khandwa, Ratlam, Dewas, and Indore districts. This zone includes 11 Integrated Tribal Development Project (I.T.D.P.), 4 Modified Area Development Approach Pockets (MADA) pockets and one cluster. The total population of this zone according to 1991 Census is 42,21,836, out of which Scheduled Tribe population is 29,03,137, forming 68.76 per cent of the total population. The percentage of Scheduled Tribe population living in this zone to the total Scheduled Tribe population in the State is 18.85 percent. As compared to other zones, the western zone has the largest proportion of Scheduled tribe population. Nevertheless proportion of Scheduled Tribe population in Dhar and Maheshwar Integrated Tribal Development Project is less than 50 per cent. As these areas were declared as scheduled Areas under the Constitution of India they were included in the clusters tribal areas of this zone. Leaving aside these two areas, Integrated Tribal Development Project's,

Modified Area Development Approach pockets and clusters form 50.13 per cent (Pamakhedi cluster district khandwa) to 92.02 per cent (Airajpur Integrated Tribal Development Project). The density of population per sq. km. ranges between 75 in Alirajpur Integrated Tribal Development Project of Jhabua district to 197 in Badwani Integrated Tribal Development Project.

Physical features

Though, the general topography of the region presents some varied features, the tribal areas in this zone consists a contiguous tract of hilly and sterile land. Jhabua district lies in the mountaineous region of Malwa and greater part of Dhar district lies in the Deccan trap. The Narmada valley of area lying in the centre of the zone mostly in Khargone district is between 500-1000 ft above sea level. This hilly area lies between 1000 to 2000 ft above sea level. Many small rivers flow from north to south to join Narmada and Chambal rivers. Lying in the centre of the zone, the Vindhya range forms the watershed from where these small rivers flow. The zone gets an annual rainfall from 70-80 cm with the exception of Southern Khargone where the rainfall is considerably less. The eastern portions of Dhar and Khargone and western parts of Ratlam and Jhabua get 80-90 cm rainfall, annually. As compared to the neighbouring Malwa region the climate in the region is subject to greater extremes of heat.

Soil

Black soil with clay texture is found in Dhar, Khargone and parts of Jhabua. Red soil with loamy texture is found in western fringes of Jhabua and Sailana. Red and brown soil is found in Jobat and Alirajpur tehsils. Land along the banks of river Mahi in Jhabua and Sailana (Ratlam) is fertile, otherwise there is very high degree of soil erosion as the area is hilly and unfertile. As found in Malwa, in Dhar district soil in high level tracts is of high fertility. Most of the country in the lower tracts is covered with forests. The land lying along the river bed is good for agriculture. The land in tribal areas of Khargone district consists of rough and hilly tracts which is very poor and not suitable for agricultural purposes.

Land use pattern

There are two agricultural seasons locally known as Kurai and Choumasa i.e. rabi and kharif. The kharif season starts from June-

July with the coming of monsoon and continues till the beginning of October or end of September. The rabi season ends in February and March beginning from October and November. Juar, maize, paddy, pulses, oil seeds and cotton are the main crops in kharif season. In rabi season, the main crops are wheat, grain and sugarcane.

Forest

The forest in this zone is of mixed type. The proportion of forest area in relation to the total area has come down to 9 per cent in Dhar and 9.38 per cent in Jhabua. Teak, salai, dhawada, anjan, babool, tendu, saja, ber, karonda, etc. are found in patches, in Alirajpur area majua tree is found. Teak forests in Khargone district are mainly confined to Vindhya and Satpura hills. Teak forest ranges from 20-90 per cent in this area. Occupying mostly unsuitable areas like hill tops and upper slopes, the mixed forest patches are dotted all over the area. Kullu gum, honey wax, palma rose oil and tendu leaves are the important minor forest produces of the area, 25 per cent of kullu gum of the state is produced in the forest of Khargone district.

Economy

In the areas included in this zone detailed geological investigations have not been undertaken. The economic possibilities of mica and managanese found in Jhabua district have still to be worked out. In Dhar district iron ore and limestone ore are found. However, in Khargone a very small quantity of iron ore is found. There does not seem to be any bright prospect of mineral extraction or industries based on them. In Khargone, good quality of fodder grass in bundled by machines for export to neighbouring districts of Maharashtra. Salai, a soft wood species grown in the zone is supplied to NEPA mills for manufacturing of paper. Tribals derive substantial supplementary income from the collection of gum. With the help of the local tribals large scale trading of kullu gum is done by the forest corporation.

CENTRAL ZONE

Population

This zone consists of 14 districts namely Betul, Chhindwara, Seoni, Mandla, Dindori, Balanghat, Jabalpur, Katni, Hoshangabad,

Harda, Sehore, Raisen, Narsinghpur and Damoh. It consists of largest number of Integrated Tribal Development Projects, i.e. 15, 12 Modified Area Development Approach Pockets, and 4 Clusters. The zone has a total population of 41,12,914 out of which 24,00,496 are tribals, forming 58.36 percent of the total population of the zone. The tribals living in the zone form 15.59 per cent of the total population of the state. The density of population per square km. is 59 (Amarwara tahsil) and 159 (Saunser tahsil). The population is dispersed in a large number of small villages scattered over extensive areas. About 40 per cent of the population lives in villages having less than 500 people per village. The number of these villages is 7223.

Physical features

In the east, north-east and south-east the zone is bound by the Maikal hills. However, a larger part of the zone is covered by the Satpura range. Mahadeo hill lies in the western portion of the zone. The average altitude is between 2000-3000 ft above sea level and about two-thirds of the zone is covered by the hills mentioned above. The total area of the zone is over 52082 sq. km. Some southern areas of Chhindwara, Balaghat and Betul districts lies in the Godawari catchment area. The rest of the zone falls in the catchment area of Narmada. In the western portion of the zone the Bengaga originate from the Mahadeo hills while Narmada with it tributaries like Banjar, Sone and Johila with its tributary, originate from the Maikal nill. The rainfall in Betul and Chhindwara is between 100-120 cms.

Soil

In the eastern and southern region Mandla has red soil mostly sandy in texture and clay in the central region. However, northern Mandla has black soil with clay texture. In Chhindwara the soil is red, interlinked mainly with clay and loam. Varying in depth according to the altitude, Betul and Bhainsdehi tahsils have black soil with clay loam. The eastern portion of Betul has red soil with skeletal texture. Large scale land-development works need to be undertaken before agricultural development can take place, as soil erosion is acute in Mandla, Chhindwara and Betul. Moisture retention in the soil is poor in Betul, Chhindwara and Mandla. Portions of Mandla, Chhindwara and Betul are very infertile and can hardly sustain intensive cultivation. However, other areas namely Bhainsdehi tahsil of Betul district, Dindori and Mandla districts have better potential and can be taken up for intensive agricultural development.

Land use pattern

Both rabi and kharif crops are grown in this zone. Jawar, kodon-kutki and oilseeds are the principal crops in the tribal areas of Betul while Baihar and Mandla have paddy as their main crop. Wheat is the main rabi crop while the Jawar is the main kharif crop in tribal areas of Chhindwara district. Both rabi and kharif crops namely wheat, gram, masoor, kodon-kutki are grown in Lakhanadon. Oilseeds like rape, mustard, sesame are sown in Lakhanadon together with tuar and gram. The net area sown is 40.90 per cent of the total area sown in Chhindwara district. The percentage of irrigated area to total area sown is 5.19 per cent while percentage of double cropped area to net area sown is 9.29 per cent. Per capita net area sown is 0.48 hectares. The gross value of agricultural produce is Rs. 60.26 per hect.

The percentage of net area sown is 31.79 per cent in Mandla district. Double cropped area to net area sown is 22.22 per cent. The percentage of irrigated area to net area sown is 0.71 per cent. The gross value of agricultural output is Rs. 504.98 per hectare. Per capita net area sown is 0.48 hect areas.

Wheat, kodon-kutki and rice are the main crops grown in Mandla. In Mandla and Shahdol districts 23.34 per cent and 35.53 per cent areas are under rice cultivation out of the total cropped area respectively. In these districts the areas under kondo-kutki are 26.57 per cent and 22.27 per cent of the total cropped area respectively. Wheat is cultivated in 13.86 per cent area in Mandla district. In Mandla oilseeds and pulses are grown over 15.92 per cent and 14.53 per cent area. While in Shahdol the oilseeds and pulses are grown over 13.6 per cent and 10.94 per cent area.

Forest

In Chhindwara and Mandla districts forests (all types) account for 26.77 per cent and 12.0 per cent of the total area. In Mandla, Betul, Seoni and Chhindwara, teak forests and found. In Mandla and Balaghat districts extensive sal forests are found. In Balaghat, Mandla and Chhindwara mixed deciduous forest occupy a large area. Bamboo, saja, tendu, dhawra, beeja, lodia, mahua, palash, harra, anwala are common species variety of the trees found.

However, the tribals benefit from these forests as labourers. Greater employment can be provided to the tribal people if processing and timber industries are organized locally. Lakh, harra, gum, khair and mahua are the minor forest produces of the zone. From the forests of Mandla and Chhindwara large quantities of harra is collected. 35.45 per cent tanning material is contained in the shell of harra fruit. Extraction of tanning and tanic acid can provide gainful employment to the tribals. In Betul and Chhindwara, karaya gum which is used in food, cosmetics, textiles and other industries is found in limited quantity. Rosa grass is found in Betul from which oil can be extracted. The minor forest produce found in the zone if organized properly can contribute substantially to the income of the tribals.

Economy

Coal, manganese, graphite and fire-clay are found in different districts in the zone. The tribals are mostly employed as unskilled seasonal labourers for the extraction of these minerals. However, the tribals of the zone are cultivators as well as agricultural labourers and also work as labourers in mines.

THE NORTH-EASTERN ZONE

Population

The north-eastern zone includes the 11 districts viz. Shahdol, Umaria, Sidhi, Rewa, Sagar, Satna, Panna, Sheopur, Shivpuri, Chhatarpur and Guna. The tribals in this zone are dispersed except of course in the districts of Shahdol, Umaria Sidhi and Sheopur. In these districts, there are Integrated Tribal Development Projects seven in number. In rest of the districts, there are MADA pockets and clusters. Thus, there are 13 MADA pockets and two clusters. The total population of the zone is 22,12,212 out of which 12,28,308 are tribals forming 55.52 per cent of the total population. The tribals of the zone form 7.98 per cent on the total population of the State.

Physical features

Shahdol and Umaria, being the predominant tribal districts of the zone, are very much akin in topography and physical features to Mandla district which lies in its neighbourhood. The soil of the district is mostly red with sandy texture. In north-west portion of the district, it has extensive black soil tracks with clay texture.

Land use pattern

Net area sown in Shahdol district is 34.05 per cent of the total area. Percentage of double cropped area to net area sown is 0.81 per cent. Per area sown is 0.44 hectare. Per hectare value on agricultural output is very low i.e. Rs. 435.64 only. Paddy, kutki and wheat are the main crops.

Forest

In Shahdol forests (all types) account for 39.30 per cent of the total area. Shahdol has sal and mixed deciduous forests. Lac is cultivated and Khair trees are also found large number quantities of Harra is collected but lac industry is in complete decay.

Economy

Though coal, bauxite, and fire clay are also found in the district, the tribals are dependent mainly on agriculture and agricultural labour for their livelihood.

Except for Shahdol, Umaria and Sidhi the tribals in rest of the districts of zone are secluded in isolated pockets. These pockets do not offer good opportunity of making a livelihood as land and forest resources are poor. The tribals raise single crop, work as agricultural labourers, collect minor forest produces for their livelihood.

THE EASTERN ZONE

Population

The eastern zone includes the districts of Sarguja, Korea, Raigarh, Jashpur, Bilaspur, Korba and Janjgir (champa) (7) districts. It has 8 Integrated Tribal Development Projects, and 4 MADA pockets. The total population of the zone is 42,78,890 out of which the tribal population is 23,90,491 forming 55.87 per cent of the total population. The Scheduled Tribes population in the zone forms 15.52 per cent of the total Scheduled Tribes population of the State. Villages in the zone are smaller and each village having less than 500 people. Such villages form 70 per cent of the total villages in the zone. In these villages about 38 per cent population resides. In bigger villages mixed population resides and the tribals live in smaller villages in the interior.

Physical features

The area in this zone consists numerous hill and undulating plateau. The total area of this zone is 38.382 sq. kms. Half of the area of this zone approximately forms an irregular rectangle. It is bound on the south-east and east by plateaus of Hetghat hills Manpat and Zamirpat in south-west and north-west by the Maikal range of Satpura hills. The average altitude is of 1000-2000 ft. but the plateaus of Manpat and Zamirpat and Hetghat hills is situated on the average altitude of 2000-30000 ft. with cliffs rising to over 3000 ft. In the western corner of the zone there are a number of hill ranges from 1800-2500 ft. above sea level. Most of the areas of the zone fall in he catchment of Mahanadi. Main tributaries of Mahanadi are Hasdeo and Mand which originate in Sonhat and Manpat plateau of Surguja. Average annual rainfall varies between 120 cm to over 160 cm annually: Raigarh and Sarguja, the northern and extreme eastern part of the zone falls under the drainage system of Son. Kanhar and Rihand are the main tributaries of Son river.

Soil

Matasi soil is good for paddy cultivation. This soil is found in the eastern half of Sarguja district, Gharghora and Dharamjaigarh tehsils of Raigarh district. In other areas of the zone Kanhar, Dorsa, Bhata and Matasi is found.

Land use pattern

Net area sown is 38.55 per cent in Raigarh district. Percentage of gross area irrigated to total area under crop is 3 per cent in Raigarh district. However, percentage of double cropped area to total area under crop is 7.74 per cent. Net area sown per capita is 0.40 per cent hectare. The tribal areas in Gharghora, Dharamjaigarh and Jashpur are hilly and have little irrigation facility. Therefore, the per capita of the net area sown is very low, so also the gross value of agricultural output. 24.82 per cent area in Surguja is net area sown of the total area of the district. Per capita net area sown is 0.40 per cent per hectare while percentage of double cropped and gross irrigated areas to net area sown are 16.47 per cent and 1.02 per cent. Paddy, Kodon-Kutki, oilseeds and pulses are the main crops in Surguja and Raigarh districts. In Raigarh rice and kondo-kutki are grown, in 63.78 per cent and 8.72 per cent area respectively. In Sarguja rice and Kodno-kutki are grown over 46.60 per cent and 4.95 per cent area. Kodon-kutki are grown in considerable quantities in the hilly areas. In Raigarh and Sarguja specially in the hilly area a lighter plough known as 'Churia Hal' is used. Oilseeds and pulses account for 11.8 per cent, 12.61 per cent and 9.03 and 12.98 per cent of the total cropped are in Sarguja and Raigarh districts, respectively.

Forest

Surguja has larger area under forest i.e. 48.0 per cent of the total area of the district as compared to Raigarh in which forest accounts for 17 per cent area. Generally a mixture of semi-Evergreens and Deciduous forests are found. Sal and mixed forests are the two groups broadly found in the zone. Sal is the dominant species of the area. However Bija, Saja, Dhaura, Bhirra, Tendu and Salai are the other important tree associates. In patches soft wood species are also found. Eucalyputs and teak are being replaced by mixed forests which are less valuable. Bamboo of good quality is found in Sarguja. However, the timber of the zone finds its market outside. Mahua, tendu leaves, kattha, gum and Harra are produced in considerable quantities. Other minor forest produce of the area are mahua flower and seeds, honey, hides and horn bhilwa fruits, bahera anwala, and kosa cocoons, etc. Bidi making from tendu leaves, manufacture of katha by handi system and processing of gum has been taken up as cottage industry.

Economy

Iron ore, coal, lime-stone, gold, mica and laterite are found in Raigarh district. Bauxite estimated to have a total reserve of 5.20 lakh tons is found in high lands and moral plateau in Jashpur district. Due to lack of transport facility the mining industry did not prosper. However, jute mills are situated in Raigarh district. There are several bidi factories and rice mills. Small-scale cottage industries like manufacture of buckets, trunks, soap, utensils are flourishing in the zone. Tusser cocoon and cloth production is a traditional industry in Bilaspur district. Rearing of tusser silk worms and tusser silk weaving gives employment to a sizable number of tribal population. The tribal also get employment in coal mines found in korba region. Spread in an area of 200 sq. miles these mines are being worked by National Coal Development Corporation (*NCDC*). Limestone forms a part of continuous out crop which extends in Raigarh, Durg and Raipur districts. The zone has good bauxite reserve in the Phutka hills which is estimated as 4.0 lakh tons.

SOUTHERN ZONE

Population

Nine districts, namely Bastar, Kanker, Dantewada, Raipur, Dhamtari, Mahasamund, Durg, Rajnandgaon and Kawardha are included in this zone. Total population of the zone is 34,35,905. Out of which the tribals are 22,04,014 forming 64.16 per cent of the total population of the zone. The total tribal population living in the zone forms 14.31 per cent of the total tribal population living in the state. There are 10 I.T.D.P's, seven MADA pockets and two clusters in this zone. The proportion of tribal population ranges from 51.77 per cent (Gariaband) to 82.14 per cent (Bijapur I.T.D.P.).

Physical features

The important rivers in this zone are Tandula in Balod tahsil of Durg district, Mahanandi and Dudh in Raipur district and Tal Kotri, Sabri and Indravati in Bastar and Dantewada districts. The total area of the zone spreads over 48790 sq. kms. The highest peak in the zone lies in Dantewada district being about 4000 ft. above sea level known as Bailadila or the "Bullock Hump". The average height is between 1000-4000 ft. above sea level. Except, in south Bastar and Abujhmarh where it is over 160 cms, the zone has an annual rainfall ranging between 140-160 cm. The southern part of the zone lies in the catchment area of Godawari and the northern part lies in the catchment area of Mahanadi.

Soil

Kanhar, Matasi, Dorsa and Kanhar are the soil types found in the zone. Kanhar type of soil is found in Durg district which is suitable for wheat cultivation but not for paddy. Matasi, yellow soil does not retain moisture but with a heavy rainfall gives a good out turn of paddy. Kachanar is low lying sandy soil adjoining the head of a river. Dorsa is a mixture of Kanhar and Matasi.

Land use pattern

In undivided Bastar district (figures of newly formed district i.e. Dantewada and Kanker are not available) area sown is 19.65 per cent. Area irrigated to total area under crop is one per cent only. The per capita net area sown is 0.46 hectare as the population is sparse. Percentage of double cropped area to net are sown is 5.20. Depending almost entirely on rainfall in September/October the double cropped area shows great variation. Except for a little wheat in Durg, the main crop in Bastar, Dantewada, Kanker, Durg Rajnandgaon, Raipur, Dhamtari and Mahasamund districts is rice. Traditional crop kondo–kutki are also grown in Durg and Bastar districts in 8.4 per cent and 19.2 per cent of the total cropped area. Pulses and oilseeds are grown in about 7.38 and 33.39 per cent of the total cropped area in Durg and 6.62 per cent and 7.77 per cent in bastar districts. As the cultivation is not advanced in hilly areas kondo, kostra kutki, Madia are grown in considerable quantities. The agricultural implements are of primitive type therefore paddy is generally sown by broadcasting method. In Abujhmarh area of Bastar district shifting cultivation is in vogue. A holding of less than 10 acres is uneconomical because it is situated in an hilly area and lacks facility for irrigation. The tribals can grow only one crop in this area. There are substantial number of agricultural labourers. In Bastar, Raipur and Durg districts the percentage of tribal agriculture labourers to total workers is 18.87 per cent, 40.03 per cent and 20.96 per cent, respectively. Intensive cultivation can be ensured only when large scale land development activity is taken up. In Durg and Raipur districts the net area sown is 63.95 per cent and 41.45 per cent of the total area respectively. 39.13 per cent in Durg and 33.6 per cent in Raipur is the area sown more than once. In Raipur and Durg districts the percentages of double cropped area and gross are irrigated is 16.6 per cent and 39.27 per cent, 13.9 per cent respectively. In Raipur and Durg districts per capita net area sown is 0.34 and 0.42 hectares respectively. The tribal areas are covered with forest and are hilly therefore, the above figures represent only the partial position. In the tribal areas the per capita net area sow and area sown more than once are considerably lower.

Forest

Bastar district (undivided) has the largest forest area, i.e.,

64.39 per cent of the total area. Raipur and Durg come after Bastar as these districts have 39.79 per cent and 11.75 per cent forest area to total area respectively. Having good quality of teak and sal forest specially in Batar the orest in this zone are quite rich. Sal covers most of the area while teak dominates the southern portion. Saja, sarai, tendu, the common tree associated to teak as well as sal is also found. Big size tree is extracted by contractors as processing facilities are not available. As sal is found in abundance, bulk supply of railway sleepers is made from these forests. Bamboo is also in abundance which is used locally. In case the market is assured the manufacture of bamboo baskets can be taken as a cottage industry.

Economy

As the agriculture is not very well developed the production accounts for consumption that too only, partially. The forest though rich do not provide sufficient employment and income to the tribals. Bartar economy is still pevalent but to the disadvantage of the tribal people. High priced minor forest produces namely chironje, Harra, kosa, etc. are bartred with low priced commodities namely salt, sugar, utensils, etc. For the extraction of iron ore, found in plenty in the zone, iron ore industry, railway line, etc. were established which helped the rapid industrialization of the area. Due to illiteracy the tribals could not take advantage of the industrial developments. The training establishments had to be made for the new concerns but the tribals could not take advantage of these training establishments. Therefore, the outsiders, took the advantage of these trading establishments.

ZONEWISE DESCRIPTION OF THE SCHEDULED TRIBES

Western Zone

The Bhils

The Bhils are concentrated mostly in the districts of Dhar, Jhabua, Khargone, Badwani, Khandwa, Ratlam and Indore. Bhil has been derived from the Dravidian word 'bil' or 'vil' meaning a bow which the Bhils use as their principle weapon. As per 1981 Census the Bhils alongwith their sub-tribes viz. Barela, Patelia and others number 2500,530 (25 lakh) and stand as the third largest tribe of the country the first two being the Gond and the Santal respectively. The Bhils are reported to be armed men of the erstwhile smaller princely states of Jhabua district. They used to commit robbery and dacoity in the neighbouring states and take shelter in the erstwhile princelv states of their abode. This must have resulted in their having criminal tendencies, even now making them indulging in crime, in some areas.

The Bhilalas

Separate population figures of the Bhilalas are not available, as they have been grouped with the Bhils. The Bhilalas have come into being from the alliance between the immigrant Rajputs and Bhils of erstwhile Madhya Bharat region. The Bhilalas claim themselves to be the Rajputs and hold estates in Malwa and Nimar.

Central Zone

The Bharias

The Bharias have many things in common with the Gonds as they have lived side by side. They are found mostly in the districts of Bilaspur, Jabalpur and Chhindwara. The Bharias have been declared to be the most primitive tribal group in Patalkot. As reported in the 1981 Census their number was 1,95,490. But in Patalkot where they have been declared to be the most primitive tribal group they number only 2,012, or 238 families.

The Dhobas

The Dhoba tribe is often confused with the dhobi or washerman. In Census operations they have been grouped with the Gonds, hence, their population is not known. The Dhobas are found in Mandla and Balaghat districts.

The Dhurvas

The Dhurvas including Parjas were 1,408 only in 1981 Census. They are the third largest tribal community of Bastar, after Maria and Muria. The Dhurvas are found in erstwhile Jagdalpur, Dantewada and Konta tahsils of Bastar and Dantewada districts.

The Gonds

As per 1981 Census, the total population of the Gonds in Madhya Pradesh was 53,49,883 (53.50 lakhs). The Gonds are numerically the largest tribe not only in M.P. but in the country. In the past the Gonds ruled the Gondwana territory in the state. The Gonds inhabit mainly the Vindhyas and Satpura on either side of the river Narmada. There are over 55 sub-tribes recognized to be Scheduled Tribes along with the Gonds. The Gonds speak Gondi which belongs to Dravidian family of languages.

The Kalangas

In the Census, the Kalangas have been grouped with the Gonds therefore, their exact number is not known. They are found mainly in eastern Chhattisgarh, especially in the area adjoining Sambalpur district of Orissa. They belong to the Dravidian tribe and took up military service and adopted the name Kalanga which may have been derived from Kalinga. The Kalangas could also be a branch of the great Kalinga tribe of Tamil Nadu.

The Korkus

The Korkus are akin to the Korwas and are an offshoot of the Munda or Kolarian tribe. The Korkus live in satpura and Mahadeo hills. Their population has reduced from 1971 Census. According to 1971 Census their population was 20,7192 but in 1981 Census they are only 6,6781. They are found in Khandwa (E. Nimar), Hoshangabad, Betul and Chhindwara districts of erstwhile Mahakaushal region. The Korku tribe is divided into two groups namely Raj and Potharia. The Raj Korku consists of the land owning members from whom the Brahmins accept water. These two divisions have been replaced by four sub-castes with territorial names like Muwasi, Bawari, Ruma and Pondoya. The Korkus are related to the Nihals who are said to be a mixture of the Korkus and the Bhils.

The Murias

As in case of Marias, the Murias have been lumped together with the Gonds therefore, their exact population is not known. The Murias are found in Bastar only. In Bastar, Muria is generally used to mean an aboriginal. Their names may have been derived from Mur, the palash tree or a root. In Bastar also they are found in Kondagaon and erstwhile Narainpur tehsils.

The Nagarchis

The Nagarchis are considered to be a branch of Gonds, whose occupation is that of a musician. The population of the tribe is not known separately as they have been grouped in the Census with the Gonds. The Nagarchis are a lesser known tribe scattered over a large area in the districts of Chhindwara, Seoni, Mandla, Balaghat and Durg. They have also been reported in Bhandara district of Maharashtra.

The Nihals

The Nihals also called Nahals are said to be a mixture of the Korkus and the Bhils. In 1981 Census, the Nihals have been grouped with the Korku, Bopchi, Mowasi, Nihal, Nahe and Bondhi. As the population of this tribe has been grouped with other tribes therefore, their population has increased from 5082 (1971 Census) to 6,6781 (1981 Census). The Nihals are found in the districts of Betul, E. Nimar and W. Nimar. Their family names is same as those of the Korkus. The Nihals have two sub-divisions namely Korku and Marathi. The Marathi Nihals are more Hinduized and disclaim any connection with the Korkus.

The Ojhas

The Ojhas are considered to be a sub-tribe of Gonds. They are soothsayers and minstrels of the Gonds. They derive their name from the word 'Ojh' meaning entrail; their original duty having been to examine the entrails of the victims immediately after it has been slain as offering to the Gods. The exact number of tribe is not known today but in 1911 they numbered about 5000, spread in Mahakaushal region.

The Pardhans

The traditional occupation of the Pardhans is to act as the priest and the minstrel of the Gonds. However, they are considered to be inferior branch of the Gonds. The population of the Pardhans has also declined. As per 1971 Census their population was 69,633 including 'Patharis' and 'Sarotis' but has been reduced to 18,234 as per 1981 Census.

North-Eastern Zone

The Baigas

The baiga tribe has been recognized to be the most primitive tribal group in Madhya Pradesh, in the districts of Mandla, Balaghat, Dindori, Bilaspur, Shahdol, Umaria and Kawardha. Their total population according to 1981 Census is 2,48,949 out of which 1,34,357 i.e. 53.97 per cent is the primitive tribal group living in the districts mentioned above. The Baigas have seven sub-division viz. Binjhwar, Bharotia, narotia or Nahar, Raibhaina, Kathbhaina, Kondwan or Kundi and Gondwaina. The Baigas are considered to be a branch of Bhuiyas of West Bengal and Bihar.

The Kols

The Kols have taken their name, from the Kolarian family of tribes. According to 1981 Census, the total population of the tribe including the Dahaits was 12,3811. They are principally concentrated in Jabalpur and Katni districts. The Kols are mainly labourers. There are two important divisions of the Kols known as 'Rautal' and 'Rauteles'. The Rautia consider themselves to be superior to Rauteles and practise hypergamy with them. They eat with Rauteles at wedding feasts only and not on any other occasion. Other divisions of the Kols are Dussehru of Rewa, the Thakuria and the Kagwaria.

The Paos

The Paos are found mostly in three districts namely Chhatarpur, Satna and Shahdol. They are also known as Pabra. Their population according to 1971 Census was 23,074 which is reduced to 7,223 in 1981 Census. In Shahdol their population was much more i.e. 20,864 according to 1971 Census.

The Saharias

The name Saharia has been derived from the Persian word *Sehar* which means the inhabitants of jungle. They are also called Sosia or Sor and are found principally in Morena, Shivpuri and Guna districts in the erstwhile Madhya Bharat region of the state. Their total population as per 1971 Census was 2,05,427 which increased to 2,61,821 as per 1981 Census. The Saharias have been declared to be most primitive tribal group in the state. Through a special Census their population has now been estimated to be 4,17,171.

Eastern Zone

The Agarias

The Agarias are a sub-tribe of Gond. Their population according to 1981 Census was 55,757 persons. They are mostly found in

Shahdol, Raipur, Bilaspur and Mandla districts. They specialize in making articles of daily use, agricultural implements and show pieces from iron ore. They used to smelt crude iron ore in traditional forms of Bhattis, but now are using iron for making articles.

The Bhainas

As per 1981 Census, the total population of the Bhainas was 39,136. They are concentrated mainly in Bilaspur district and its surrounding areas. The Bhainas also work as village priest and magician. Their close connection is also established with the Baiga and Kawars. In Mandla, the Baiga tribe has two divisions known as Rai or Raj Bhaina and Kath Bhaina.

The Dhanwars

The Dhanwar tribe is also known as "Dhanuhar", which means a bow-man, as they used to obtain their livelihood from hunting through bow and arrow. They are concentrated in forest and hilly tracts of Bilaspur district. They are an offshoot of either the Gond or Kanwar tribe or could be a mixture of both. According to 1981 Census their population was 34,386.

The Kawars

As per 1981 Census, the population of the Kawar tribe was 5,62,200. They trace their origin from Kauravas of Mahabharata. They are divided into Cherwa, Rathia, Tanwar or Chattri. They live in the hilly areas of Chhattisgarh north of the Mahanadi in the districts of Bilaspur, Raigarh and Surguja.

The Khairwars

The total population of Khairwar tribe according to 1981 Census was 14,374. The tribe is found mainly in the districts of Bilaspur, Surguja and parts of erstwhile Vindhya Pradesh. They used to derive Khair from catechu tree. Therefore, they are known as Khairwars.

The Kharias

The population of the Kharia tribe, which is Kolarian in origin was 23,228 according to 1971 Census but this has come down to 6,891 persons as per 1981 Census. The Khairas are found in Bilaspur, Raigarh and Surguja districts. They are akin to Mundas and Savaras. The Kharias earn their livelihood as cultivators, labourers and collectors of minor forest produce.

The Korwas

The Korwa tribe belong to the Kolarian family of tribes. This tribe is concentrated principally in Bilaspur, Sarguja, Raigarh and Jashpur districts. Their population has also declined, according to 1971 Census there were about 67,303 Korwas (including Korakus) which were reduced to 15,340 in 1981 Census. The Korwas living on the hills known as Pahari Korwas, have been declared as a most primitive tribal group. According to special survey in the year 1992-93 their population was 27,953. They speak a dialect of their own known as Korwa which is closely related to Asuri and resembles, to Mundari and Santhali. The tribe is divided into two sub-divisions viz. Diharia or Kisan Korwa (cultivation) or Pahari Korwa of the hill. The Pahari Korwa are also called Bewaria, since they practise Bewar or shifting cultivation.

The Majhwars

The Majhwar tribe also known as Majhi or Manjhiya have originated from the Gonds, the Mundas or the Korwas. Their population which was 33,489 in 1971 Census has declined to be 6,509 only, in 1981 Census. The Majhwars live principally in Raigarh and Sarguja districts. The word Majhi means a head man of tribal sub-division.

The Mundas

The Mundas are a mixed group as their list of sub-tribe include the Khangar, Kharia, Mahali. Oraon and Sanwar all of which are the names of separate tribe. The Binjhwar and Nagbanshi Mundas belong to the aristocratic group of the tribe. Their population declined as they numbered 14,007 as per 1971 Census but only 1,579 in 1981 Census. Though quite small in number in the state, the Munda is a great tribe of Chhotanagpur which has given its name to the Munda family of tribes. They are found principally in Raigarh district.

The Nagesias

The population of the Nagesia tribe has also declined, it was 60,513 in 1971 Census but only 14,471 in 1981 Census. The Nagesias are found in Jashpur tehsil (now district) of Raigarh and

Sarguja districts. The tribe derives its name either from the word 'Nag' meaning a cobra or 'Nagbasia' meaning the original settlers of Chhotanagpur. The Nagesia is considered to be an offshoot of Mundas.

The Oraons

The Oraons are commonly known as 'Dhangar' which means a farm servant. The Oraons call themselves 'Kurukh'. This tribe is an important Dravidian tribe and live mainly in Raigarh and Sarguja districts. The dialect which they speak is known as Kurukh hence the Oraons call themselves 'Kurukh'. Their population has declined substantially, as per 1971 Census of the population of the Oraons was 3,70,652 but it has come down to 88,819 as per 1981 Census. The percentage of literacy among the Oraons is quite high as compared to other tribes. Their occupation is cultivation and agriculture labour. Subsidiary occupations are occasional labour, breeding cattle, fishing, keeping poultry, etc.

The Sawars

The Sawars number 59,535 in 1971 Census and 63,773 in 1981 Census. They are known by different names in different parts of the state. In Bundelkhand they are called 'Savaras'. Their other names are Savaras, Sabras and Sabhia. The tribe is also found in the adjoining area of U.P., Orissa and Andhra Pradesh. The tribe is considered to be a branch of Munda of Kolarian tribe. In Madhya Pradesh they speak the local dialects.

Southern Zone

The Abujhmarias

The Abujhmarias are a sub-tribe of Gonds, living in Abujhmarh area of Bastar and Dantewada districts. Their population as per special survey conducted in 1992-93 is 17,016 persons living in as many as 150 villages. The Abujhmarh area is spread over nearly 15,000 sq. miles. The villages of the Abujhmarias shift as per area of the shifting cultivation. Abujhmarh area is covered with a number of hills but thin forest. The Abujhmarias have also been declared as the most primitive tribal group and an Abhikaran (Agency) has been registered in Narainpur for their development. The Abujhmarias visit a weekly market in Chhote Dongar for the sale of their minor forest produces and purchase of the commodities of their daily use. Otherwise they have very little contact with the outside world.

The Bhattras

The population of Bhattras according to 1981 Census is 1,17,297. They live mostly in Bastar and South of Raipur. They are divided into three sub-divisions viz. Pit, Amnait, and Sen Bhattras. The Bhattra are employed mostly as domestic servants or village watchmen. The word Bhattra stands to mean a servant.

The Binjhwars

The Binjhwars are considered to be an offshoot of the Baigas of Balaghat and Mandla districts. They live in the districts of Raipur and Bilaspur. They are considered to be land-owning section of the Baigas. Their population according to the 1981 Census was 92,079. The Binjhwars are divided into four sub-divisions viz. Birjhia, Binjia, Sonjhare and Binjhwar. The Sonjharas collect gold ores from the river bed and make articles of gold.

The Bhunjia

The population of the Bhunjias according to 1981 Census was 9,524. This tribe inhabits the areas of ex-zamindaris of Bindranawagarh and Khairiar in Raipur district. They are divided into two sub-divisions namely Chaukhutia and Chinda. The Chaukhutia Bhunjia was born as a result of relations between a Gond woman and Halba man. It was said that the Chinda Bhujias have descended from the Baigas. Various names of the Chaukhutia Bhunjias are of Gondi origin.

The Halbas

As per 1981 Census, the population of Halba tribe was 2,36,375. The tribe is found in Raipur and Bastar districts (undivided). They are mainly cultivators and agricultural labourers and occupy a high position in the tribe living in Bastar. They are divided into Bastaraha, Chattisgariah and Marethia.

The Kamars

As per 1981 Census the total population of the Kamars was 17,517 which has come down to 13,110 as per special survey conducted in 1992-93. The Kamars have been declared to be the most primitive tribal group in Gariaband tahsil of Raipur district.

However they are found in former zamindaris of Bindranawagarh, Suarmarh and Phingeshwar, in the Nagri and Sihawa tracts in Dhamtari district.

The Khonds

The Khonds live mostly in eastern portion of Raigarh and southern portion of Raipur districts. They are also known as Kands. In Raigarh they are found in large numbers in the area of former Sarangarh state, in Raipur they are concentrated mainly in the ex-zamindari of Khairiar. They also call themselves, Kuiloka or Kuienju which may possibly be derived from 'ko' or 'ku' a Telugu word for a mountain. They are also found in Bihar and Orissa. The population of Khonds has also declined as compared to 1971 Census. In 1971 they were 6,899 and in 1981 the population has come down to 1,670 persons only.

The Gadbas

The Gadba tribe belongs to Mundari or Kolarian group and is found in Bastar district. They speak a dialect of their own which is known as Gadba or Gadbi. The word Gadba denotes a person who carries loads on his shoulders. However, some of them are cultivators and labourers and some are employed as watchmen. The population of Gadba was 3,254 as per 1981 Census.

The Dorlas

The Dorlas are a sub-tribe of Gond found in southern portion of Bastar district. The river Kolab or Sabri, divides, the district from Orissa forming the eastern border of Dorla tract. The Dorla tract extends southwards upto Konta and in the west, the Dorlas are distributed over the adjoining tahsil of Bijapur. As they have been grouped with the Gonds, their population is not available, separately.

The population of the tribe in 1971 was 69,633 (including the Patharis and the Sarotis) but reduced to 18,234 in 1981.

The Saharias

The Saharias, also called Sosia or Sor, are found principally in Morena, Shivpuri and Guna districts of the old Madhya Bharat region of the state. Their total population was estimated at about 2,05,427 in 1971 and 2,61,821 in 1981 Census. The Saharias have been declared to be the most primitive tribal group in the state. Through a special Census their population is now 4,17,171. The name Saharia probably means inhabitants of Jungle (from the Persian word *Sehr*).

The Savars

The Savars are known by different names in different parts of the state. In Bundelkhand they are called Saonras. Their other names are Savaras, Sabras and Sabhra. The Savars numbers 59,535 in 1971 and 63,773 in 1981 Census.

The tribe is also found in the adjoining areas of Uttar Pradesh, Orissa and Andhra Pradesh. The eastern branch of the tribe in M.P. is separated from the western branch by a wide expanse of territory. There are diverse opinions about the origin of the name 'Savar'. The tribe is considered to be a branch of the great Munda of Kolarian tribe but in Madhya Pradesh they speak the local dialects.

Demographic Features of the Tribals

The tribals are not only different from other general groups in terms of social structure but also in demography. Barring exceptions, in some tribes the sex-ratio is in favour of women. Widow remarriage is permissible. The size of the family is large.

Rural-Urban Concentration

As per 1991 Census 7,46,000 tribals (4.9 per cent) of the total lived in the urban areas. Rest 95.10 per cent lived in the rural areas. The urban areas attract the tribals for employment etc., therefore, there is a steady increase in the proportion of urban population. As reported by the 1961 Census, the percentage of tribal population in urban areas was only 1.1 per cent it has increased now to 4.9 per cent.

The scenario of concentration of rural-urban population differs from district to district. In Mandla only 1.5 per cent tribals live in urban areas whereas in Bhopal the percentage is 72.0 per cent. The tribals have been attracted towards the cities basically to earn wages. Therefore, the proportion of the tribals in the industrially growing cities i.e., Indore (32.7 per cent), Gwalior (25.7 per cent) and Ujjain (25.4 per cent) is higher and growing.

Sex-ratio: Number of females to every thousand males is called sex-ratio. As per 1991 Census there are 985 females per

1000 males among the STs. This sex-ratio is quite high as compared to the sex-ratio in general, i.e., 931, amongst the Scheduled Caste 915, and in non-Scheduled Tribe population 916.

There is a clearcut impact of immigration on the sex-ratio amongst the tribes. In cities, the sex-ratio amongst the tribals is 902 which is akin to the non-tribal population, i.e., 893. This indicates the trend that tribals come to cities for employment with less number of women folk. In rural areas, the sex-ratio among the STs is 989 as compared to the general population which is 925.

Variation in sex-ratio has also been found in different age groups. As per 1981 Census, there are 1130 females for 1000 males in the age grop of 60. This shows that longevity among women is more in this age group. More or less the same trend is reflected in the age-group of 0-4 i.e., 1019. But it declines in the age-group of 10-14 and 15-19, it comes down to 942 and 966 respectively. In working population (20-49) however, it increases to 1,009. Most probably the males have to struggle hard therefore the population declines.

Sizeable variations in sex-ratio are also found in different tribes:

More than 1000	Bhaina, Bhattra, Binjhwar, Birhul, Gond, Halba, Kamar, Kawar, Mawasi, Nagesia, Oraon, Pradhan, Sawar, Bhunjia, Khond, Munda, Saote.
950-1000	Agaria, Baiga, Bharia, Bhil, Domar, Dhanwar, Gadaba, Khairwar, Kol, Korku, Kanwar, Manjhi, Majhwar, Mina, Panika, Saur, Sonr.
Less than 950	Korku, Keer, Kolam, Parja, Andh.

The sex-ratio varies from tribe to tribe. Among the Gonds, the tribe having largest population, the sex-ratio was 1011 as per 1981 Census. The sex-ratio varied in rural-urban setting too. Among the Gonds in urban areas it was 875 and in rural areas it was 1016. The Kanwars too are a large tribe, the sex-ratio among them was 1013. The sex ratio among Halba is 1034, Bhattra 1013, Binjhwar 1019, Oraon 1027 and Sawar 1027. These are among the 18 largely populated tribals of the state. In the remaining 11 Scheduled Tribes, the sex-ratio is decreasing, prominent among them are the

Bhils and the Bhilala amongst whom the sex-ratio is 978. Among Baiga, Bharia, Kol, Korku, Agaria, Panika and Dhanwar tribals, the sex-ratio is between 975 to 1000. But among Saharia it is 953, Saur 966, Sonr 934 less than 975. It may be mentioned that these tribals live in those areas where sex-ratio is less even in general population. There are tribals viz. Korku, Keer, Kolam, Parja and Andh among whom the females are quite less in number.

Age composition. The analysis of the figures given in the table below shows that the trend of age composition among the tribals and the general population that is, male and female is the same. Among the tribals as well as in general, both male and female, the maximum population is in the age-group of 0-14. Next below this is in the age-group of 20-49 years. There is a sharp decline in the population after the age-group of 0-14 to 15-19. In the old age-group, i.e., 60+ the population is around six per cent.

Age-Group Distribution Amongst the Tribals of M.P. 1981 census (1991 census not available so far)

Age-group Persons	*Male*	*Female*	*Percentage of tribals*
0-14	41.61	41.78	41.42
15-19	8.70	8.84	8.57
20-49	37.32	37.10	37.54
50-59	6.25	6.54	5.97
60+	6.12	5.74	6.50
Total	100.00	100.00	100.00

Decadel Growth Rate (1961-91)

The decadel growth rate has been compared in the last three decades amongst the tribals. The total population of the Scheduled Tribes in 1961 Census was 66,78,410. It increased to 83,87,403 during 1971, the population further increased to 1,19,87,031 in 1981 and it is 1,53,99,034 during the year 1991. The decadel growth rate, thus has been 25.59 per cent during 1961-71, 42.9 per cent during 1971-81 and 28.47 per cent during 1981-91. The decadel growth rate in general population in the state, during this period has been 28.7 per cent during 1961-71, 25.3 per cent during 1971-81 and 26.8 per cent during 1981-91, the list of the Scheduled

Tribes was revised in the year 1976 doing away with the area restrictions. By and large, the tribal in one pocket was declared as a Scheduled Tribe in the whole state, therefore, the population increased in 1981 Census. There was a decline in the proportion of the STs in the total population during 1971 from 20.63 per cent in 1961 to 20.11 per cent in 1971. But in 1981, it increased to 22.97 per cent and it is 23.27 per cent in 1991. Sharp rise in the proportion of STs during 1971-81 is due to the fact that the list of the Scheduled Tribes was revised doing away with the area restrictions and declaring them as a Scheduled Tribe in the whole of the state.

Difference in the growth rate of different tribes during 1961-81 has been as follows:

Tribe	*Population*			*Percentage (increase during)*
	1961	*1971*	*1981*	*1961-81*
1. Gond	30,94,613	38,51,261	53,49,883	72.9
2. Bhil-Bhilala	12,29,930	16,18,794	25,05,888	103.3
3. Kawar	3,28,713	4,30,493	5,62,200	71.0
4. Saharia	1,74,320	2,05,427	2,61,816	50.2
5. Baiga	1,44,005	1,76,394	2,48,949	72.9
6. Halba	1,30,123	1,73,374	2,36,375	81.7
7. Bharia	1,22,904	1,17,795	1,95,490	59.1
8. Kol	3,86,009	4,78,081	1,23,811	-67.9
9. Bhattra	72,274	71,145	1,17,297	52.3
10. Bhinjwar	43,804	57,013	92,059	88.6
11. Oraon	2,83,073	3,70,652	88,819	-68.6
12. Sour	16,576	N.A.	68,034	310.4
13. Korku	1,60,675	2,17,917	66,781	-58.4
14. Sawar	48,584	59,535	63,773	31.3
15. Agaria	11,793	17,548	55,757	372.8
16. Panika	36,498	43,988	52,979	45.2
17. Sonr	17,541	N.A.	48,657	117.4
18. Dhanwar	21,137	24,161	34,386	62.7
Total	66,78,410	83,87,403	1,19,87,031	79.5

Thus, the growth of population amongst the Bhil-Bhilala, Halba, Binjhwar, Agaria and Sonr is more as compared to the decadal growth rate in general population. In contrast the population of Saharia, Bharia, Sawar and Panika has increased at a slow rate.

The population of Kol, Oraon and Korku tribes have decreased instead of increasing.

Marital Status: Marriage is an important institution amongst the Scheduled Tribes. Different types of marriages are prevalent. Marriage institution will be discussed here as an important demographic indicator. It may be mentioned here that conditions of marriage vary from tribe to tribe and area to area.

Among the male 40 per cent and among the female 55 per cent are married. Age of 99 per cent unmarried females is less than 19 years which shows that among the STs child marriage is less prevalent. The percentage of married boys and girls in the age-group of 10-14 years is only 3.9 per cent and 8.12 per cent respectively.

The universality of marriage amongst the Scheduled Tribes is clear from the fact that in the age-group of 15-49 years 79 per cent males and 90 per cent females are married at one time or the other. The percentage of married people amongst the Scheduled Tribes is more as compared to non-tribals. Widow and widower remarriage is prevalent. Therefore the percentage of widows and widowers in the tribal population is quite less. Among these people 2/3 females and 3/4 males are in the age-group of over 50 years, age in which the males and females do not remarry. Divorce and separation is more among the STs, as compared to the general population. Among the females the percentage of divorce is 1.59 per cent and amongst the male it is 1.17 per cent. The comparative picture in general population is 0.80 per cent and 0.83 per cent respectively. It is clear that divorce and separation are easily granted among the Scheduled Tribes.

Position of Marriage Among the Scheduled Tribes as Compared to General Population

Marital Status	*Sex*	*Percentage in total population*	*Total S.T.*	*Total Non-S.T.*
1. Percentage of married people in the age-group of 10-14 years.	Female	13.27	8.12	14.84
	Male	5.50	3.90	5.59
2. Percentage of married people in the age-group of 15-49 years.	Male	91.24	79.15	94.66
	Female	91.36	90.20	91.72
3. Percentage of Widower/ Widows	Male	5.65	5.58	5.67
	Female	13.79	13.72	13.81
4. Percentage of Divorce and Separated	Male	0.98	1.59	0.80
	Female	0.91	1.17	0.83

The Problems as Faced by the Tribals

The tribal communities occupy a unique position in Indian society. They are one of the earliest inhabitants of the country and have contributed to the variety and richness of its cultural forms. They have preserved a distinctive lifestyle over the centuries and stand out in sharp contrast to the general rural masses. They remained comparatively isolated in the past and enjoyed a more or less self-sufficient economy. In pre-independent India, the policy towards the tribal community was either that of compassion, or isolation. It was only in independent India that the problems of the tribals attracted the attention of the government and provision of special protective measures was made in the Constitution.

Ever since the people came in contact with the tribals, it was tried to study their problems. The Britishers were very much concerned with the problems of the tribes, therefore a special officer was appointed to investigate the conditions of the aboriginal tribes in the province particularly in the partially excluded areas W.V. Grigson was appointed as a special officer (1st May, 1940). The Gazette extraordinary announcing his terms of reference explained that for the past some time Provincial government had under consideration the measures necessary to improve the conditions under which this large element of the provincial population exists. The government therefore considered that the whole question should form the subject of a systematic and co-ordinated inquiry conducted by a special officer.

Shri W.V. Grigson submitted his report which was published in book form under the title Aboriginal Problems in the Central Provinces and Berar. The problems enunciated in this report were 'Loss of aboriginal land and debt', Agriculture-low yield, land reclamation, soil conservation, veterinary, health and medical relief, excise policy, and forest policy, education, law and justice.[3]

The vast and sparsely populated tribal area also posed problems before the administration. Due to ignorance of tribal languages, their culture in general and problems, the officers posted in tribal areas were not in a position to establish contacts with the tribals and gain their confidence. The officers/officials were quickly transferred from the tribal areas. This tendency also debarred the officers/officials in establishing good contacts with the tribals.

After Independence, the country committed itself to a Constitution. The concern of the constitution of India for the tribal population is illustrated by the provision in Article 339 that the President shall appoint a Commission at the end of ten years from its commencement to report on the administration of what are known as the scheduled areas and the welfare of the Scheduled Tribes in states. The Commission examined the problems of the Scheduled Tribes in great details and submitted its report to the President of India. This Commission will hitherto be referred as Dhebar Commission.

The Dhebar Commission has pointed out the 'lack of understanding'— on the part of non-tribals and government officials, politicians, landlords, money-lenders, forest contractors, administrators etc. as number one problem. The tribals live at widely different stages of development. In fact they may be divided into four categories—those who are living in the remotest corners of the country and for the reason are almost in primitive stage—they are designated to be the most primitive tribal groups. A few of them are at the shifting cultivation stage, quite a few of them have taken to regular agriculture. A good number of these have already been assimilated. The differences in physical environment also call for separate treatment. Before anyone can successfully tackle the problem, the person must be sensitive to understand the tribal people in the context of their urges and aspirations together with the rational behind them. The tribal people are prepared to make an entry into that area with other members of the family.

The only thing that they expect is that the changes should not destroy the harmony of their life, and the contracts should not result in suppressing their distinctive personality.[4]

Apart from these basic consideratio, s there is the problem of integration and development. The most difficult part of national unity is emotional integration and that of development is the psychological aspect. Despite a lack of clarity about the basic approach, the difficulties of distance, both physical and mental and the inadequacy of resources, it can be said that there has been a definite impact on the tribal mind. While there is dissatisfaction, it is true there is also contentment. Besides difficulties and tensions, there is improvement in the tribal.

There are other aspects of this problem. They can be summed up as 'protective' and 'development aspects'. The protective aspects relates to the protection of the rights of the tribes in land and forests and the right to be safeguarded against usurious or exploitative elements. The developmental aspects relate to positive welfare schemes. It is impossible to minimize the magnitude of what remains to be done in these two fields.

The Constitution deliberately laid emphasis on both these aspects, but the state government has still to translate that emphasis into action. Even in the scheduled areas there are glaring deficiencies, and the situation outside them is naturally worse for there is much more difficulty. The problems of plain tribals and the hill tribals differ. Broadly speaking, the plain tribals have not received much attention.

The sectors responsible for making a living of the tribals, e.g. agriculture, animal husbandry, handicrafts, etc. also suffer from many problems. Other sources of employment-labour, markets and money economy and bonded labour also pose a number of problems before the tribals as well as administration. Drinking water and treatment of diseases are also big problems in tribal areas. Consumption of liquor to which the tribals are used to traditionally, poses a number of problems now. Education which is of great necessity to the tribals suffers from many problems. These problems are a great source of discontentment among the tribals. This portion has been discussed in great details in Chapter III.

The present educational system sponsored by both official and non-official agencies aim at increasing general awareness, enlarging the world view of the people, as well as equipping him for getting some gainful employment so that he can make his living. The percentage of literacy amongst the tribals compared to the general literacy is as follows:

Comparison in the Percentage of Literacy in the Total and Tribal Population

	Total			*Tribal Population*		
Year	*Total*	*Male*	*Female*	*Total*	*Male*	*Female*
1961	17.13	27.00	6.70	5.09	9.25	0.97
1971	22.14	32.70	10.92	7.62	13.05	2.18
1981	27.87	34.49	15.53	10.68	17.74	3.60
growth during						
1961-81	62.70	46.3	31.8	109.8	91.8	27.1

Due to various problems, the tribals of M.P. are far behind in education as compared to the general population. However, a few tribal viz. the Oraon and Halba who have come in contact with well educated general population and missionaries have picked up education very well. In 1981 Census, among the Halba the percentage of literacy was 28.8 per cent and among Saharia it was lowest i.e. 2.74 per cent, among Oraons it was 22.6. These two communities have maintained their leadership in education amongst the tribals of M.P.

The tribal children start participation in their household chores including earning livelihood from the very beginning. When they come to the school their participation in the household chores is disrupted. Therefore, the children and their parents both find school as disrupting their daily households chores.

Administration of Justice

S.C. Roy wrote on the administration of justice in tribal area, the British system of law and administration has further tended to impair the social solidarity of these tribes and has weakened the authority of the social heads or panchayat and the respect they formally commanded. Until recently, when government orders validating tribal customary laws regarding succession and inheritance were promulgated, the courts often disregarded the customs against inheritance by daughters and applied to them the Succession Act quite inconsistent with the fundamental structure and ideas of kinship of the tribes. Until recently, where rules against alienation of ancestral lands were promulgated by Government, the ancient tribal customs regarding such alienation was utterly disregarded.

To sum up, the tribal problems can be viewed from two angles, from the society at large and from the viewpoint of the tribals. The above description has been given from the viewpoint of the society at large. From the tribals viewpoint their problems are–means of livelihood due to deforestation at a very great speed, dispossession of land, drinking water, health and to some extent the insensitive administration and outsiders who come to them for their own benefit and exploit them.

REFERENCES

1. Vidyarthi, LP, (Ed) *Applied Anthropology in India* 1968, p. 261.
2. Singh, KS,–*Colonial transformation of the Tribals Society in Middle India*, 1978, p. 12.
3. Grigson, W V, *Aboriginal problems in CP and Berar,* 1944, p. 408.
4. Elwin Verrier, *A New Deal for Tribal India,* 1963, p. 3.

N.B. The Statistical figures in this chapter have been taken from:

(a) Census of India 1991:

(b) Gazetteers of the respective districts published by the District Gazetteers Department, M.P.

Population figures of the tribes have been taken from Census of India 1981. The tribewise figures from 1991 Census are still not available.

3

Condition of the Tribes Prior to Independence Under British Rule in Central India

A study of the life of the tribal people before independence has its difficulties, for the areas they inhabited were inaccessible, making it difficult to establish contacts with them. However, a few officers, anthropologists, welfare workers and Missionaries who maintained constant touch with them, left valuable accounts which depict the conditions under which they used to live. Depending on these sources, a brief account will be presented here and the policy that governed the tribal people before independence will be discussed.

British Policy of Isolation

Earlier, a description of the tribes has been given. This description gives an insight into their isolated life and struggle for existence. The tribal people living in their remote hills and forests for many centuries led a life of their own, generally uninfluenced by the main currents of development outside. It was with the entry of the missionaries into these areas that the officers of the administration started paying some attention to them. But this contact was superficial and prompted them to come to some equally superficial conclusions. The foremost of which was to isolate these people from the rest of their countrymen and separate the tribal areas from the purview of normal administration. The people in the plains were either too subdued or too ignorant to mind what happened. If the administration contributed to the difficulties of the tribal people by its policy of isolation, the people of the plains added to the problem by their conscious or unconscious neglect.

The Government of India Act, 1919, continued the provision of administering the tribal areas separately from the rest of the provinces. With the growth of the freedom movement there was increasing anxiety on the part of the British to isolate the tribes from political contagion.

Simon Commission in 1929 suggested that the administration of the tribal areas should be undertaken by the Centre. This required security of land tenure, protection from economic exploitation, freedom to pursue their traditional method of livelihood and ancestral customs. The commission also suggested that these tracts be classified into two categories "Excluded" and "Partially Excluded" areas.

The government's decisions on the recommendations of the Simon Commission were embodied in the Government of India Act, 1935. Sections 91 and 92 of the Act provided for the declaration by an order in council of "Excluded Areas" and "Partially Excluded Areas". Any act of the federal or the provincial legislature would apply to these areas only on the direction of the Governor who was empowered to make such exceptions and modifications as he considered necessary. Reservation of seats for tribals was made in the Legislature of Madras, Bombay, Bihar, the Central Province, (one of the constituents of present M.P.) Assam and Orissa. In drawing up the scheme, it was indicated that the areas to be placed in the category of "Excluded Areas" must be as limited as possible. In regard to areas classified as "Partially Excluded", any area having a preponderance of tribals sufficient to make possible the application of special legislation and administrative treatment was to be included. Accordingly, the frontier and border regions in Assam, Laccadive and Minicoy Islands and, Lahul and Spiti areas were declared "Excluded Areas" and huge tribal tracts in the provinces of Madras, Bombay, Bengal. United Province, Bihar, Central Province and Orissa were made "Partially Excluded Areas".[1]

The British system of law and administration did nothing to bolster and much to damage the social structure of these tribes and weakened the authority of the social heads of panchayats and the respect they formerly commanded. The tribal people were not adequately represented in the legislatures and the local bodies. In the Central Province and Berar, where the tribals numbered as much as 20 per cent of the population only one seat was reserved for them in the Legislative Assembly. In the Central Assembly out of the total number of 250 seats, not a single seat was reserved for the tribals.

The British policy as we have seen, provided for a sort of protection largely through isolation. After the formation of popular ministries in 1937, committees were appointed in the provinces of Bihar, the Central Province, Orissa, Bombay and Madras to enquire into the conditions of the tribals although they had only a limited responsibility for the "Partially Excluded Areas". The Second World War and the consequent resignation of the popular ministries, however, postponed the adoption of any new policy for tribal welfare, until independence.

The policy of exclusion from legislation resulted in exploitation by zamindars, landlords, money-lenders and contractors. These contacts with the non-tribals were not only unwelcome but also pugnacious to the tribes and in the words of Mr. Dhebar, "They added to the strain of fighting a lonesome battle against ruthless natural erosion, denudation of hills and erratic rivers".[2]

The British programme of conservation of the forests dislocated the tribal economy with a force which they were unable to bear. The frustration and suspicion of the people being denied access to forest which formed their sustenance can be vividly imagined. This suspicion was mainly in direction of the forest contractor who carried the profits of the forest produce which resulted in their sordid exploitation. This economic exploitation which reduced them to a state of penury, with lowest level of literacy, combined with the British desire to make inroads in their social and religious institutions, "led to an interesting variety of reactions including hostility as well as attempts to use some Christian tenets in anti-foreign way".[3]

From 1870-80 onwards there was a tightening of control on forest zones for revenue purposes. Shifting cultivation, essential in the poorest rural society was banned or restricted in reserved forests and on top of this attempt was made to monopolize forest wealth through curbs on use of timber and grazing facilities.

The tribal response to all these included uprising against the English in various parts of the country. These uprisings were mainly against the economic exploitation, social humiliation which the tribes—who were proud as Lucifer about their heritage had to suffer and to certain extent a reaction to the mood prevailing in the country against the Britishers. Another reason was the nervousness on the part of the tribes who had not embraced Christianity, due to the feeling that they would be discriminated against their Christian brethren.

Land and Forest—the Twin Needs of the Tribals

All students of tribal economy agree that the two things of greatest significance to the tribals are land and forest. As the Rev. W.J. Culshaw writes:–

"The most powerful motive in Santal life is possession of the land which they till...No motive is so strong in a tribal people as the preservation of the life of the tribe and its mores and a Santal's land not only provides economic security, but is a powerful link with his ancestors; and this applies to newly entered no less than the old, for they will not take possession till the spirits approve. The land is a part of his spiritual as well as his economic heritage".

The forests constitute an equally important source of livelihood. The tribals once roamed the forest areas at will and were the sole beneficiaries of the forest produce.

Basis of British Policy

A study of the efforts made by the British Government to meet these two primary requirements reveals that as they proceeded from a policy of isolation and status quo, the tribals had to remain at the mercy of petty officials and usurers and nothing positive by way of rehabilitation and development was achieved.

The whole basis of the British administration in India was to support its supporters. These vested interests were shrewd enough to benefit from every act and omission of the British rulers. It will be quite relevant here to discuss the status of the means of livelihood of the tribals then. This will help in understanding the causes of rebellions of the tribals against Britishers described later.

State of Agriculture in Tribal Areas

The practice included small land-holding continuously encroached upon all sides, poor quality of the soil and in many cases primitive methods of cultivation, were responsible for low agriculture yields which were not adequate to sustain the people throughout the year. They had, therefore, to supplement this insufficient food supply by consuming locally available fruits, roots, wild vegetables and berries. The tribal people raised only food crops for domestic and local consumption. Cash crops, as a rule, did not find a place in their economy. Agricultural production was usually supplemented by animal husbandry, rearing of pigs and poultry farming.

In Assam, Bihar, Orissa, Andhra Pradesh and parts of M.P., shifting cultivation was widely practised. The area cultivated was established by old tradition and agreement among the various families who maintained the integrity of their boundaries which were marked off by streams, hills or trees. In parts of Assam, the Hills of 'jhuming' cultivation were selected annually by the council of village elders in consultation with the priests as jhuming was a co-operative enterprise. The various agricultural operations involved, such as clearing the forest, burning the trees, sowing or dibbling the seed, weeding, fencing and reaping, were done by everybody at the same time and were preceded by appropriate religious ceremonies.

Animal Husbandry

In addition to these agricultural pursuits, some tribal groups followed a pastoral economy, a classic example being that of gond-guaris of the erstwhile Bhopal state. Their entire way of life was built on buffaloes and their milk products which were exchanged by them with their neighbours for other necessities of life. The Bhutias of north Uttar Pradesh and parts of West Bengal followed a mixed agricultural and pastoral economy. Traditionally, they were graziers, stock-breeders, agriculturists and traders. The Gujjars and Gaddis of Himachal Pradesh and Punjab reared goats, sheep and buffaloes and were entirely dependent on them and their products for their livelihood. They were obliged to lead a nomadic life on account of the persistent need for finding new pasture lands and fodder for their herds. By virtue of their nomadic habits, both men and animals suffered on account of the indifference, neglect and sometimes opposition of the government functionaries.

Handicrafts

The tribals were adept in preparing articles for their daily use, themselves. The tribal people, in many parts of the country have always distinguished themselves as good craftsmen. The Nagas, the Khonds, the Mishmis, the Abors, the Khamptis, the Kacharis and the Mompas of NEFA were among those known for their skill in handlooms and handicrafts. The Korwas and the Agarias of M.P. were known as iron smelters though their techniques were not up-to-date. The Tharus of U.P. manufactured utensils, baskets, musical instrument, ropes, mats and even weapons. Some of the tribes of South India made excellent bamboo articles. The Urali Kurumbas of Kerala made a living from the earthen pots which they bartered for foodgrains. The Betta Kurubas of Mysore excelled in bamboo and cane work. The Kotas, neighbours of the Todas of Nilgiris, have for generations been the artisan tribes par excellence. They are herdsman, blacksmiths, carpenters, potters, rope and umbrella makers, all combined into one. They are also known to be good jewellers. The Gadaba women attained great proficiency in weaving bark-fibre cloth on their loin-looms, and they dyed them with various vegetable dyes.

The handloom fabrics produced by the tribals of Assam, Nagaland, Manipur and Tripura, have always been acclaimed as of a very high quality. In the villages, every home had its loom. In Kemeng, the Mompas made carpets, mats and saddle-bags, and attained a high degree of artistic beauty and technical skill. In Siang and parts of Lohit, the Adis manufactured serviceable cotton blankets and wove their own clothes.

Wood-carving was another art practiced by the tribals for a long time. The Baigas and Gonds of Madhya Pradesh used to do excellent carving on wooden doors. The Murias of Bastar carved the pillars of their dormitories and made wooden masks for their dancers. The Santals, Garos and Nagas also used to do excellent wood-carving.

No other class of people suffered as a result of the policy of callous disregard towards cottage and village industries and arts and crafts in the days of the British power as much as the tribals. They were denied the requisite incentives; an atmosphere was created which made them feel that their arts were good for nothing. The restrictions imposed by the forest authorities, which denied them the raw materials for their arts and crafts, greatly contributed to the decline of the industry and is still a major obstacle to its development.

Other Sources of Employment

A socio-economic survey of tribal labour in the Tata Iron and Steel Company refers to the migration of Kol families from M.P. for work in plantations. It is reported that the Kols were preferred to other labourers on account of their larger output of work at a lower wage. In a family of four or five persons, two stayed behind at home to enable the rest to migrate. Between 1840 and 1870, the overseas migration of these labourers reached the figure of 55,000. The demand for tribal labour probably arose from the disappearance of Negro slave labour from plantation work in the European farms overseas. When the British Parliament, in 1834 abolished trade in slave labour from its colonies, there was fear that work and profits would come to an end. Then India was tapped as an alternative source of labour. The available records show that the journey from India was miserable beyond description leading to the death on an average of 15 persons a day. Referring to this emigration, Sir Grierson in 1882 reported, that the Province of Bihar has contributed nearly one half of the Calcutta emigration; the North Western Provinces and Oudh come next; the number from Central India is very small and Western Bengal stands third. It may be said generally that the easiest recruiting grounds in the Bengal Presidency were Bihar and Chhota-nagpur, the so-called 'Junglies' or Hill Coolies, probably for the most part Oraon Kols the natives of India, as Colonel Dalton calls them, being much sought after.'

In Bengal, Bihar and Madhya Pradesh, an important source of large-scale employment for the tribal people was the coal, iron and manganese mines and ancillary industries. The Santals have always been considered good pick-miners and coal-cutters. It was estimated that in the manganese mines of Madhya Pradesh about 50 per cent of the labour force was tribal. The iron and steel industries in Bihar also provided employment to Santals and Hos. The bulk of unskilled labour attached to the Tata Iron and Steel Company was provided by the tribal people. The advent of industrialization in the tribal areas established a kind of "tribal urban continuum".

The tea plantations in Assam and Bengal resulted in the migration of a large number of tribal families from the states of Orissa, Madhya Pradesh and Bihar. Several hundred tribal families of Kerala and Madras found employment in the coffee, tea and rubber plantations in the south.

Working conditions for the tribals employed in the tea gardens were, in the initial stages, extremely hard. As a result of their employment in industries and plantations, their economic condition improved to some extent; this small gain was offset by addiction and extravagance. It also resulted in a rapid process of de-tribalization.

Markets and Money Economy

The introduction of a money economy in the tribal areas has been of comparatively recent origin, for marketing as an institution was formerly very rare in most of the tribal areas. There was a weekly market or seasonal fair which enabled the tribal to barter his produce for his requirements. Gradually, money-lending by non-tribal people crept in and soon assumed formidable proportion. Writing in 1895 on the conditions of the Warlis, Thakurs and Kolis, Mr. J.P. Orr stated that, "The necessity of some policy or other in this direction arises from the notorious fact that by various means, the least iniquitous of which is cajolery, Brahmans, Parsees, Prabhus and Marwadis are getting hold of all land and rack-renting the resident cultivators. The Mahalkari of Umbergoan assures me that not 10 per cent of the Warlis and Kolis, whom he knew as holding large estates two decades back, can claim a single acre as their own today and on local inquiry I find the statement entirely corroborated".[4] Similar conditions prevailed in varying degrees throughout other tribal areas.

Bonded Labour

Money-lending gave birth to the obnoxious system of slavery, known variously as Sagri, Gothi, Hali, Vetti, etc. mostly in the central and southern zones. The misery of the Gothi knew no bounds. The service rendered was usually counted only towards the interest and he was merely given some food and clothing. In many cases the dependents of the Gothis had to serve the descendants of the creditor in lieu of the family debt, thus keeping the system of serfdom perpetually in existence. There was also a system of transferring the Gothi to another person who paid the outstanding debt.

Diseases, Traditional Medicinemen, Drinking-Water Supply

The monographs left by administrators and anthropologists suggest that the tribal people generally led a healthy life though some of them, of course, suffered from manifold diseases like malaria, yaws, scabies, leprosy, tuberculosis, venereal diseases and black-water fever. The incidence of malaria was high in almost all the tribal areas, particularly in the Bastar, Mandla, Chhindwara and Betul districts of Madhya Pradesh, throughout the Agency Areas of Andhra Pradesh and Wynad and the Nilgiris in the South. Yaws was prevalent in a virulent form in Bastar, Andhra Agency and in Orissa. Endemic goitre was common. It is stated by many authorities that the spread of venereal diseases and tuberculosis in the tribal areas was the result of outsiders entering into their areas.

The tribal people depended for the prevention and cure of their diseases on their traditional priests and medicinemen. They also used herbal remedies. Except for a few sporadic efforts by the government and Christian missionaries, no organized endeavour seems to have been made before independence to provide medical services in tribal areas.

Supply of drinking water has always been a serious problem in the difficult terrain of the tribal areas. This has been one of the reasons for the spread of intestinal diseases.

Consumption of Liquor

On the consumption of liquor, the observations of Mr. D. Symington in 1938, on the tribals were as follows:

"The Bhils and other aboriginal and hill tribes do themselves untold damage by their addiction to drink. Births, marriages, deaths, panchayat meetings, the presence of guests, festivals, etc., are all taken advantage of as excuses for drunkenness. The women and children are encouraged to drink too. I do not consider the position in this respect to be hopeless. I have every where found a dawning idea of the serious losses which the habit causes them and a desire, albeit perhaps a faint one to be cured of this level. Hitherto it has been accepted as axiomatic that the aboriginal cannot be made amenable to prohibition (a) because of his "religious" belief in the efficacy and necessity of liquor for all his ceremonies, and (b) because of his many facilities for illicit distillation. The former contention is losing its force, but the latter is at present true".[5]

The excise policy of the British administration in making the sale of liquor a monopoly and a source of revenue to the State had devastating effects on the tribal people.

Education

The Census figures of 1931 disclosed that among the tribals the literacy percentage was very low. Some details are given below :

Province	*Total Tribals*	*Tribals (literate)*	*Percentage*
1	*2*	*3*	*4*
Assam	9,92,390	14,094	1.4
Bengal	5,28,037	3,874	0.7
Bihar and Orissa	20,48,809	11,834	0.5
Central Provinces	13,51,615	6,769	0.5

As far as literacy was concerned, the condition of the tribal people was worse than that of the Scheduled Castes. The late Shri A.V. Thakkar observed in 1941:–

"Educational grants to aboriginal areas have been meagre and inadequate hitherto. Middle school, high school and college education among the Adivasis is, of course, negligible, if not altogether zero. We can find a few aborigines who have received or are now receiving University education. At present many Christian mission organizations and a few non-Christian Indian Bodies are conducting schools for aborigines with government aid in most cases. Their work, commendable as it is, appears to be only a drop in the ocean".[6]

Missionary activity had already begun to undermine their traditional tribal institutions such as the dormitories in the areas the missions operated. This was bound to lead to a vacuum resulting in general frustration. Mr. J.P. Mills, I.C.S., in his book, *The Rengma Nagas*, said that by preventing the converted Nagas from attending the dormitories, the Baptist missionaries made them run the risk of cultural disintegration. He felt that in the absence of provision for extensive or intensive training at home, other types of training only helped in creating tensions between parent and child.

Communications

The policy of isolating the tribals adopted by the British government was largely effected by their deliberate efforts in not developing communications in the tribal areas which remained cut off from the main currents of Indian civilization. The few roads that were constructed were for security purposes and to enable contractors to exploit the forest produce.

Administration of Justice

On the question of the administration of justice in the tribal areas, it is pertinent to quote the remarks of the late Shri S.C. Roy:–

"The British system of law and administration has further tended to impair the social solidarity of these tribes and has weakened the authority of the social heads or panchayats and the respect they formerly commanded. Until recently, when government orders validating tribal customary law regarding succession and inheritance were promulgated, the courts often disregarded the customs against inheritance by daughters and applied to them the Succession Act quite inconsistent with the fundamental social structure and ideas of kinship of the tribes. Until recently when rules against alienation of ancestral lands were promulgated by Government, the ancient tribal custom against such alienation was utterly disregarded".[7]

Representation in Legislatures

The tribal people were not adequately represented in the legislatures and on local bodies. There were only 24 tribal representatives in the Provincial Legislative Assemblies under the Government of India Act, 1935, against a total of 1,535 members. In the Central Provinces and Berar, where the tribals numbered as much as 20 per cent of the population, only one seat was reserved for them in the Legislative Assembly. Madras and Bombay also had only one seat apiece. In Bihar there were seven. In the Central Assembly, out of a total number of 250 seats, 105 were general, 82 were for Mohammedans and 19 were reserved for the Scheduled Castes. There was no provision of a seat for the tribal people.

The depressive and exploitative state of affairs mentioned resulted in distrust, disbelief in the minds of the tribal people. This state of affairs resulted into rebellions important of which are described below:

Tribal Rebellions against the Britishers

One of the early attempts made by the British to deal with tribal areas was when they entered Chhotanagpur in Bihar about the middle of the eighteenth century. The entry was resented and there was series of disturbances in 1789, 1801, 1807, and 1808 which had to be put down with the help of the armed forces. Lands were granted to the retired soldiers at the foot of the hills thus making a ring fence of loyal military men to encircle the tribals. A system of paying pension, which then amounted to Rs.15000 per year continued for about a century.

In 1831-32 followed the great uprising occupying the north-eastern side of the state viz. Rewa, Satna and Chhatarpur districts which was the result of discontentment among the tribal people against the settlement of their land with Hindus, Muslims, and Sikhs who had come from other parts of India. Other forms of oppression falling heavily on tribal cultivators were arbitrary enhancement of rents, forcible extraction of begar, and forcible dispossession of their Khuntkatti land. Khuntkatti land is that land which is cleared by the tribals of the forests for agriculture purposes. The suppression of rights was followed by a number of agrarian reforms to prevent tribal land from passing into the hands of non-tribals. The most important administrative reform was regulation XIII of 1833 as a result of which Chhotanagpur was declared a non-regulated area, as it was considered that the regulations which were intended for the non-advanced districts of Bengal and Bihar were not suited to it. These reforms and administrative steps, however, more or less remained on paper as the tribals were totally uninformed about them and even if they knew, they were too isolated to take any advantage of them.

Santal Rebellions

The Indian mutiny of 1857 was preceded by Santal Rebellion in 1855 which was excited by the oppression of the money-lenders and rapacious landlords. The rebellion was put down mercilessly by the British. The following passage from Thompson and Garrat's '*Rise and fulfillment of British rule in India*' is significant: "Inside India the Santal Rebellion of 1855 at the time was taken as a potent threat and aroused much of the alarm and savagery of repression which were to blaze out less than two years later. The Santal aborigin who in a state of nature live by the chase, a people of extreme simplicity and lovable were suffering from Hindu infiltration.

This meant change of habits and a whole train of perplexities. Their lands became alienated they were entangled in debts to people far clever than themselves. They were under foolish local officials who would not help them. The facile reply that the Santals should appeal to the civil courts, or prove their charges of oppression before the criminal courts was the answer of the father who should offer his son a stone when he asked for bread.

No one dreamt of insurrection by a race of gentle and harmless people with courts of justice ever open to them.

Then without warning a Santal inundation swept over the outlying regions of Bengal, spreading to within a hundred miles of Calcutta leaving open skulls of European and Indian alike, pouring out poisoned arrows, burning huts and bungalows. All ended, as it was bound to end in massacre and executions".[8]

In 1869 and 1870 there was unrest in Dhanbad between the Zamindar of Turli and Santal on the question of enhancement of rent and forest rights but the matter was settled by the intervention of Colonel Dalton, an exceptional official with great understanding of the tribes.

Rebellions in Madhya Pradesh

The Armed rebellion of Bastar, 1910. During the long minority of the successor Rudra Pratap Deo from 1891 to 1908 the administration remained entirely in the hands of officals of the British Government. Two of these were Englishmen, Colonel Fagan and Mr. W.V. Gayer who worked as administrators during this period for eighteen years. When the ruler was installed in power in 1908 he was required to act in consultation with his Diwan, RB Panda, Baijnath, an extra Assistant Commissioner from the Central Provinces. Not long afterwards in the beginning of February 1910 to be more precise, when Mr. EADC Brett the Political Agent was touring with the Diwan, the South-western part of the state, there was an armed rebellion of the Marias, Battras, Parjas and Bison horn Marias. Mr. (afterwards) Sir BP Standen, Chief Secretary to the Chief Commissioner of the central provinces narrated in his admirable report dated 29th March 1910 to the Government of India the causes and course of rebellion and the measures taken to suppress it. According to Mr. Standen, the rising began with arson, robbery, and violence towards foreigners who were savagely beaten and in some cases murdered. Their women folk being striped and turned out naked, it was in short a movement of Bastar state for Bastar forest dwellers. The political agent's view that the grievance of the aborigin might have been largely genuine was endorsed, but it was also pointed out that there were precedents for calling in of the aborigins to take side in royal intrigues; that the idea of persuading them to do so occurred repeatedly in the accounts of such intrigues; that though, they habitually carried arms to kill games, they were very peaceful and retiring but excitable and greatly under the influence of their hereditary leaders and that Lala Kalindra Singh who had been increasing his influence over them for 30 years could have had no difficulty in getting up the rising.

In his famous book *'The Maria Gonds of Bastar,'* W V Grigson, the administrator of Bastar has given a good account of the causes of "rebellion..." But Mr. Gayer was succeeded by an

Indian superintendent who held charge for the last few years of the minority and then continued till 1910 as Raja Rudra Pratap Deo's Diwan. He had served successfully as Diwan of Kalahandi state and his intentions were admirable. Unfortunately, he was unable to control his subordinates to see that his excellent orders were enforced. He was responsible also for two unpopular initiatives. The first was a policy of instituting new primary schools all over the state. The masters assisted by attendance peons bullied the ryots into sending their children to school where they levied forced labour and exhorted free supplies.

The second was reservation of a large area of the state forests, a measure necessary to check the wholesale destruction of valuable timber by the aboriginals practicing shifting cultivation. But bound by its very nature and its interference with long cherished rights to arouse suspicion.

It called therefore for the great tact and the people should have been carefully prepared for the measure, and protected from any avoidable hardship in its execution. Instead it was carried out abruptly. Every village in the reserved areas was destroyed, though provision ought to have been made for forest village as a source of forest labour, and if this had been done few of the villages need have been disturbed; the old village land still often remain treeless in the forest, and in recent years it has been necessary to try and attempt settlers back to found much needed forest villages. Oppression by state officials and by immigrant settlers, excessive levy of forced labour and supplies, unpopular new measures and the apparent blindness of the Raja and his Diwan to popular grievances produced deep discontent, which was worked up by Lal Kalendra Singh, the first cousin and former Diwan of Raja Bhairam Deo in the hope of securing the succession for himself. The Marias Bhattras and Parja of Jagdalpur tahsil and some of the Bison Horn Marias and others in Dantewara tahsil and further south broke into rebellion in which the Murias of Antagarh and Kondagaon joined, only the Zamindars and the Marias of the Abhujhmar hills abstaining. The tribes converged on Jagdalpur, the Diwan who had been touring the south fled into the Chanda district. A half battalion of regular Punjabi troops and a large detachments of armed Central Provinces police soon suppressed and disarmed the rebels. A few ring leaders who had been guilty of cruel murders of isolated state officials were hanged and several hundred men flogged, a punishment really more humane for such primitive men than imprisonment. Lal Kalendra Singh and a few of his associates were banished. The Raja was deprived of powers and an experienced Englishman Mr. James May was appointed Diwan. The rebellion had been marked by keen hostility towards the immigrant exploiters and a movement to keep Bastar for Bastaris.

Sardari Agitation of 1887

Sardari agitation was against compulsory labour, periodical contributions, illegal enhancement of rent by landlords. In 1890, the Lt. Governor Sir Stewart Balley held a conference in Ranchi which resulted in measures intended to stop agrarian discontent. The position however did not improve.

Simultaneously, there were large scale conversions to Christianity as many of the tribals believed that by becoming Christians they would be protected from their landlords by the missionaries. At the same time, such a mass conversion created a sense of nervousness among those who were not converted, who thought that the British Government would protect the Christians, but would leave their non-Christian brethren at the mercy of their landlords.

The Birsa Movement

In 1885, Mundas again revolted under the leadership of Birsa Munda. He exercised extraordinary influence over the Mundas and the Oraons through his new religion which was a mixture of Hinduism and Christianity. The Birsa Movement was directed both against the Hindu landlords and money-lenders and the Christian missionaries. After the revolt was put down, it was decided to prepare a complete record of rights to give protection against exploitation by non-tribals. The inception of settlement and survey observations in Ranchi district was thus a direct outcome of the Birsa Movement. Now a yearly prize of one lakh rupees has been kept to be awarded to that person who does social service among the tribals, after the name of this leader.

Other Revolts due to Land Alienation

Exploitation of tribals was the cause of many other disturbances, such as the Rampa Rebellion in East Godavari, the Bastar rising of 1911 and the civil disobedience by the Kond Maliahs of Orissa and by the Tana Bhagats in 1920. In comparatively recent times also, in the Adilabad district of Hyderabad, many Gonds and Kolmas rebelled in 1941 as a result of the alienation of land and forest reservation rules.

However these uprisings could not achieve anything substantial as regards the upliftment of the tribal people. Very few if any of the grievances were redressed. Government sought to tighten control over the administration of the area. Infiltration of Christian missionaries increased, with some good results such as increase in literacy and they provided the window through which the tribals could have a glimpse of the outerworld.

Conclusion

This review of the conditions of the tribals before independence goes to show that the policy of isolation and drift meant nothing more than a maintenance of status quo. It resulted in reducing the tribals to a state of penury in most part of India. They were at the lowest level of literacy except in certain parts, their lands were heavily encumbered and a good portion had already passed into the hands of non-tribals. Their rights in forest were definitely encroached upon. Outside elements introduced for the purposes of government and forest work continued to exploit them. On many an occasion the tribals rose in revolt and on many an occasion reforms were ordered but all these proved futile.

REFERENCES

1. The Government of India's Dispatch to Secretary of State, No. 1 of 1935, 24th Dec. 1935.
2. Report of the Scheduled Areas and Scheduled Tribes Commission—Shri U.N. Dhebar, Vol. I, 1961, p. 22.
3. Sarkar, Sumit, *Modern India 1885-1947*, p. 44.
4. Orr, J.P. as quoted by the Scheduled areas and the Scheduled Tribes Commission popularly known as Dhebar Commission, 1961, p. 27.

5. D. Symington as quoted by Dr. Verrier Elwin in, 'A New Deal for Tribal India', p. 13.
6. The Scheduled Areas and the Scheduled Tribes Commission, 1961, p. 29.
7. The Scheduled Areas and the Scheduled Tribes Commission, 1961, p. 30.
8. Thompson and Garrat, "Rise and fulfillment of British rule in India." as quoted in the Scheduled Areas and the Scheduled Tribes Commissions report, 1961, p. 23.

4

Tribal Development—The Constitution and The Scheduled Tribes

Constitutional Safeguards

The independence on 15 August, 1947 brought a new era to the people of India. It led to the formation of a Constitution (1950) for the nation which guaranteed to all its citizens Justice—social, economic and political, liberty of thought, expression, belief, faith and worship, equality of status and opportunity; and to promote among them fraternity assuring the dignity of the individual and the unity and integrity of the nation.

For the first time in the administration of the tribal people, the Constitution placed the responsibility of their welfare on the popular governments, through the President and the Governors. The result was far reaching and momentous.

The former policy provided for a sort of protection achieved largely through isolation even though many protests were raised against it. Despite their isolation and their comparatively poor economic condition, many of the tribals were already showing keen desire to move forward and develop economically, politically and socially. There were several reasons. The welfare of Scheduled Tribes had engaged the attention of national leaders. It was one of the points in the constructive programmes of the Indian National Congress. Gandhiji himself emphasized the need to develop the tribes living in inaccessible places so as to ensure their integration with the rest of the country.

Although, the public remained ignorant or misinformed about the tribal people, the ground was prepared for the new attitude and policies of recent years. Shri A.V. Thakkar and other social workers did pioneering work among the tribes. The name of the late Sarat Chandra Roy will long be remembered in Chotanagpur as a champion of tribal rights. Christian missionaries in certain parts, especially in Assam and Bihar, did much to rouse the tribal people to a greater desire for progress. A few eminent British officials such as the late Sir W.V. Grigson, and Dr. J.H. Hutton made important suggestions for the welfare of the tribes and worked for their welfare for many years. A number of Indian anthropologists even at this stage drew attention to the need of the tribes; on a more popular level translations of their songs and stories revealed that they had a rich view of poetry and this gradually paved the way to a proper appreciation of tribal culture.

It was, however, only with the attainment of Independence, that India, which was gradually becoming conscious of her tribes became fully aware of her responsibilities towards them. Indeed one of the first acts of Constituent Assembly was to appoint what was known as the "Excluded and the Partially Excluded Areas" (other than Assam) sub-committee with Shri A.V. Thakkar as its Chairman.

The most important findings of this committee which was accepted by the Constituent Assembly was to establish the principle that the new democratic state has a responsibility for the welfare of the tribal people and the development of the tribal areas, however, remote and inaccessible they might be. The tribal problem thereby became an intergral part of the development of the Indian people as a whole.

The sub-committee emphasized that "the great need of the aboriginal was protection from exploitation of his agricultural land and virtual serfdom under the money-lenders".

It also sounded a note of caution. The tribes themselves are for the most part extremely simple people who can be and are exploited easily by plains-folk resulting in the passage of land formerly cultivated by them to money-lenders and other erstwhile non-agriculturists. The tribes have their own customs and way of life with institutions like tribal and village panchayats or councils which are very effective in the smooth running of village administration. The sudden disruption of tribal customs by exposure, to the impact of a more complicated and sophisticated manner of life is capable of doing great harm. Considering past experience and the strong temptation, it is essential to provide statutory safeguards for the protection of land which is the mainstay of the aboriginals economic life and for his customs and institutions which, apart, from being his own, contains elements of value.

A novel emphasis made by the sub-committee was to stress the importance of the tribals living in the plains, outside the "Excluded and Partially Excluded" areas and interspersed with the rest of the population. They had previously been greatly neglected, failing to attract the attention of academic anthropologists. The sub-committee urged that any scheme which confirmed attention to the tribals living in excluded or partially excluded areas would be, and that all tribals where they were found should be brought within the contemplated constitutional arrangements. This was a significant change from the policy hither to be pursued and focussed the attention of the government on the necessity of viewing the tribal problem as a whole.

The sub-committee, however, realized that it would not be possible for geographical and other reasons to give the same protection to the tribal people living in the plains as could be given to those in the excluded and partially excluded areas.

Keeping in view the facts mentioned above, the following provisions were made in the Constitution to provide protection from exploitation by the so-called advanced people and give incentives for adopting various measures of development.

The generous heart of a new and resurgent India was expressed in the moving words of Article 46 of the Constitution.

"The state shall promote with special care the education and economic interests of the weaker sections of the people, and in particular, of the Scheduled Castes and the Scheduled Tribes and shall protect them from social injustice and all forms of exploitation."

Article 164 sub-para provides for the appointment of Minister in charge of tribal welfare in the states of Bihar, Madhya Pradesh and Orissa. Besides tribal welfare these Ministers can also hold the charge of Scheduled Castes and the Backward Classes development and the other.

Other Articles empower the President to make arrangements for the implementation of this high ideal. Article 244, empowers him to declare any area, which has a substantial population of tribal people, as a Scheduled Area under the Fifth Schedule or in Assam, Tripura, Meghalaya and Mizoram as Tribal Areas in Sixth Schedule. Under the Fifth Schedule, the executive power of the state extends to the Scheduled Areas but the government is vested with the authority to modify state and the central laws and to make regulations for their peace and good government. The Scheduled Areas of the State is given in Annexure No. II. In all states having Scheduled areas a 'Tribes Advisory Council' has to be set up. The Governor has to submit periodical reports to the President. It is also provided that the executive-power of the Union shall extend to giving of directions to the state for the administration of the said areas.

Article 275 of the Constitution provides for supplemental financial assistance to the states for the implementation of various schemes for the development of the tribal people in line with the constitutional provisions.

Articles 330, 332 and 334(a) provide for the reservation of seats for the Scheduled Tribes in the House of the People and the Legislative Assemblies for a certain period. Article 335 provides for the reservation in services.

Article 338 provides for the appointment of a special officer to investigate all matters relating to the safeguards provided for the Scheduled Castes and the Scheduled Tribes under the Constitution and report to the President upon the working of those safeguards at such intervals as the President may direct and the President shall cause all such reports to be laid before each House of the Parliament.

Under Article 339, the President may appoint a commission to investigate the conditions of the Scheduled Tribes and level of their development.

Under Article 342, statewise list of the Scheduled Tribes

could be declared. List of the Scheduled Tribes in the States is in Annexure No. III.

As per constitutional provisions, it is quite interesting to know the names of the persons who held the charge of the Minister of tribal welfare in M.P. Late Raja Naresh Chandra Singh of Sarangarh was the first Minister in charge of tribal welfare under the able guidance of Pt. Ravishankar Shukla, as Chief Minister.

Shri Goverdhan Das Khandelwal

Shri Bhanu Pratap Singh Komakhan

Shri Vasant Rao Uikey

Dr. Bhanwar Singh Porte

Smt. Kamla Devi

Shri Arjun Singh (C.M.)

Shri Manju Rai (S.M.)

Shri Motilal Vora (C.M.)

Smt. Jamuna Devi (S.M.)

Shri Kishan Lal Kurre (Dy. M.)

Shri Shiv Bhanu Singh Solanki

Shri Govardhan Netam (Dy. M.)

Shri Baliram Kashyap

Shri Shivpratap Singh (S.M.)

Shri Haridas Bhardwaj

Shri Kanti Lal Bhuria

Shri Ganpat Singh Uikey (S.M.)

(Abbreviations C.M.—Chief Minister, S.M.—State Minister Dy. M.—Deputy Minister).

The record pertaining to the period held by each minister is not available before 1985. After 1985, however, the charge held by each minister is given of. Two chief ministers viz. Sarvshri Arjun Singh and Motilal Vora held the charge of the Minister tribal welfare also.

The Fifth Schedule: Under Fifth Schedule of the Constitutior two important provisions have been made:

1. Constituting the Tribes Advisory Council, and

2. Submission of the periodical reports on the administration of the Scheduled area by H.E. the Governor.

An important provision has also been made to make new laws or modify old and existing one in so far their application to the Scheduled Area of the state is concerned. The provision has been made with the sole objective of ensuring peace and good government for the tribal people.

1. The Tribes Advisory Council

Rules have been framed for constituting the Tribes Advisory Council. As such there should be 20 members in the Council composed of 15 elected members of the Legislative Assembly; Five members to be nominated from the social workers and other eminent persons from amongst the tribes or persons working for their development.

At least two meetings should be held each year. In the meeting of the Tribes Advisory Council, policy matters relating to the development of the Scheduled Tribes should be discussed and finalized. All the development mechanism adopted or likely to be adopted should be discussed.

A study was conducted by the Government of India on the working of the Tribes Advisory Council in the states. The observations in the study is quite revealing. It has been observed from the minutes of these meetings that instead of discussing the policy matters the members find it convenient to discuss the problems of their areas and make complaints about the public servants. This defeates the very purpose of constituting the Tribes Advisory Council.

Different governments, have different attitudes towards the Tribes Advisory Councils. The BJP government under Shri Sunderlal Patwa did not bother for the Tribes Advisory Council. But the present Congress government under the Chief Ministership of Shri Digvijay Singh not only is fixing and convening regular meetings of the TAC but is also taking care to carry out the advice it gives. This may be due to the fact that the tribals, have voted for the Congress party in majority and brought them in power.

2. Submission of the Periodical Reports on the Administration of the Scheduled Areas

The Governor of the state submits annual report on the administration of the Scheduled area. The tribal sub-plan area extend to 35 districts whereas the Scheduled area extends only to 21 districts. The Tribal sub-plan area is more akin and nearer to the existing administrative structure. Therefore, the departments from where the feedback comes for the report on the administration of the tribal areas, finds it more convenient to report the progress of the tribal areas as a whole and not the Scheduled Area in particular. As the Scheduled Area and the existing administrative units have not been dovetailed therefore, the report which is being sent to HE the President of India is the progress report of the development schemes of the tribal sub-plan areas and not the report of the Scheduled Tribal Area. It may be mentioned that the Scheduled Area is predominantly tribal and backward area which needs special care and approach for development.

The report is not in terms of qualitative assessment of the impact of the development schemes on the tribals and administration of Scheduled Area but a collection of statistics pertaining to the financial and physical achievements. As Jawaharlal Nehru, the late Prime Minister of India had said, "the development of the tribal people should be judged not in terms of achievements of the physical and financial targets but in terms of the quality of life of the tribal people involved.' This view he had expressed while writing the foreword of the book *Philosophy for NEFA* written by Dr. Verrier Elwin[1].

Funds under the Article 275 of the Constitution. Under this provision, supplementary funds are provided to the states for the development of the Scheduled Tribes. It is not always understood that these special provisions are intended to supplement and not to supplant the general welfare programmes which are directed to the entire community of which Scheduled Tribes are only a part. In earlier plan periods, (upto Fifth Plan) the Government of India had left the utilization of these funds entirely to the state government. When it was found that the fund were used for other purposes beside tribal development, the Government of India issued strict guidelines for the utilization of these funds. The guidelines provide that the funds could be used for family oriented economic benefit schemes up to 75 per cent, 25 per cent funds could be used for the infrastructural development incidental to family oriented economic development schemes of the tribal areas of the state.

The programme of giving grants-in-aid to states envisaged under Article 275 is based on the following considerations:

1. Though, the subject for which grants are given is primarily a state responsibility, the state government are often short of funds and unless the Union helps them the tribal programmes may not be fully implemented.
2. The Union Government has an equal concern to ensure that Welfare services, development activities are mainly of a certain standard throughout the country.
3. The Union Government further has an added advantage in being able to co-ordinate welfare activities in the states and to improve the quality of the performance through their technical advice.
4. Through a programme of matching grants, the State government can be persuaded to earmark a portion of their own revenues for welfare work.

This grant has to be distributed amongst various states, therefore, certain criteria have been evolved to determine the size of this grant to various states.

1. Population of the Scheduled Tribes in each state and the extent of the Scheduled areas.
2. Level of development reached by state government to contribute 50 per cent from their general revenue specifically for the welfare of the Scheduled Tribes.

The plan periodwise allocations and utilization of funds in the state of M.P. has been given in Chapter-IV.

The State Government of M.P. has not been quite rigid in following the guidelines of the Central Government in the utilization of SCA funds. The funds have been given to different departments of the state government on whom the responsibility of identifying family or economic development programmes lay. These departments failed to identify such programmes and spend the amount on different construction activities. Construction activity is quite easy to carry out as it also fulfils the vested interest of the people who are interested in construction.

The funds are released to the general kitty of the state government. The finance department takes the amount into its ways and means position and releases the funds as per their convenience and not as per the requirement of the tribal people.

A number of committees and commissions have been set up to study the utilization of these funds. These commissions and committees have studied the total utilization processes and found that to a great extent the funds have not been used for the purpose for which they are released. It has been suggested that the funds instead of being given to the general kitty of the State Government, should directly be .placed at the disposal of the nodal department responsible to co-ordinate the development activities meant for the tribal people with other departments.[2] The financial year should begin from June-July, the actual months of starting development works and not March-April as at present.[3] The funds should be made non-lapsable at the end of the financial year so that the balance could be utilised next year.[4]

It has also been suggested that a strong machinery should be set up to watch the programme of various schemes. The basic problem to be tackled is that funds should not be spent for purpose other than for which it has been meant.

As per special provisions relating to certain classes (part XVI) in Article 330, 33 seats have been reserved for the Scheduled Tribes in the House of the People i.e., Lok Sabha.

75 seats are reserved for the Scheduled Tribes as per Article 332 in the Vidhan Sabha. This forms 23.43 per cent of the total seats. In the present day of caste-class politics these people form a solid chunk from a single community to help a particular party.

Reservation in Services

Looking at their backwardness and injustice done to them from ages their claims have been granted as per Article 335 of the Constitution for different services and posts. As per Madhya Pradesh Lok Seva (Anusuchit Jatiyon, Anusuchit Janjatiyon Aur Anya Pichhada Vargon Ke Liya Arakshan), Adhiniyam, 1994. 18

per cent in the class I and II services and 20 per cent in class III and IV have been reserved for the Scheduled Tribes.

With a view to watching the implementation of this Act in letter and spirit a standing committee has been made of the following members.

1.	Minister of Scheduled Castes and Scheduled Tribes	Chairman
2.	Five members of the Madhya Pradesh Legislative Assembly to be nominated by the speaker out of which, one each shall be a member belonging to the Scheduled Castes and Scheduled Tribes	Member
3.	Secretary in charge of the General Administration Department	Member
4.	Secretary in charge of the SC, ST and Backward Class development	Member Secretary

The standing committee will perform the following functions, viz.

(a) Review the implementation of the provisions of this Act and rules made there under.

(b) Suggest measure for the removal of difficulties in implementing the provisions of this Act and the rules made.

(c) Such other functions as the state government may from time to time assign to the committee.

The state government shall prepare an Annual Report on the working of this Act and lay the same before the Legislative Assembly.

As per these provisions the representation of the Scheduled Tribes in the services are as follows:

As per information made available by the General Administration Department in all there are 35,220 posts reserved for the Scheduled Tribes out of these, 28,033 posts are filled in and 7,187 posts are lying vacant. The following departments have filled in all the posts in the reserved category available to them:

	Department	*No. of Posts*
1.	Women and Child Development	13
2.	Co-operation	149
3.	Tribal and Scheduled Castes Welfare	4310
4.	Urban Welfare	2
5.	Revenue	1816
6.	School Education	9161
7.	Narmada Valley Development	226
8.	Labour	135
9.	Commerce and Industries	239
10.	Transport	73
	Total	16124

However, 30 departments could fill up only 10,509 posts, nearly 60 per cent of the total posts, i.e., 17,696 available. Departmentwise details are given in Appendix–I. Maximum vacancies in public health and family welfare department i.e., 4,318 posts. Candidates having degree in science and other technical subjects are required for these posts. As these are not available it is difficult to find suitable candidates for them. The departmentwise position as on 1-10-96 is given in the Appendix–II. Departmentwise, Service classwise vacancy position is as follows :

Class I	262
Class II	1,305
Class III	5,330
Class IV	290
Total	7,187

Thus, maximum vacancies exist in class III because candidates having requisite qualification are not available. Though, there are less number of posts available in class II and I but in these categories also, it is quite difficult to get the candidates having requisite qualifications.

With a view to removing the backlog, special recruitment

drives have been conducted by various departments. Even then it has not been possible to fill in the vacancies. On the one hand the Scheduled Tribes and Scheduled Castes candidates are registered in the Employment Exchange, on the other, the posts reserved for them are lying vacant. It may be possible that the ST, SC candidat may not have the requisite qualifications, so they may not be selected. But there are ITIs and the vocational training centres which can train the ST candidates for the jobs. If there is a better co-ordination amongst the departments having vacant posts and the coaching and training institutes the situation can definitely improve.

As per provisions in Article 338 of the Constitution Commissioner for the Scheduled Castes and the Tribes is to be appointed. The first Commissioner was Shri L.M. Shrikant. A routine report was submitted till Dr. B.D. Sharma was appointed who made tremendous changes and improvement in the report to include the real problems as are being faced by the tribals and their remedial measures statewise. He made it obligatory on the part of the state and central government to lay these annual reports in the Parliament as well as the Legislative Assemblies for the discussion by the members. However, after 65th Amendment of the Constitution, the post of commissioner has been merged with that of the commission for the Scheduled Castes and Tribes. The commission has seven members including the Chairman and the Vice-Chairman. Shri Hanuman-thappa is at present the Chairman of the commission.

Under Article 339, the President may appoint a commission to investigate and report the conditions of the ST and SC. The last commission appointed by the President of India was in the year 1960, under the Chairmanship of Shri U.N. Dhebar. The commission submitted its report in the year 1961. Thereafter no commission has been appointed.

Under Article 342, statewise list of the Scheduled Tribes have been prepared. After the framing of the Constitution in 1950 the list was revised in 1956 on the occasion of the reorganization of the State of M.P. and then in 1976. The list has been circulated vide Government of M.P. GAD (Tribal and Scheduled Castes Cell) No. 49/1907-1 dated 31st January, 1978. As per this list there are 46 communities included as the Scheduled Tribes. This list cannot be said to be the all inclusive exhaustive list of the tribal communities in the state. There are many more communities who want to be included in this list so that they can enjoy the benefits given to the Scheduled Tribes. Some are taking advantage of similarities of names and want to use this to be admitted to the Scheduled Tribes rank.

As per GAD circular No. F 7-1/1/aa pra/91 dated 20-02-1991 issued by the Government of Madhya Pradesh the following officers have been nominated to issue the certificates for the tribal people.

(1) Collector, Additional Collector, Deputy Collector, SDO, Sub-Divisional Magistrate, City Magistrate.

(2) Tahsildar.

(3) Naib Tahsildar.

(4) Project Officer, Major and Medium Integrated Tribal Development Project.

These officers have been instructed to adopt such a procedure which will guarantee the issue of the certificate to the real tribal people and not to the fraudulent ones but many fake tribals manage to take certificate. Government of India, Ministry of Welfare have issued guidelines for the issue of the certificates.

A person who wants the certificiate should by birth belong to the same community. It should be ascertained that his parents also belong to the same community, the person should be domicile of the State. Contrary to the Scheduled Castes he may belong to any religion. He should be a resident of that particular area from where he wants the ST certificate.

In case a person migrates to a State where he is not recognized as a Scheduled Tribe his status as a ST will depend upon the position of the ST to the State he belongs.

The tribal position does not change by marriage. The child gets the status and tribal position of parents who adopt them. Every care has to be taken to see that all the formalities in this case has been followed. As per Hindu Adoption Act 1956, the child belongs to the parents who adopts him. However no adoption is valid if it is the case of a 15 years boy/girl and he is married. After adoption the boy or girl in question should not have any relationship with parent of their origin.

Acts and Rules for Protecting the Interests of ST

The State Government of M.P. is quite concerned about various problems faced by the tribals. To help the tribals in getting relief from those problems a numbers of Acts have been passed. A list of which is given in Appendix-III.

These Acts relate to indebtedness, land alienation, legal aids, giving possession of alienated land, financial relief to helpless and distressed STs. One commission named as Anusuchit Janjati Ayog has been established to work as watch dog for the interest of the STs, review the development scheme for them and submit its report to the government with suitable recommendations.

Appendix No. I

Position of Reserved Posts Filled Departmentwise

Sl. No.	*Departments*	*Filled in Posts upto Sept. 1996*	*Vacant Posts as on 1-10-1996*
1.	Public Health and Family Welfare	1,913	4318
2.	Agriculture	381	786
3.	Higher Education	967	706
4.	Manpower Planning	423	330
5.	Public Works Department	673	160
6.	Panchayat and Rural Development	618	188
7.	Water Resource Department	1,074	161
8.	Veterinary Department	598	811
9.	Public Health Engineering	252	67
10.	Culture	68	50
11.	General Administration	110	41
12.	Commercial Taxes Department	218	54
13.	Public Relation	47	34
14.	Dairy	34	33
15.	Forest Department	811	23
16.	Rehabilitation	—	21
17.	Fisheries	147	11
18.	Housing and Environment	51	14
19.	Engineering	29	12
20.	Home Department	173	8
21.	Mining	37	7
22.	Social Welfare	72	5
23.	Law and Legal Aid	2	3
24.	Food and Civil Supplies	67	3
25.	Jail	829	30
26.	Parliamentary Affairs	1	2
27.	Local Self-Government	26	1
28.	Planning, Economic and Statistic Department	284	1
29.	Sports and Youth Welfare	6	1
30.	Rural Industries	598	34
	Total	10509	7187

Appendix No. II

Vacancy Position in Different Departments Under Special Recruitment Drive

Sl. No.	Name of the Departments	I	II	III	IV	Total	Particulars
1	2	3	4	5	6	7	8
1.	Public Health and Family Welfare	64	449	3560	245	4318	In class III Health Dai Assistant Surgeon
2.	Agriculture	—	55	733	—	788	Mainly Rural Extension Officer Development Officer
3.	Higher Education	31	675	—	—	706	Asst. Professor Librarian
4.	Manpower Planning	155	6	145	24	330	
5.	Public Works Deptt.	—	1	157	2	160	1. LDC 2. Tracer 3. Cartographer
6.	Panchayat and Rural Development	—	4	184	—	188	Assistant Engineer and Others
7.	Water Resource Deptt.	—	1	160	—	161	Stenographer
8.	Veterinary Deptt.	—	71	10	—	81	Grade 3
9.	Public Health Engineering	—	8	59	—	67	Assistant Engineer
10.	Culture	—	6	44	—	50	Artist
11.	General Administration	—	—	41	—	41	Stenographer
12.	Commercial Taxes Deptt.	—	—	54	—	54	
13.	Public Relation	—	—	34	—	34	
14.	Dairy	1	2	30	—	33	
15.	Forest Deptt.	—	—	23	—	23	
16.	Rehabilitation	—	—	8	13	21	
17.	Fisheries	10	—	—	1	11	
18.	Housing and Environment	—	2	12	—	14	
19.	Engineering Deptt.	—	1	11	—	12	
20.	Home Deptt.	—	5	3	—	8	
21.	Mining	—	6	1	—	7	
22.	Social Welfare	—	3	2	—	5	
23.	Law and Legal Aid	—	—	3	—	3	

1	2	3	4	5	6	7	8
24.	Food and Civil Supplies	—	2	1	—	3	
25.	Parliamentary Affairs	—	—	1	1	2	
26.	Local Self Government	—	—	—	1	1	
27.	Planning Economic and Statistic Department	—	1	—	—	1	
28.	Sports and Youth Welfare	—	—	1	—	1	
29.	Rural Industries	1	7	23	3	34	
	Total	262	11305	5330	290	7187	

Appendix No. III

Various Acts and Rules Pertaining to the ST applicable to the State of M.P.

Sl.No.	*Name of Acts/Rules*	*Purpose*
1.	The M.P., Anusuchit Jati Aur Janjati Rin Sahayata Adhiniyam 1967 (Amend 33/72)	To provide relief to the ST/SC families from indebtedness and to free them from the clutches of the money-lenders
2.	The M.P. Gramin Rin Vimukti Tatha Rin Sthagan Adhiniyam, 1973	To provide relief to the members of ST/SC, small and marginal farmers and landless labourers and to impose punishment including imprisonment to those who are found guilty for violating the provision of the Act.
3.	M.P. Samaj ke Kamjor Vargon Ke Krishi Bhoomi Dharkon Ka Udhar Dene Valon Ke Bhumi Hadapne Sambandhi Kuchakron Se Paritran Tatha Mukti Adhiniyam, 1976	To better the economic conditions of holders of agricultural land of the weaker section of the society by providing further relief from agricultural indebtedness by nullifying the land grabbing designs reported to in many a form by money lenders of money while and after extending credit to them and matters connected therewith.
4.	The M.P. Anusuchit Janjati Sahukar Viniyam, 1972	To make it compulsory for the persons carrying on business of money-lending in the scheduled area to obtain money-lenders licenses, thus binding the money-lenders to charge reasonable

Sl.No.	Name of Acts/Rules	Purpose
		rate of interest. The records of the money-lenders shall be subject to scrutiny by the persons/agencies made competent under the Viniyam.
5.	The M.P. Samaj ke Kamjor Vargon ke liye Vidhik Sahayata Tatha Vidhik Salah Adhiniyam, 1976	To provide Judicial assistance in the form of legal aid and legal advice to the weaker sections of the people with a view to bringing the system of justice within their reach and thereby making the legal process a surer means to social and economic justice and for matters ancillary thereto.
6.	The M.P. Vassthan Dakhalkar (Bhumiswami Adhikaran Ka Pradan Kiya Jana) Adhiniyam, 1980	To provide for the conferring of Bhumiswami Rights on landless persons in respect of dwelling house and sites on or appertainent to agricultural lands in non-urban areas in the state of M.P.
7.	The M.P. Lok Adhikarhon Ke Madhyam Se Bees-Sutriya Karyakaram ka Karyanvayan Adhiniyam-1989	To provide for implementation of 20 point economic development programme through public agencies and matter ancillary thereto.
8.	The Anusuchit Jan Jati Ayog Adhiniyam (amended)	To provide for the establishment of Anusuchit Jati, Anuchit Janjati and Pichada Varg Ayog for the state and to regulate its duties and functions. The commission shall act as watch-dog for the protection offered to the members of the SCs, STs and OBCs, under the constitution and under any other law for the time being in force.
9.	The M.P. Nagariya Kshetron ke Bhoomihin Vyakti Pattadhriti Adhikaron Ka Pradan kiya Jana Adhiniyam, 1984	To provide for the conferring of leasehold rights on landless persons in respect of sites for dwelling house in urban areas in the state of M.P.
10.	The M.P. Anusuchit Janjati (Kanooni) Sahayata Niyam 1960	To provide help to poor and resourceless ST, families to seek justice in the courts of law.

Sl.No.	*Name of Acts/Rules*	*Purpose*
11.	The M.P. Harijan Adivasi Rahat Yojana Niyam, 1979, (amended)	To provide immediate financial aid to poor and helpless ST and SC families in distress.
12.	The M.P. Asyaprashyta Nivaranarth Antarjatiya Vivah Protsahan Yojana Nigam	To recognize and honour the inter-caste marriage in order to eradicate the observance of untouchability.
13.	The protection of Civil Rights Act, 1955	To prescribe punishment for the (preaching and practice of untouchability) for the enforcement of any disability arising therefrom and for matters connected therewith.
14.	The M.P. Scheduled Area (Restriction on Research Survey, photography, films etc.) Rules, 1982.	To provide restrictions on irresponsible display and mis-representation of tribal values and their mode of culture.

REFERENCES

1. *Philosophy for NEFA*, Elwin, Verrier, Dr. Foreword (1958).
2. Report of the Scheduled Areas and the Scheduled Tribes Commission, New Delhi, 1961, p. 83.
3. *Op. cit.,* para II (c) p. 82.
4. *Op. cit.,* para II (b) p. 82.

5

The Tribal Development Strategy Before and After Tribal Sub-Plan Concept

In the earlier chapters, the tribals, their habitat, demographic characteristics, problems faced by them have been discussed. The British policy of administration and the condition of the tribes before independence have also been given in details. The constitutional safeguards and various rules and acts made have also been described.

Now, after independence the central and state governments have become conscious of their responsibilities towards the development of the tribes. The welfare and relief measures taken by different constituent states before reorganization of M.P. have been shown in this chapter. After reorganization of the state and before adopting the tribal sub-plan strategy, special development agency had been evolved. The priorities of the programmes and strategy during different plan periods have also been discussed.

After adopting the tribal sub-plan strategy, the delineation of the tribal sub-plan area, special implementing agency, monitoring mechanism have been given in details in the present chapter. The primitive tribal groups are most vulnerable among the Scheduled Tribes. Their welfare and development measures are also given in this chapter. The Madhya Pradesh Scheduled Tribe Development Corporation specially set up for economic development of the tribals has also been discussed in this chapter.

Evolution of the Special Implementing Agencies

Development of Scheduled Tribes is a constitutional responsibility as mentioned in the Constitution. The Fifth Schedule envisages a special type of administration for the peace and good government of the Scheduled areas. The Governors of the states have been given special powers to frame laws, rules and regulations to safeguard the interests of the tribal people. The Governor can-frame new acts/laws or prohibit the application of certain laws, both state and central or amend them in so far as their application to the Scheduled areas is concerned.

The State of M.P., has been constitued after merging four states viz. Mahakoshal, Madhya Bharat, Vindhya Pradesh and Bhopal. Every state was working for the tribal development in its own way. In Mahakoshal, 30 tribal welfare centres were established. In every centre, there was a middle school, and a hostel. Under one centre five to six primary schools were also opened. With every middle school, a small farm, cottage industries training centre, a co-operative society and a veterinary unit was attached. At the end of the plan period 782 primary schools, 61 middle schools and 61 hostels were there in this state. One important institution i.e., the Tribal Research Institute, which was supposed to do research work among the tribes, provide training to the workers in the tribal areas and evaluate the tribal development programmes was opened at Chhindwara, in 1954.

In Madhya Bharat, 16 community development centres were opened. A balwadi, a primary school, a hostel and a cottage industry training centre was opened, some health facilities were also provided. A number of incentives were given for attracting children towards education. Quite a good number of economic development programmes were also undertaken. With a view to encouraging the handloom activities, four handloom training centres were opened. Besides all these, four bee keeping training centres, 13 industrial training institutes, five poultry farms were also opened. Emphasis on well and road construction was also given.

In Vindhya Pradesh, priority was given to the spread of education, provisions for free education was made for tribal children. Students were provided scholarship, books and uniforms. Night schools and Ashrams were opened. In all, 78 multipurpose co-operative societies were opened. Measures were taken to rehabilitate the landless, facilities for health, drinking water and roads were provided.

In Bhopal, two ashrams by Government and one by Rajya Adivasi Seva Sangh was opened. Ten new primary schools were also running. Agriculture co-operative societies were opened. Tribals were given loan for housing and wells were constructed for drinking water.

After reorganization of the state i.e., in 1956 it was tried that all the activities running in different erstwhile states were run properly. But it was quite difficult to integrate them. As more widely covered programmes were allowed to continue some of the programmes viz. the community welfare centres in old V.P. region which had become irrelevant were discontinued.

An important institution viz. the special multi-purpose tribal development block was established for the tribal areas during the Second Plan period. Maximum number of blocks were in M.P. Statewise position was as follows:

1. Madhya Pradesh	10
2. Bihar	8
3. Assam	7
4. Maharashtra	7
5. Andhra Pradesh	4
6. Orissa	4
7. Rajasthan	1
8. Manipur	1
9. Tripura	1

The speciality of staffing pattern in a SMPT block was the following additional staff which was posted over and above the ordinary (CD Block).

Assistant Engineer	1
Overseer	1
Soil Conservator	1
Extension Officer	1
Medical Officer	1
Compounder	1
Midwives	2
Head Clerk	1

These blocks, had 23,540.58 sq. miles area and had a population of 16.85 lakhs, of which 12.1 lakh i.e. 71.0 per cent were tribal. The average coverage in each block works out to 182 villages with a population of 39,193 spread over an area of 547.45 sq. miles.

Looking at the success of these blocks, it was decided to open more blocks in the country. The name was changed from special Multipurpose Tribal Development Block to simply Tribal Development Blocks. In Madhya Pradesh, initially 71 tribal development blocks were opened but now there are 174 TD blocks.

The objectives behind opening these blocks were defined as follows:

"To promote all sided development of the village (tribal) community including their economic, social, political, cultural and moral development in particular:

(a) To develop a spirit of community life among the people by promoting co-operation and mutual sharing, leading ultimately to voluntary community ownership of the basic needs of production, such as land, and fulfilment by the village community of responsibility for the welfare, employment and livelihood of all its members.

(b) To make the village self-sufficient, in the primary needs of life, such as food, clothing, and shelter and to promote the development of each village along with the development of the local area of which it forms part, and

(c) To develop self-reliance in the individual so that the people are able to manage and run their affairs themselves and make the village self-governing units."[1]

In order to implement these objectives, the whole country was divided into blocks. Each of the community development blocks contains about 100 villages covering an area of 150 sq. miles and a population ranging between sixty and seventy thousand. Before entering on the intensive or first stage, every block except the tribal development blocks had a pre-extension phase of one year during which the programme is exclusively confined to agriculture development. Then followed a period of intensive development for five years. On completion of that period the block enters the second stage during which development was continued with a relatively reduced budget. These blocks were opened in all rural areas throughout the country whereas the tribal development blocks (formerly called Special Multi-purpose Tribal Blocks) were opened where there is predominantly tribal population. Since in the tribal areas the population is sparse and the terrain often difficult each tribal development block is planned to cover about 25,000 persons as against 65,000 in a normal block. To encourage more intensive efforts in these blocks, the Ministry of Home Affairs contributed in the second phase an amount of Rs 15 lakh per block in addition to the usual Rs 12 lakh available for a stage one block. The administrative structure of the Tribal Development Blocks was also different as two officers instead of one were provided in Tribal Development Blocks with the following services:

1. Rural Engineering
2. Medical Officer
3. Compounder
4. Mid-wives, six as against four in normal blocks.

Thus, for taking up more constructive works in tribal areas engineering staff and for carrying of health activities more medical staff was provided.

The Community Development Evaluation Mission in India organized in 1958-59, by the United Nations Technical Administration characterising the community development movement as one of the major experiments of the 20th century says in its review "The Community Development programme is intended to meet all these problems (ignorance, illiteracy and poverty of the rural population) through an integrated comprehensive approach which is simultaneously economical and socially aimed at both future production and current welfare. Its theory is that change cannot take place in an isolated fragment of society, but must be a total process involving the total persons and the entire community. The energies upon which it depends are mainly those of the people; the chief source of capital upon which it must draw is the surplus labour of the village."[2]

This project to develop the neglected villages of India,

especially as it affects tribal India, is of great importance. A development block has an average 20 technicians and about a dozen trained gram sevaks and gram sevikas. Never before in India's history has such concentrated attention been paid to the economic and technical needs of rural people. The following table indicates the number of workers who were employed in the exclusive work of blocks.

Extension Staff in Position
(As on the 30 Sept. 1960)

(a)	Block Development Officer	3,172
(b)	Extension Officer (Agriculture)	3,161
(c)	Extension Officer (Animal Husbandry)	1,840
(d)	Extension Officer (Co-operation)	2,577
(e)	Extension Officer (Village Industries)	1,658
(f)	Extension Officer (Panchayats)	1,654
(g)	Social Education Organizer (Male)	3,359
(h)	Social Education Organizer (Female)	1,549
(i)	Overseer	2,426
(j)	Gram Sevaks	30,853
(k)	Gram Sevikas	2,775
(l)	Progress Assistant	1,754
	Total	56,778

The programmes of the TD blocks, benefiting about 5 per cent of the total tribal population of the country in the Second Plan covered about 39 per cent of the total tribal population at the end of the Fourth Plan.

There has been considerable criticism of the work of the SMPT blocks. These blocks were slow in getting started and tended to introduce, unmodified programmes designed for other parts of India with special reference to tribal needs.[3]

In its resolution No. 20/1770/58-SCT-III of the 1st May, 1959 the Ministry of Home Affairs, Government of India accordingly appointed a committee to examine the work and programmes of these blocks. The Chairman of the committee was Dr. Verrier Elwin, quite famous for his work in the tribal areas and tribal people. The committee had four members including the chairman and one officer on special duty as its secretary. The term of reference of the committee was :

1. To study the working of the SMP blocks, and
2. To advise the Government of India how to implement the intensive development programmes of blocks more effectively and give the programmes a proper tribal bias.

The Committee[4] studied the working of these blocks and found that the norms of the area and population fixed for these blocks have not been followed. The basis of coverage was an area of 200 sq. miles with a tribal population of 25000 and per capita outlay of expenditure of Rs. 108. However, in actual practice most of the states ignored this and considerably increased the coverage to an average population of 39,193, an area of 454.45 sq. miles and per capita outlay of only Rs. 68.00. In many blocks the proportion of tribal to non-tribal was far too high. Some of the blocks were far too big, Bagicha SMPT block was 1052 sq. miles in area.

The schematic budget has, in practice proved an obstacle to the adaptation of the programmes to urgent tribal needs. The schematic pattern tends to set a rigid pattern which results in lop-sided expenditure. Although, the state governments and to some extent the PEOs have been empowered to transfer funds from one head to another within the same block. But this power has rarely been used.

There has been little attempt to build programmes on a tribal foundation: there were practically no ideas in most of the blocks of developing people along the lines on their own traditions. The officials never tried to learn the local language.

The psychological effect of so much money available and the difficulty of spending it creates a sense of guilt and strain among the block officials and invites them often to put up schemes which appear to be based not so much on the actual needs of the people as on feeling that the money must be spent at any cost.

Far too much is being spent on construction programme and elaborate buildings are being created partly to get rid of the money available where much simple and more economic buildings would do.

An even more serious consequence in the growth of what an experienced officer called 'a chain of falsehood' whereby far too optimistic reports are submitted by village level worker to his immediate superior.

The committee reported the views of one experienced development commissioner by saying that too much misguided goodwill, too much money, not enough care in drawing up programme, excessive zeal, theoretical and amateurish pressure from top and destruction of self-reliance are some drawbacks. Are we, he asked 'simply to spend money in a hurry or do we really want to fulfill our basic aims?'

The Renuka Roy Committee has remarked that 'it is now clear to any serious student of working of plan schemes that overdoing or unduly hastening the process and pace of development often leads to passivity, a disposition to accept but not to do'. It is no use trying to hustle the tribal areas, however, desirable it may be that they should rapidly develop along with the rest of the country. Experience has shown that this just will not happen, and it would be better to be practical and realistic and accept the fact that, however, much money may be provided, the progress that may well be expected in an already developed area within five years will take ten or fifteen years among the tribes. This does not mean, however, that we should not attack malnutrition exploitation and disease by every means in our power and as speedily as possible.

These considerations suggest that the entire tribal area should go forward, not piecemeal but together, that there should be much greater attention to real priorities such as agriculture, health and communications, and that it would be better to spread our resource over a wider area than to concentrate them on pockets which may be wrongly selected.

Many of the blocks were slow in starting. Some blocks were opened without even a PEO to supervise the work. In others there was no medical officer or no one to look after cottage industries, cooperation, social education and so on until after two or three years. In several cases, there were disputes about the location of the blocks headquarters and in one place the site was twice changed before the block officials settled down to their permanent home. Members of the staff, many of whom came from urban surroundings, found themselves confused and lost in the unfamiliar setting of hills and forests.

The tribal people themselves neglected and isolated for so long, did not always welcome the newcomers. In a block, they once threatened to kill the development officials, and for long time refused to give them any place for their buildings, since they were afraid that the entire scheme was based on some sinister plot to alienate the tribal land and to introduce permanent settlers. In two blocks in M.P., it has been reported that the people begged the officials to go away and leave them alone. There was an atmosphere of bewilderment and even suspicion at the sudden invasion of so many officials, for it seemed incomprehensible to the tribal mind that after so many centuries of neglect, government should suddenly take an interest in them.

The committee, therefore, suggested that all the drawbacks mentioned must be removed and the experiment of SMPT blocks, limited to a select area must be extended to the whole tribal area by carving out special tribal blocks with 25000 individuals in area of 200 sq. miles with 55 per cent as tribal population.

In respect of tribal development the late Prime Minister of India Pt. Jawaharlal Nehru had laid down Panchsheela or the five guiding principles while writing foreword for the book of Verrier Elwin *Philosophy for NEFA, 1958*. "We cannot allow matters to drift in the tribal areas or just not take interest in them. In the world of today that is not possible or desirable. At the same time we should avoid over administering these areas and in particular sending too many outsiders into tribal territory.

It is between these two extreme positions that the work of tribal development has to function. The avenues of development should however, be pursued within the broad framework of following fundamental principles:—

1. People should develop along the lines of their own genius and we should avoid anything imposing on them. We should try to encourage in every way their own traditions, arts and culture.
2. Tribal rights in land and forest should be respected.
3. We should try to train and build up a team of their own people to do the work of administration and development.

Some technical personnel from outside will no doubt be needed especially in the beginning. But we should avoid introducing too many outsiders into tribal territory.

4. We should not over-administer these areas or overwhelm them with multiplicity of schemes. We should work through, and not in rivalry to their own social and cultural institutions.
5. We should judge results not by statistics or the amount of money spent but by the quality of human character that is evolved."

In the community development programme the development of the tribals was given special treatment either through the special multi-purpose tribal development blocks or tribal development blocks. The pattern of schemes, priorities, and mode of implementation was uniform to all the blocks, the staff both technical and non-technical were posted in these blocks from outside. Progress was judged by the statistics and not by the quality of life evolved as laid down by the Hon. Prime Minister. In respect of certain scheme it is said that their implementation was far from the reality.

From the First Five Year Plan to the Fourth-Five Year Plan the main thrust on tribal development activities was education together with health, animal husbandry and community welfare. Educational activities included opening up of primary, middle, higher secondary schools and ashrams i.e. residential schools. Looking to the socio-economic background of the tribes incentives in the shape of scholarship, stipend for the hostels and ashrams, books, slates were given. Mid-day meals programme with the help of the CARE (Co-operative of American Relief Everywhere) was implemented. During the First Plan period area organizers mostly at the tahsil levels were posted with all the power. To assist them were the circle organizers. But in the year 1962, district organizers at the district level were appointed to co-ordinate the tribal development activities in the distt. and assist the collector in implementing them.

In the beginning of the Fourth Plan period it was felt that the programmes should be more focussed and should aim at all round development of the Tribal areas with focus on the tribal population. The programmes should be as per the needs of the tribal area, and the tribal people. The block was thought to be a smaller unit for planning any activity.

As mentioned, schemes pertaining to the economic aspects, human resources and area development were formulated and implemented. The emphasis, however, was different in different plan periods due to various policy decisions both at the centre and the state level. But the patterns of the schemes remains the same. With a view to understanding the point clearly it is necessary to divide the period in two phases. One Pre-Tribal Sub-plan Strategy and secondly, the Tribal Sub-plan Strategy.

Pre-Tribal Sub-plan Period: (1947-74)

Before tribal sub-plan strategy, areas, mostly at the tahsil, places were delineated and Area Officers known as Area Organizers were put in charge of that area. To assist him, Circle Organizer was posted. The Area Organizer was responsible for implementing development schemes in that area to the tune of funds allotted. He could sanction schemes to the extent of budget allotment received. The Circle Organizer was an important functionary in the field who assisted the Area Organizer and disbursed the pay of the staff.

The Area Organizer was the whole and sole for the implementation of the scheme at field level, independent of the Collector. At the state level the Director of Tribal Welfare assisted by four deputy directors was posted with no staff at the district and divisional level. During this period, the activities for the tribal development was limited to the community welfare centres under Circle Organizer.

On the recommendations of Norohna Committee (1964) the state government took a decision to transfer the educational institutions in Tribal areas from state education department to tribal welfare department. This was done to promote the growth of education amongst the tribal Number of institutions run by the tribal welfare department is given in Appendix No. 1.

As the activities of tribal welfare department, especially, educational activities increased, post of District Organizer at the district level, and that of Deputy Director at the Divisional level was created to co-ordinate the activities. Shri B.K. Dube, IAS, played an important role for the Department during the period

1962 to 1967. He worked as Director and Secretary Tribal Welfare Department and also as the Chairman and M.D. of the Tribal Co-operation Development Federation. In addition to the hostels and ashrams which the department was already running, the mid-day meals programme was also run by the department. At the district level the departmental staff was brought under the Collector but at the divisional level the officers of the department were not under the Commissioner but directly under the Director.

The tribal life depended to a larger extent on the forests, collection and sale of minor forest produces being an important activity. But the traders and money-lender, exploited them on this count. The Forest Labour Co-operative societies were formed at the field level. In addition to these, the multi-purpose co-operative societies were formed which ran their business on their own without bothering for profit or loss. Tribal Co-operative Development Corporation, later on, known as Federation was formed as an apex body which would organize the working of the co-operative societies. The societies at the base level worked as its grassroot institution.

The Federation took up commercial activities especially, purchase and sale of minor forest produces, trade in petrol pumps, a few production units engaged in the manufacture of soap and oil. In all these activities the Corporation incurred heavy losses due to various reasons, therefore, it was decided to be liquidated. The liquidation process is still going on. It has not been finalized as yet.

The Tribal Sub-plan Period i.e. 1974 to 1997, Fifth to Eighth Plan

The Evolution of Tribal Sub-plan Concept during Fifth Plan

The work done in respect of tribal development during all the four plan periods was reviewed and it was found that though the Constitution provided a flexible policy frame it could not be applied to provide maximum gains to the tribal people. Tribal development can no longer be left to be dealt with piecemeal at the convenience of a multiplicity of organisations, subject to availability of men and material and the vagaries of out of context policy decisions. Tribal development should be treated as an integrated part of socio-economic development... It should be accorded a high priority in the programmes of every department in view of its urgency and multi-organizational character for there is a danger that short fall in our programme may throw out of gear the entire scheme."[5]

It was admitted that the forces which were being generated by the new process were so unfamiliar to the tribal communities that they would still require protection and a policy of controlled and guided change at different points. This was in contrast to the advanced areas where it could be expected that purposive intervention at one point could itself lead to general upward movement. In case of simple tribal communities such a choice is generally not available. On the other hand there may be completely unpredictable reactions which may be detrimental to the local community. For example, opening up of a road in general areas stimulates economic activity and benefit the whole or section of areas, on the other hand, it may simply mean the withdrawal of the community from the roadside giving way to others.

Tribal Development Administration during the fifth Plan

A new strategy for administrative structure was contemplated during the Fifth Plan when the tribal sub-plan set up was promulgated in the country. At the Centre, Dr. B.D. Sharma, an IAS officer, helped in the policy formulation. He opined "In any strategy of development, the first crucial step is to neutralise the adverse forces so that the people can enjoy the fruits of their labour. In view of the present situation, protection must be the agenda of development programmes. Apart from state protection, measures are necessary to create capabilities in the community itself so that it may face the new situation on its own, and be able to counter adverse forces. This is possible through sensitizing the people to the new situations and educating them for the change."[6] The responsibility so envisaged could be shouldered through a suitably designed and adequately motivated administration.

As the tribal areas are very big depositories of natural resources its exploitation in both national and tribal interest is quite necessary. The tribal areas are underdeveloped so also the people, therefore a sensitized development administration is also necessary.

Detailed guidelines were issued by the Ministry of Home Affairs, which said that "A sub-plan should be drawn up for these areas which may present an integrated view of their problems, the broad objectives and stratigis an outline of the various programmes physical inputs, financial outlays, legislative and administrative frame. All activities of a government and semi-government organizations financing and credit institutions, and special sectoral programme may be fully integrated in the sub-plan which should present a total picture of the development of the region."[7]

Preparation of sub-plan and project formulation will be two distinct exercises, although preliminary steps for preparation of projects will have to be taken concurrently.

Both long-term and short-term objectives of the sub-plan were decided. The long-term objectives of the sub-plan were:

(i) To narrow the gap between the levels of development of tribal and other areas; and

(ii) To improve the quality of life of the tribal communities.

Among the immediate objectives were, checking the exploitation in all forms, speeding up the process for social and economic development, building up the inner strength of the people and improving their organizational capabilities.

It was in this context that the Fifth Plan attempted to present a special policy frame for the development of tribal areas in the form of sub-plan. The sub-plan envisaged a total picture of development. The guidelines of the Planning Commission largely states that all activities of the government and semi-government organizations, financing and credit institutions and special sector programmes must be fully integrated. A wide frame encompassing all the aspects of tribal life, was therefore provided. It was, in fact, an attempt to articulate the constitutional provisions in the form of specific programmes. The policy frame emphasised that the approach to tribal development should not be bound by precedent as a rigid normative formula. It was therefore, suggested that the entire legal, administrative and institutional as also inter-sector and intra-sectoral priorities should be reviewed keeping the welfare and development of the tribal people in mind.

The new strategy for tribal development was thus essentially an attempt to appreciate the problem of tribal development in totality. It proposed to comprehend the entire process from the people's point of view and trust the validity of any programme and utility of any organization in that light. It was found that functional specialization and developmental apparatus had become extremely complex. Once a programme was finalised, it acquired an individuality and the ultimate goals got displayed by intermediate target. In the tribal context simple socio-economic situations required suitable programmes which could be comprehended by the people. Similarly, a simple administrative apparatus could attend to the assigned tasks without much difficulty. Therefore a system was devised through which the complex matrix at the national and the state level could get translated in simple terms at the field level. The most important feature of the new strategy was the recognition of the fact that there was no uniform solution to the varied problems of the tribal areas and the tribes which were at different levels of socio-economic development.

During the Fifth Five Year Plan, the need for streamlining administration with the decision to substantially step up developmental efforts in tribal areas was fully appreciated. The first step in this direction was to cover all the tribal majority areas under the Fifth Schedule so that its provisions could be used for making necessary changes in the administration, as also in the laws, if necessary, since all authority for administrative action is ultimately derived from law. Second, a number of policy implications of the new thrust in relation to administrative system were made explicit so as to provide suitable guidelines for future action.

Some of the important elements can be summarized as follows: (a) As regulatory and the developmental administration are so intimately intermixed in the tribal areas, the administrative system should be holistic, responsible for all aspects of tribal life. (b) Since the tribal economy is simple and largely undifferentiated the administrative system should also be simple. The line of authority should be clear and responsibilities specific. The organizations in these areas should be multi-functional covering a large spectrum of related needs of people so that necessary services can be provided at a limited number of points. (c) No rule and procedure should be allowed to come in the way of any action designed for the welfare and development of the people. It is the rule and the law which should get amended, rather than compromising the peoples, interest. (d) Formal distinctions between the variety of programmes, due to their sources of funding, like plan and non-plan, or sponsoring organizations, like the central government, state government or different departments should not be allowed to appear at the operational level, and all of them must get moulded in a simple frame in which priorities are determined with reference to the conditions in the areas and needs to the people there. (e) A high quality of personnel at all levels should be ensured, weeding out the undesirable elements which may have already forced their way in these areas. Selected personnel should be placed and provided with suitable incentives and physical facilities.

In streamlining the development administration, the first issue is to define the basic unit of administration. It may be recalled that even though the district has continued to be the pivot of general administration, Development blocks established in the early 50's have come to be recognised as the units of development administration. The blocks in the tribal area which are known as Tribal Development blocks (TD Blocks) are of smaller size in view of the difficult terrain and sparse population. An average block in the country covers an area of about 250 sq. kms. and a population of 50,000. The tribal sub-plan for the tribal majority areas comprise about 800 blocks in all. It was realized that with such a large number of small units, a Tribal Development block may not be viable, as a unit for planning and development. Moreover, if the administration was to be charged with the responsibility for comprehensive development, it ought to have adequate stature and competence comparative to the level of responsibility. It was clear that it would be difficult to create strong structure like that at the block level.

On the other hand a district could not be taken as a unit for tribal development since in most cases only parts of districts comprised tribal majority areas and included in the sub-plans. It was, therefore, decided to carve out a new unit for tribal development programme which is known as Integrated Tribal Development Project (ITDP). It comprises a number of blocks which are grouped together taking into consideration the administrative boundaries, geographical features, natural resources endowment, social and economic conditions of the people.

An irrigation scheme, may benefit the people of more than one block, similar may be the case of roads, bridges, educational institutions, therefore bigger areas were to be carved for planning, implementation and monitoring the scheme. The concept of Integrated Tribal Development Projects (ITDP) which are bigger than TD blocks, but are at the tahsil level were proposed to be carved out.

1. All the tahsils having more than 50 per cent tribal population.
2. Part block areas having more than 50 per cent tribal population even though they cover more than one tahsil.
3. Contiguous areas having a total of 10,000 population with more than 50 per cent tribal population, such pockets were carved out and were known as pockets under the Modified Area Development Approach (MADA).
4. Contiguous areas having a total of 5,000 population with more than 50 per cent tribal population were known as clusters.

In pursuance of the principle of simple and unified administrative structure a body has been created known as project implementation committee for each ITDP comprising the Collector of a district as the chairman, heads of various development departments as members and the project administrator as the secretary. The project authority is responsible for implementation of the programme. A Project Advisory Committee known as Parijoyana Salahkar Mandal has been constituted and made responsible for preparing the plans of development for the project area.

The Advisory Committee comprises, the Collector, representative of the people, of financing and other institutions and project administrator. Thus, the regulatory and development functions coalesce at the project level and all aspects of people's life touched by the modern system directly or indirectly are expected to come under its purview. Within this frame the various developmental programmes, irrespective of their sources of funding and sponsoring organizations are expected to converge at the project level from where they are passed down to the implementing agency in a common mould, all differences having been ironed out by adopting them suitably. An ITDP authority cannot take a formal stand that a problem faced by the people in an area is outside their purview, even though it is possible that the project may not have adequate resources or expertise to solve it at a given moment. The ITDP is expected to initiate action and mobilise necessary support as soon as it takes up a problem of vital concern to the people.

The tribal sub-plan programme strategy included development schemes—economic, area, human resources; protective measures in the shape of Acts, executive orders etc. and relief works. These were to be planned at the Integrated Tribal Development Project (ITDP) level and monitored also.

In the year 1971-72 however, before issuing, the guidelines for the formulation of ITD projects by Government of India, Konta and Dantewara projects were prepared to develop the area with focus on the development of the tribals on pilot basis. As per guidelines and norms issued by the Ministry of Home Affairs and Planning Commission, Government of India, the Tribal Sub-plan area was initially delineated into 42 Integrated Tribal Development Projects (ITDPs)—31 major and 11 medium projects. The major project were those, the total population of which was more than three lakhs and medium projects whose population was below three lakhs. The whole TSP area was declared as Scheduled Area (July, 1976). All the macro projects covered one or more than one tahsils except Shahdol and Pushprajgarh tahsils falling in north-eastern zone, all the seven projects of Bastar District falling in southern zone, Ambikapur and Surajpur ITDPs (Surguja district in eastern zone). This exercise was done to incorporate all the TD blocks and part of CD blocks having 50 per cent ST population. All the medium projects covered part tahsils except Karhal TD block and Sailana (Sailana and Bajna) TD blocks. With a view to covering remaining tribal areas Modified Area Development Approach (1980) was adopted in which pockets of 10,000 population was carved, 50 per cent or more population

MADA pockets were identified. Jawad Manasa pocket in Mandsaur District was not approved as it presented a dispersed picture.

During Sixth Five Year Plan period two major ITDPs of West Nimar and Betul districts viz. Sendhwa and Bhainsdehi were bifurcated from Barwani and Betul ITDPs. Thus total 44 ITDPs were identified before MADA exercise was done. After 25 MADA pockets were annexed to 16 ITDPs, 18 new ITDPs were formed with 32 MADA pockets, the number of ITDPs rose to 62-38 (Major) 8 (Medium) and 16 (Minor). As this bufurication was not approved by the Government of India additional funds by way of special central assistance was not provided. However, in January, 1988 approval of the Government of India was taken for 44 major ITDPs, five medium, 39 MADA pockets and eighth clusters. The funds from special central assistance started coming.

As there was no agency at the divisional level for tribal development, in the year 1989 ten Adimjati, Anuchuchit Jati Kshetriya Vikas Pradhikarans were established at Revenue Divisions headquarters, viz. Bhopal, Indore, Ujjain, Jabalpur, Rewa, Sagar, Bilaspur, Raipur, Bastar and Gwalior. The Pradhikarans were supposed to supervise the planning, implementation and monitoring of the tribal development schemes through the projects. In each Pradhikarans two bodies were constituted—one responsible for the implementation of the schemes under the chairmanship of the commissioner. This body was composed of the officers. Another body Paryavekshan and Salahkar Samiti—supervisory and Advisory body was responsible for the supervison, monitoring and advice for the implementation of the programmes. Funds were also kept at their level to supplement the programmes run at the project levels. Due to lack of proper delegation of powers and earmarking of funds at the Pradhikaran level these bodies had no impact on the development programmes. Therefore, these bodies were dissolved w.e.f. 30-10-96. The Pradhikarans have been abolished mainly because the Panchayati Raj has been established in the state. Under the three–tier Panchayati Raj institutions—the Gram, Janpad and the District Panchayats are important functioning institutions. They have no role to play at the divisional level. The final authority in the Panchayati Raj system is at the zila i.e. district level. The commissioners of Revenue Divisions have been made responsible for the monitoring of the development programme as in case of other development activities in the Division. List of ITD Projects, MADA pockets and clusters, zonewise is given in Annexure IV.

It was also intended that perspective development plans will be prepared on the basis of which development programmes for each project will be taken up. The development programmes could not be prepared as per objectives, mainly, due to two reasons, firstly, status notes giving socio-economic details of the tribal people and tribal areas was not prepared. Thus, the problems of the Scheduled Tribes could not be delineated. Secondly, technical personnel with sufficient experience of working in tribal areas were not available. Therefore, the area specific micro level development plans could not be prepared.

Approach, Strategy and Priorities of Tribal Development during Different Plan Periods

Before reorganization of the State of M.P. each constitutent state had taken up programmes of development for the tribals in their own way. After reorganization of the state the All-India pattern of tribal development especially SMPT and TD blocks was taken up as has been described above in detail.

After adopting the concept of tribal sub–plan i.e. from the Fifth Plan period, the approach, strategy and priorities of the programmes were decided. During the first tribal sub-plan area was delineated forming ITDP's giving a structural base to the projects. Before finalising strategy and priority of development for the plan period, 'core' programme in respect of agriculture, education, health, drinking water and communication were taken up.

During the Sixth Plan period, the broad approach of TSP strategy continued shifting the priorities to development of education, generating employment, improving the quality of life through providing hygienic drinking water, health measures etc. and development of adequate infra-structure and minimizing exploitation.

Sixth plan was the formative period for TSP. The administrative structure, planning process, implementation and monitoring were streamlined. Linkage among different sectoral programmes were decided considering the local needs of the people and area.

TRIBAL SUB PLAN/SCHEDULED AREA
IN
MADHYA PRADESH

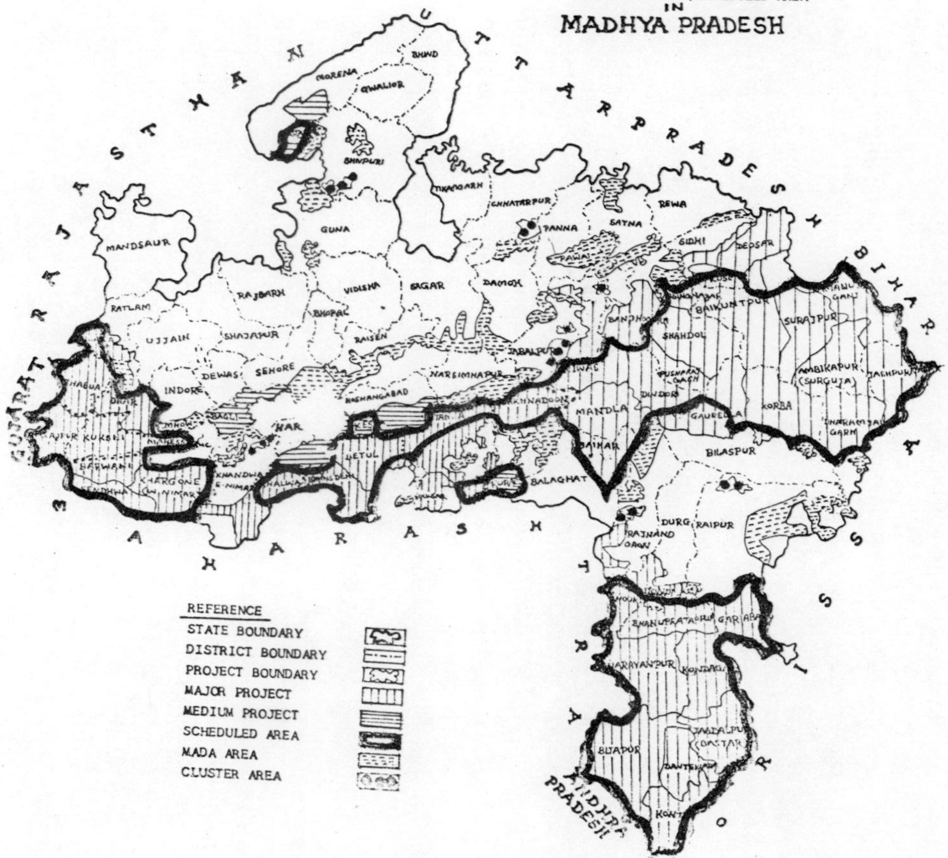

Quantification of funds for tribal sub-plan was raised, financial and budgetary mechanisms were evolved and procedure of implementation streamlined.

The Seventh Plan period witnessed the Third tribal sub-plan of the state reflecting the fine orientation to the planning process. The tribal sub-plan of this plan period laid greater attention and priority on (i) employment oriented and poverty alleviation sectoral programmes, (ii) ensuring income generating assets of permanent nature to the Scheduled Tribes, (iii) taking greater care of dispersed tribes by taking them under the umbrella of tribal sub-plan, (iv) ensuring maximum use of science and technology, inputs in tribal economy to improve the quality of life, (v) universalisation of primary education, and (vi) raising quantification for tribal sub-plan area.

On the eve of Eighth Five Year Plan a fresh stock of tribal problems and tribal development approach in Fifth, Sixth and Seventh Five Year Plan were taken. Three–tier Panchayati Raj systems is being launched in the state and the tribal development is being greared to this system. The lacunas in different areas were noted and analysed.

The tribal sub-plan strategy is continued in Eighth Five Year Plan i.e. Fourth the tribal sub-plan. Ratifying the guidelines given by the working group on tribal development constituted for Eighth Five Year Plan and the approach paper issued by the Planning Commission the tribal sub-plan was prepared laying focus on the following priorities (i) to make the programmes more result oriented and purposeful, (ii) filling the gaps of last three plans, (iii) raising the tribal sub-plan quantification through pool system, (iv) identify agriculture and minor irrigation as two key areas of investment taking minor irrigation programme in the shape of a movement, (v) to allocate funds to a judicious mix of beneficiary oriented schemes, (vi) narrowing the gap between different groups of tribal communities, (vii) emphasis on development of education among vulnerable group's and dispersed tribals, and (viii) decentralization of planning process and accordingly designing the administrative set–up and stringent implementation of protective laws and measures.

Pool system: Under the tribal sub-plan strategy each sector (development department) was supposed to contribute to the tribal development, funds from its kitty, at least in the proportion of ST population in the state. Though the proportion of the population of the ST has varied from Census to Census and in the latest Census i.e. 1991 it is 23.27 per cent but the decision of keeping sectoral plan funds at least in the proportion of ST population continued.

Though the tribals would benefit from economic, area, infrastructural and human resources development plans taken up in tribal sub-plan area with focus on tribals, a number of schemes creeped in the tribal sub-plan which were not directly beneficial either to the tribal area or to the tribals through the system of percentage quantification. Thus, under Narmada valley development, major irrigation schemes, spreading of high tension line under energy, the tribals did not benefit directly. Similarly from the police housing under which government houses are built for the police personnel posted in the tribal areas the tribals are in no way benefitted. But the funds under these were shown for the tribal development. All these schemes which were not benefitting the tribals were highly criticised at different tribal forums, mention may be made of Tribes Advisory Council (TAC), Akhil Bhartiya Adivasi Vikas Parishad etc.

Taking in view the above draw–backs in quantification, rationalisation of schemes under TSP was done. Detailed sector–wise review included in TSP budget during 1988-89 for the development of ST was done and 130 schemes pertaining to 24 sectors which were not beneficial to ST were deleted and alternative schemes were taken up. On October 4, 1988 the State Cabinet took a decision that the size of the tribal sub-plan should no doubt be at least in proportion to the ST population of the state. But the quantification should not be sector–wise but the entire allocation under tribal sub-plan should be carved out from total state plan as a pool. The tribal welfare department will then decide looking to the priorities and needs of the tribal schemes to be taken and funds allotted accordingly to that particular sector.

Though this decision was taken as long back as 1988-89 but it could be implemented during the year 1994-95 when 10 per cent of the total tribal sub-plan money was earmarked as a pool from which the tribal welfare department could allocate funds looking to the priorities of tribal development. During the year 1995-96 the pool amount was 15 per cent of the total tribal sub-plan. During the year 1996-97 the entire amount under the tribal sub-plan was kept as a pool and the tribal welfare department allocated funds from this pool to the schemes from the point of view of the priorities of tribal development to different sectors. This system was already being adopted in respect to special central assistance which is received from Government of India as lumpsum amount by the state government.

Initially during the plan period and then in each annual plan, financial ceilings to each department/sector is made on the basis of which budget provisions are included. In the budget allotments given under schemes to concerned sectors and the expenditure is made by each sector out of that allotment. Budget provisions made, allotments released and expenditure incurred sector-wise and scheme–wise in terms of financial and physical achievements have been discussed in detail in Chapters Sixth and Seventh.

Monitoring

At the state level, The Tribal Welfare Department (TWD) is responsible for the administration and development of tribal areas and also of the dispersed tribal population outside the areas of tribal concentration. The various state departments are responsible for planning and implementation of progress in their respective speciality.

The T.W.D. functions as the nodal Department. In M.P. the nodal role of the T.W.D. has been reinforced by creating a seprate budget demand for the tribal areas which comprises the outlays for all the developmental activities in that area. Thus, by virtue of authorization of expenditure by the *state legislature* on all activities in the tribal areas to the T.W.D. the final responsibility and answerability in relation to all the developmental activities rests with the T.W.D. All other departments are expected to function under the overall guidance of Tribal Welfare Department.

While protective measures against alien exploitation in various forms like usury, land alienation, marketing and so on are essential a major issue in the simple tribal situation is protection against the malfunctioning of the administrative system itself. Consequently, regulation to the effect that no liability shall accrue to a tribal if the intended benefit of a scheme does not reach him provided it is not a case of malafide on his part, is essential during the crucial transitional period.

The project administrators monitor the work of different departments at the project level. At the divisional level, till 30-10-96 the Regional Tribal Development Authorities used to monitor the tribal development programmes. Even a body consisting of the representatives of the people also used to monitor the programmes. However, the responsibility of monitoring the tribal development programmes has now been shifted to the divisional commissioners.

As the tribal development programmes are being implemented by different departments it is very necessary to have an effective monitoring system. Every department, while conceiving a programme for the tribal development develops inbuilt system of monitoring, in the programme itself. The senior officers above the implementing and extension officers not only supervise the programmes but monitor the day to day working. The senior officers interfere wherever possible for correcting the programmes so that the programmes are run as per the objectives defined. The work of the village level workers are monitored by the agriculture extension officers.

The Ayog (Commission) as Monitoring Body

M.P. Anusuchit Jati, Anusuchit Janjati Tatha Pichda Varg Ayog Adhiniyam, 1983, has been repealed in 1995 and M.P. Anusuchit Janjati Ayog Adhiniyam 1995 has been passed.

Objective. Adhiniyam provides for a Ayog to look after the interests of Scheduled Tribes in the following manner:-

(i) To act as a watchdog for protection given to STs under the Constitution and other laws framed for this purpose.

(ii) To recommend to the state government for taking steps to include specific tribes or groups or part of such tribes or groups to be included in the Constitution (STs) Order 1950.

(iii) To monitor the implementation of developmental programmes for Scheduled Tribes and to recommend suggestions for improvement.

(iv) To advise on reservation of STs for admission in educational institutions and public services.

Impact of the Act

Ayog constituted under the Act has recently submitted its first report for the year 1996-97.

Various departments have been asked to act upon the recommendations of the Ayog. The report will be laid on the table of Vidhan Sabha during its next session.

The Primitive Tribal Groups

With a view to giving special attention to certain tribal groups looking at their backwardness the concept of declaring certain tribal groups as special primitive tribal groups was evolved by Government of India. The Government of India issued directives vide their letter No. 20018/5/81–TDA dated 27th April, 1980 for the identification of primitive tribal groups.[8]

Three criteria for the identification of the primitive tribal groups have been evolved. These are as follows (i) use of technology, which is of pre-agricultural level, (ii) low level of literacy, and (iii) population which is stagnant or diminishing. Based on these criteria following tribes have been identified as Primitive tribal groups:-

(1) Abhujhmaria, (2) Baiga, (3) Bharia, (4) Birhor, (5) Pahari Korwa, (6) Kamar and (7) Saharia.

Having identified the primitive groups an exhaustive programme for them has been formulated. Primitive groups are to be distinguished from the impoverished as the very concept of poverty may be unknown to them. Hence special programmes will have to be taken up as a part of general development in the area.

The organization of a society under SFDA/TDA model will be beneficial in the programming for primitive tribes. The society should have specific perspective plans for each of the communities so that continuity of the work to be conducted can be provided.

This programme can only succeed when a group of sensitive personnel is appointed to the task. The appointments cannot be made on functional basis, as the programmes relate to a small group numbering about 50 to 100 or 200 families. The officer will have to be school teacher and an agricultural extension officer rolled in one with adequate authority to take liaisons. They can be compensated for lack of social services or special pay can be given to them ranging between 25-50 per cent depending on the location of their headquarters.

The Project

Top priority should be given to provide protection for the existing economic activities of this group. External predatory forces sniping at their produce and leaving them bare should be warded off so that the members of the group are in a position to fully enjoy the fruits of their labour. Restoration of land should be given top priority.

The project in each group must cover the entire gestation period so that the project should come to an end only when the group has become a viable one.

In settlement programmes generally some subsistence allowance is given without any labour input which can be demoralising and misused. A mechanism has to be found where by the community should be given the feeling that they are earing their subsistence and nothing is being paid to them ex-gratia.

A programme providing working opportunity for a period of 300 days in a year on minimum wages should be formulated. The principle of converting the manpower of the group into capital assets has to be followed. Thus, the entire land reclamation work can be taken up by the beneficiary group itself.

Irrigation programmes can be taken up provided bulk of the land belongs to the primitive tribes. In the plantation programme the approach has to be to give the ownership of the trees to the tribals while the land may continue to belong to the state. Bee-keeping and similar other cottage industries may have a good potential. It may be possible for the state Government to give the contract of fishing in the tank to the tribal co-operative development corporation which can organise co-operatives of fishermen in the areas. Co-operatives for the supply of raw-materials to the primitive tribes should be arranged, which will also undertake marketing of the finished goods.

The fuel collectors are the weakest group in any community. It will be useful if a programme for fuel wood collectors is taken up which should include organization of co-operatives, provision of consumption credit and planting of special fuel wood series.

Among the primitive groups the first problem is that of health. The entire primitive tribal community should be medically checked up by a team organized by the Health Department and they should be given medical care according to a time schedule.

The tribal groups under consideration have to be equipped mentally and psychologically so that they are able to withstand the depradation among them by external agencies. This can be done by educating them in a way which does not erode their distinct personality and cultural individuality. They need to include education of a sort different from the conventional type. A suitable incentive for attendance may be given as an indirect compensation to the parents for the loss in the earnings of a family as a result of the child going away to the school. At primary level the assistance has to be mostly in kind, school uniforms, text–books and exercise books. It would be desirable to work out a system whereby children also get some nourishment.

A substantial adult education effort should be made amongst the primitive tribes. In the first instance reading material should be prepared, keeping in view their own local situation and their problems.

The above instructions were issued by the Ministry of Welfare, Government of India during the year 1977 to the state governments. The Government of M.P., however, identified these groups and launched four groups of schemes viz. Family oriented economic, community infrastructure and human resources development programmes on the subsidy and loan basis. The loan component was kept only 20 per cent and subsidy upto 80 per cent. The subsidy portion was more as compared to normal tribal groups which is only 50 per cent.

The economic development programmes included Integrated Rural Development Programme, the development of agriculture and allied activities, self–employment and family oriented income generating schemes based on subsidy and loan basis.

The Community Development programmes included distribution of uniforms and text–books, provision of health facilities, establishing agricultural farms, provisions for the ashrams, contour bunding, sericulture, bamboo plantation, distribution of iodized salt, provision of soap, employment training programmes. The infrastructure development programme include approach roads, bridges and culverts, stop dam, nishtari tanks, construction of school building, hand pump and well construction and community buildings. Under Human Resources Development programmes all the educational and training programmes are included which help in equipping a person for getting suitable employment.

During the year 1992, however, a new approach was adopted wherein Five Year Development Plans based on the actual socio-economic surveys of these groups were prepared taking into account their aspirations.

With a view to providing a very dynamic and effective administrative and financial structure separate agencies were registered for each primitive tribal group. While Kamar, Bharia, Abhujhmaria, and Birhor are located in an area of a single district, the Baiga, Saharia and Pahadi Korwa are located in more than one district – the Baiga in five districts and Saharia in all the six districts of Gwalior and Chambal divisions. It was found difficult to ensure effective administration of schemes from one place of all the districts. Even the distribution of funds was disproportionate in all the districts–giving more funds to the district in which an agency was situated.

It was decided therefore to establish an agency in a district in which the population of primitive tribal group was 20,000 or more. In fourteen districts such agencies have been established. It has also been decided to nominate a member of the primitive community concerned, as the Chairman of the agencies and persons as members. The idea is to empower the members of the community themselves so that they can decide the mode of their development.

One very important measure has been taken to issue family identity cards to each primitive tribal group family so that they can get advantage of development works easily.

In this background the spread of the primitive tribal groups and amount spent for them is outlined below. The population, as per special survey conducted during 1992 of these groups is 6,11,710 which is 3.96 per cent of the total population of Scheduled Tribes in the state. The districtwise spread is as follows:

Sl. No.	Name of the special primitive tribal group	Total population	Total families	District	Blocks	Villages
1.	Abhujhmaria	17016	4327	Bastar	1. Narainpur	235
					2. Orchha	
					3. Dantewada	
					4. Bijapur	
2.	Baiga	134357	27531	1. Mandla		
				2. Shahdol	30 blocks	1197
				3. Balaghat		
				4. Bilaspur		
				5. Rajnandgaon		
3.	Bharia	2012	238	Chhindwara	Tamia	12
4.	Birhor	935	281	Raigarh	1. Lailunga	
					2. Dharam Jaigarh	
					3. Tamnar	
					4. Patthalgaon	249
					5. Bagicha	
					6. Kunkuri	
					7. Kansabel	
5.	Korwa	27019	6142	Raigarh		
				Surguja	16 blocks	320
				Bilaspur		
6.	Kamar	13310	2867	Raipur	1. Gariaband	
					2. Mainpur	
					3. Chhura	249
					4. Nagri	
					5. Sihawa	
7.	Saharia	417171	60997	Gwalior		
				Morena		
				Bhind	26 blocks	1159
				Datia		
				Guna		
				Shivpuri		
	Total	6,11,710	1,02,383			

Quite a sizeable amount has been spent on various developmental programmes for these groups. The details are as follows:

Since Fifth Year Plan till 1994-95 the amount spent on these groups is as follows:

(Rs. in Lakh)

Sl. No.	*Agency*	*Amount received*	*Expenditure on Programmes*				
			Family oriented economic development	*Community development*	*Infrastr- ucture development*	*Establi- shment*	*Total*
1	*2*	*3*	*4*	*5*	*6*	*7*	*8*
1.	Kamar	250.56	42.87	165.87	19.38	—	228.12
2.	Bharia	120.95	20.87	27.47	34.12	25.22	107.68
3.	Abhujmaria	313.45	49.36	110.15	129.22	—	288.73
4.	Baiga	1274.42	238.60	718.11	175.28	—	1131.99
5.	Pahadi Korwa	300.00	78.33	61.35	117.38	—	257.06
6.	Birhor	68.00	19.34	17.14	21.36	—	57.84
7.	Saharia	533.41	84.45	239.88	133.38	—	457.71
	Total	2860.88	533.82	1339.97	630.12	25.22	2529.13

Out of a total of 1,02,383 special primitive tribal group families 63935 families or 62.44 per cent of the total received some kind of benefit or the other.

With a view to providing special employment opportunities the requisite qualifications for the recruitment to certain posts was relaxed as per GAD Order No. F NOC-3-17/86/3/1 dated 26 August, 1986. As such 17 Teachers and 44 peons got recruited in Pahadi Korwa area, 3 teachers and 6 peons in Birhor area, in Baiga Agency Area 210 Asstt. teachers and in Bharia, 2 Assistant Teachers got recruited.

The Tribal Co-operative Development Federation

The tribal areas have had the services of multipurpose co-operative societies and forest labour co-operative societies. These societies used to trade in minor forest produces and provide essential commodities to the tribal people. It was decided to organize an apex body to organize, co–ordinate, supervise and provide technical guidance to these societies.

Therefore, the Madhya Pradesh Co-operative Development Fedration was organized on 16-3-1960. The Federation used to function through 309 member co-operative societies.

It used to trade in the following commodities through the member co-operative society:

1. Collection and trade of forest produces: It used to collect and trade in forest produces viz. harra, mahua, gond, katha, mahul patta, sal seed etc.
2. Timber trade: The Federation used to take contract of forest coups, prepration of katha and trade in gum etc.
3. Purchase and sale of commodities of day to day use for the tribals at a reasonable price.
4. In addition to the above activities gond (gum), soap preparation and saw machine units were also taken up.

Authorized working capital of the Federation was Rs. 1.00 crore and paid up capital was 20,42,704 or Rs. 20.42 lakhs. The Federation used to organize the above activities with the help of loans and subsidies received from the government from time to time. But no fund either by way of loan or subsidy was provided by the government after 1972 with the result that the working capital of the Federation was reduced. Continuous losses everyday in different trades undertaken by the corporation also reduced the working capital of the corporation. The Federation had met losses upto Rs. 2.33 crores upto 1977. The Federation was not able to pay the salaries of its staff, pay off the liabilities of its debtors. Keeping in view all these factors, as per decision of the government of M.P. Tribal and Scheduled Caste Welfare Department, the Federation was liquidated w.e.f. 22-6-1981.

On the day of liquidation the Federation had to pay Rs. 2.58 crores by way of loan to the government, royalty of Rs. 39.96 lakhs to Forest department and Rs. 36.18 lakhs as sales tax to Sales Tax department.

Looking to the critical financial condition of the Federation it was decided by the Government to write off Rs. 39.96 lakhs as royalty to the forest and Rs. 36.18 lakhs as sales tax to the Sales Tax department.

Madhya Pradesh Adivasi Vitta Avam Vikas Nigam

Ever since the liquidation of the M.P. Tribal Co-operative Development Federation the Government of India was insistent upon opening similar organization in the state. Because no organization was left which could look after the minor forest produce and economic development programmes for the tribals. The Scheduled Caste Development Corporation which was known previously as Antyavaasai Sahkari Vikas Nigam looked after the development of Scheduled Castes in addition to that of the tribals.

Therefore, the Madhya Pradesh Adivasi Vitta Avam Vikas Nigam was organized under the Indian Company's Act section 25 with non-profit earning motive. It was registered with the Registrar of Companies, Gwalior on 29-9-94. The corporation started its self-financing schemes w.e.f. 1st April, 1995.

The corporation has been established with three sole objectives: (1) To develop the tribals, socially, economically and educationally: (2) Adopt such measures which prevent their exploitation and (3) Economically, assist the tribals so that they can rise above the poverty line.

The authorised share capital of the corporation is Rs. 50 crores, 51 per cent of which belong to the state government and 49 per cent to the Government of India. The following schemes are being implemented for the tribal beneficiaries:

1. Self-employment schemes announced by the state government from time to time.
2. Schemes in respect of small industries.
3. Cottage industries.
4. Transport.
5. Construction.
6. Providing services viz. transport, fax, health consultancy, etc. so that tribals can earn their livelihood.
7. Purchase and sales of minor forest produces.
8. All sorts of trade.

9. Schemes relating to service/repairs.
10. All kinds of shops.
11. Different kinds of contracts.
12. Any other legal activities which guaranteed the beneficiaries self-employment so that they do not remain unemployed.

Sanction of Schemes

(a) Sanction by NSFDC. After preparing the schemes it is sent to NSFDC for sanction. After sanctioning the scheme the NSFDC provides loan for implementation of the scheme at the rate of 6 per cent annual interest. 5 per cent share of the total amount of the scheme is provided by the beneficiary. The rest of the amount of the scheme is provided by the corporation. Financial assistance of the state government is taken to provide for the share of the corporation.

The proposals are sent to the NSFDC as per details given below:

(i)	Agriculture	50 per cent
(ii)	Industry	20 per cent
(iii)	Services and Transport	20 per cent

(b) NABARD Schemes—At the branch level the loan cases are prepared and sent to bank for sanction. After sanctioning the loan amount and distributing it to the beneficiaries the subsidy portion of the corporation is made available. The subsidy amount will be 50 per cent of the loan amount or maximum amount of Rs. 6,000 whichever is more. The subsidy amount is adjusted in the repayment of loan instalments by the beneficiaries.

Under NABARD scheme the cases prepared and sent for the sanction are as follows

(i)	Primary Sector	30 per cent
(ii)	Secondary Sector	40 per cent
(iii)	Tertiary Sector	30 per cent

Training—With a view to helping the tribals in earning more income a number of training schemes have been started. Some of the important training programmes are as under:–

(i) Motor driving

(ii) Trade and occupation

(iii) Trade in minor forest produce

(iv) Tailoring

Eligibility. Terms and conditions for eligibility for taking advantage of different schemes are as follows

(i) The Scheduled Tribes of M.P.

(ii) The beneficiary should not be an income-tax payee.

(iii) The yearly income of the beneficiary should not be more than Rs. 11,000. The state government fixes up the annual income of the beneficiary year to year. For getting the advantage under the scheme the annual income of the beneficiary should not be more than the annual income fixed by the state government from time to time.

(iv) The tribal beneficiaries who are not eligible for subsidies can get interest subsidy from the corporation at the fixed rate from time to time.

(v) The age of the beneficiary should not be less than 18 years.

(vi) Only those tribals will be eligible to get the benefit of the schemes on whom there is no liability of payment of bank loan.

(vii) Only those tribals will get the benefit of the scheme who have not received the advantage of any scheme of the corporation.

(viii) In the following cases the beneficiaries should either be trained or should have sufficient experience:

(a) Establishing construction units except mining

(b) Poultry farming

(c) Repair Units

(d) Services which require training

(e) In cases of jeep, taxi, and auto rickshaw, the trainees should have a driving license.

Procedure of Applying

The tribals have to apply to the branch managers of the corporations in prescribed proforma and have to produce following certificates:

(a) Tribe and caste certificate

(b) Domicile certificate of M.P.

(c) Income certificate.

(d) Training and experience certificate wherever necessary.

Selection

At the branch level a selection committee has been constituted in which one of the tribal members who is a representative of the people will be the chairman of the selection committee. One of the tribal representative of the people will be member. Collector or his representative will also be a member. The assistant zonal manager of the NSFDC Bhopal will also be a member and branch manager of the corporation will be member secretary of the committee. The committee will select the beneficiary by lottery system. The tribal female applicants and special primitive tribal groups will get preference in the selection.

Schemes run with the assistance of NSFDC

As many as 90 schemes are run with the help of NSFDC.

Schemes of NSFDC being implemented by the Scheduled Tribes finance and Development Corporation.

(a) Sechemes related to Agriculture and Allied Activities

  (i) Tractor Trolley

  (ii) Goat rearing

  (iii) Increase in productivity of agriculture

  (iv) Poultry farms

  (v) Pig rearing

  (vi) Marketing of minor forest produces

(b) Services and Transport

  (i) Mini Truck

(ii) Jeep, Taxi

(iii) Dumper

(iv) Minibus

(v) Auto Rikshaw

(vi) Truck

(vii) Bus

(viii) Cycle Rikshaw

(ix) Photocopier

(x) General Store

(c) Schemes related to Industries

(i) Brick Kiln

(ii) Printing Press

(iii) Dhaba

(iv) Carpet weaving

(v) Bamboo Basket

(vi) Broom manufacturing

(vii) Mini Rice Mill unit

(viii) Atta Chakki unit

Implementation of the schemes

In all the 45 districts the corporation has established its branches. In some of the districts the corporation has its own staff, in rest of the districts the departmental officers-project administrators/assistant commissioners/district organisers/area organisers are working as branch managers in addition to their duties. As and when the staff is sanctioned by the state government the corporation will post its own staff and the departmental officers will be relieved of their additional charge.

The branch manager will prepare the schemes at the branch level and select the beneficiaries. The schemes prepared by the corporation and the list of beneficiaries will be sent to the NSFDC and after getting sanction from national corporation the schemes will be implemented.

The specialities of the schemes being implemented

(a) The objective is not only to help the tribals economically but helping them to get relief from exploitation.

(b) Under transport not only the vehicle will be provided but routes will also be reserved.

(c) Under self–employment schemes not only raw material will be provided but also help the tribals in sale of their manufactured items.

(d) Training in different trades.

(e) Helping the trainees economically in getting self-employment. With a view to helping the tribal beneficiaries in repayment of loan along with interest, joint account in the name of beneficiary and corporations will be opened. The beneficiary in this manner will not only repay his instalment but also have full knowledge of the amount repayed.

(f) Loans will directly be sanctioned to the beneficiaries so that he is not required to go to the bank.

(g) To open branches at the block level along with the district level to help the tribal in the interior areas.

(h) The tribals will select the schemes of their choice and the corporation will prepare its project profile free of cost.

(i) The corporation will provide guidance and advice to the tribals from time to time.

(j) The amount of loan and interest will be recovered in easy instalments. The female beneficiaries and the members of the special primitive tribal groups will be given preference.

(k) In nut shell all possible efforts will be made to ensure the success of the beneficiaries.

Appendix No. 1

The schemes run by Tribal Welfare Department (Commissioner Tribal Development).

The Tribal Welfare Department runs educational institutions

in Tribal Sub-plan area as well as outside and provide a number of incentives to tribal students for education. In addition to the educational programmes certain economic development and economic assistance programme are also provided.

In addition to the educational institutions, run by the department, grant-in-aid is also given to non-governmental organizations. The Institutions run by the tribal welfare department are as follows:—

	Type of School	*Number upto 1996*
1.	Junior Primary Schools	2601
2.	Primary School	15750
3.	Primary School (under DPEP)	620
4.	Middle School	3579
5.	High School	495
6.	Higher Secondary School	468
7.	Model Higher Secondary School	12
8.	Girls Educational Complex	06
9.	Gurukul Vidyalaya	01

In addition to the educational institutions, residential institutions are also opened so that the tribals can reside in or near the educational institutions and continue their studies. Thus, upto 1996-97, 1834 pre-matric hostels (47950 seats), 107 post–matric hostels (6770 seats) and 1018 ashram school (47385 seats) were running. The students residing in these educational institutions are provided stipend at the rate of Rs 250 for boys and Rs 260 for girls.

Sports Complex. In addition to the educational and residential institutions, 25 sports complex with 2500 seats are also running. Out of these, Seven sports complexes are exclusively for the girls.

Technical Training: With a view to providing technical training to the tribals for gettig better avenues for employment, 9 ITI's for boys and 6 ITI's for girls i.e. 15 ITIs are running. During the year 1996-97 out of 2500 seats sanctioned in these institutions 1814 trainees were admitted. 15 training-cum-production centres are also being run in which 604 seats are sanctioned, upto the year 1996-97, 228 trainees were admitted:

Scholarship. With a view to assisting in continuing their studies properly the tribal students are provided with different kinds of scholarships namely state, post–matric and merit scholarships. For increasing literacy among women, scholarship is given to girls from Class IIIrd and to boys from Class VIth.

Free distribution of text books. Nationalised text-books and book sets of language and mathematics are provided to tribal students studying in the class I and II. During the year 1996-97, 292621 students of Class I and 390541 students of Class II were provided with books.

Grant-in-aid to NGO's. In the interior tribal areas non-governmental organizations are running Higher secondary, Middle, Primary schools, ashram, hostel, health centres and balvadis. There are 67 NGOs conducting 348 educational activities. During the year 1996-97 67 NGOs were provided with Rs. 1289.00 lakh as subsidy.

REFERENCES

1. Report of the Scheduled Areas and Scheduled Tribes Commission Report 1961, p. 175.
2. Report of the Community Development Evaluation Mission as quoted by the Scheduled Areas and Scheduled Tribes Commission, Report 1961, p. 174.
3. Report of the Committee on Special Multipurpose Tribal Blocks, Ministry of Home Affairs, New Delhi, 1960, p. 1.
4. Report of the Committee on Special Multipurpose Tribal Blocks, Ministry of Home Affairs, New Delhi, 1960.
5. Tribal development in V Plan, Some Basic Policy Papers, Vol. I, Ministry of Home Affairs, Government of India, New Delhi, 1975, p. 38.
6. Sharma B.D. Dr., Administration for Tribal Development, Our Tribal Heritage souvenir of National Tribal Festival, October 1989, Ranchi, p. 50.
7. Compendium of circulars/guidelines on Tribal Development, GOI, Ministry of Welfare, Tribal Development Division, New Delhi, 1990, p. 9.
8. *Op.cit.*, p. 153.

6

Impact of Developmental Programmes: Financial

The Constitution of India has laid the responsibility of developing the tribal people on the Central and State Governments. Besides, central and state governments, the non-governmental organizations have also launched development programmes for tribals.

As mentioned in an earlier Chapter, the community development programmes also covered the tribal people. Special multi-purpose Tribal Development Blocks, later on known as Tribal Development Blocks were launched specially for the tribal people.

However, it was the Tribal Sub-plan strategy which envisaged all-round development of the tribal people. After studying the problems of the tribal people four broad categories of development programmes were thought of, economic, infrastructual, human resources and other.

Under economic development programmes, all kinds of productions, assisting the tribal people in raising their levels of income-both family and individual, and self-employment schemes, by and large, were included.

The tribal areas lack basic infrastructure. Therefore, infrastructural development programmes including building of roads bridges and culverts, extension of high tension lines, developing water resources etc. were taken up.

The human resources development programme include education of all kinds--elementary, secondary, higher technical and Training of different kinds, both for preparing for different competitive examinations and taking up of jobs. Safe drinking water, Public health and family welfare are also included under this broad category of Human Resources Development.

In addition to the above, broad categories of programmes, updating and improvements in land records are also taken up which come in the 'other' category.

As mentioned in Chapter V, Pt. Jawaharlal Nehru the then Prime Minister of India had mentioned that "we should judge results not by statistics or the amount of money spent but by the quality of human character that is evolved. By 'human character evolved, he probably, meant the bestowing the boon of education on the people, thereby becoming useful citizens of the country.

All the broad categories of development programmes, mentioned above, no doubt, aim at the objective of evolving the human character. The process however, requires an analysis for understanding the impact of development programmes on the tribal people. However, from the First Plan itself amount on tribal development has been shown separately. During the First Plan, Rs. 348.04 lakhs were spent under the state sector for the tribal welfare programmes, per capita expenditure being Rs. 7.08. There was, however, no central sector programme during this period. In the second plan Rs. 489.96 lakhs were spent under both state and central sectors. Under state sector only Rs. 185.06 lakhs could be spent, out of a total allocation of Rs. 499.96 lakhs. The per capita expenditure under both sectors was Rs. 7.34. The Third Plan provision under bath the sectors was Rs. 1265.80 lakhs but only Rs. 1021.61 lakhs could be utilised. The average per-capita expenditure came to Rs. 15.30 Rs. 1706.24 lakhs were granted during the Fourth Plan under both the sectors. The state sector expenditure being Rs. 737.51 lakhs, Rs. 20.34 was per capita expenditure. The expenditure incurred in M.P. during the four plan period thus comes to Rs. 3560.85 lakhs or Rs. 35.60 crores. Under the tribal sub-plan which was adopted from the Fifth Five Year Plan period, Rs. 255.79 crores was provided from the state plan resources. In addition to this amount Rs. 50 crores were provided as special central assistance by the Government of India. In this manner, provision of funds was boosted after adopting the tribal sub-plan strategy.

From the Sixth plan onwards, the programmes included under the four major categories were identified into different schemes run for the development of the tribal people. The whole programme content was broken into 16 heads of development. These heads of development and the amount provided under each from Sixth to Eighth plan including Annual Plans 1990-91 and 1991-92 are given in Annexure No. VI-A Summary of expenditure is given below:

TABLE NO. 1

Provision and Expenditure during VIth to VIIIth Plan including Annual Plan 90-91 and 91-92

Rs. in Crore

Head of development	*Provision during Sixth to Eighth Plan*	*Expen-diture Sixth to Eighth Plan*	*Percent of expen-diture to the pro-vision*	*Percent of total provi-sion T.S.P.*	*Percent of total expen-diture T.S.P.*
1. Agricultural and allied activities	814.42	612.14	75.16	14.15	12.53
2. Rural development	645.90	556.29	87.67	11.23	11.59
3. Irrigation and flood control	1202.53	993.43	82.61	20.89	20.34
4. Energy	424.22	560.92	132.22	7.37	11.48
5. Industry and mining	189.51	152.40	80.41	3.29	2.97
6. Transport	366.12	304.21	83.09	6.36	6.23
7. Science and technology	10.46	6.83	65.25	0.18	0.14
8. General economic services	136.22	101.65	74.62	2.37	2.08
9. Social services	739.83	570.92	77.17	12.86	11.69
10. Public Health and Family Welfare	278.64	197.79	70.98	4.84	4.05
11. Water Supply, Sanitation and Housing	308.13	286.28	92.99	5.36	5.86
12. Information and Publicity	6.90	4.14	59.90	0.12	0.09
13. Welfare of SC/ST/ OBC	462.07	427.16	92.44	8.03	8.74

Head of development	Provision during Sixth to Eighth Plan	Expen- diture Sixth to Eighth Plan	Percent of expen- diture to the pro- vision	Percent of total provi- sion T.S.P.	Percent of total expen- diture T.S.P.
14. Labour and Employment	32.88	12.35	37.55	0.56	0.25
15. Social Weflare and Nutrition	32.88	12.35	37.55	0.56	0.25
16. Social Welfare and Nutrition	129.27	96.31	74.50	2.24	1.97
17. General services	2.81	0.59	21.05	0.05	0.02
Total	5750.01	4892.41	85.09	100	100

Sight difference in the figures as compared to the totals given in Annexure V is due to converting and rounding up the figures into crores).

The summary picture of the provisions and expenditure as above includes the Annual Plans 90-91 and 91-92.

The tribal sub-plan was started from the fifth Five Year Plan. But the provisions and expenditure from the Sixth to the Eighth plan have been given above. The Fifth plan provisions and expenditure have not been included as the schematic pattern was not worked out in details as during Fifth to Eighth plan, including Annual plan 90-91 and 91-92.

Sectors namely agriculture, animal husbandry, fisheries, and cooperation which have been shown during the fifth Five Year Plan have been included under agriculture and allied activities during Sixth to Eighth Plan. During the fifth Five Year Plan, health and water supply have been grouped together which have been shown separately during Sixth to Eighth Plan. As the fifth Five Year Plan was the period from which tribal sub-plan was started, separate provisions have been shown under administrative structure but has been grouped in different sectors included under Sixth to Eighth Plan. The figures could not have tallied, due to differences in grouping under the heads of development, therefore, a separate account of provision and expenditure during The Fifth Plan is given below:

TABLE NO. 2

Sectoral Breakup of the Outlay During Ist Tribal Sub-Plan i.e., Fifth Plan

Sector	*State Plan*	*Supple-mental assis-tance from GOI*	*Total state Plan+ SCA*	*Sectorwise percentage to total outlay i.e. State and SCA*
1. Agricultural and allied activities	18.17	8.4	26.21	1.24
2. Animal husbandry	2.20	2.05	4.25	1.66
3. Fisheries	1.00	0.24	1.24	0.49
4. Co-operation	6.40	8.20	14.60	5.71
5. Irrigation	20.30	2.55	22.85	8.9
6. Power	41.50	1.00	42.50	16.62
7. Communication	19.00	9.90	28.90	11.30
8. Mining and industries	5.33	0.84	6.17	2.42
9. Education	23.75	7.88	31.63	12.37
10. Health and water supply	19.04	3.81	22.85	8.94
11. Welfare of SC/ST/OBC	15.00	—	15.00	5.86
12. Nutrition	29.00	—	29.00	11.33
13. Administrative structure	5.11	5.49	10.60	4.16
Total	205.79	50.00	255.79	100.00

The priority of investment during the Fifth plan was power (16.62 per cent), education (12.37 per cent), Nutrition (11.33 per cent), communication (11.30 per cent), agriculture (10.24 per cent) health and Water supply (8.54 per cent), irrigation (8.9 per cent), Welfare of SC/ST/OBC (5.86 per cent) and cooperatives (5.79 per cent). The least amount invested was under fisheries which was 0.49 per cent of the total investment. Under administrative structure the funds provided was to the tune of 4.16 per cent.

During the period between The Sixth to the Eighth plan, agriculture production, horticulture, marketing, soil and Water Conservation, (Agriculture and Forest department) Animal Husbandry, Dairy-Fisheries, Forest, Cooperatives, Food and Civil supplies (Public Distribution System) are included under Agriculture and Allied Activities.

Under Rural Development, different programmes of poverty alleviation, land reforms, community development, and Panchayats are included.

Under Irrigation and Flood Control, Major and medium irrigation, Narmada valley development, minor irrigation or irrigation department, Agriculture department and Micro-Minor works Command Area Development are included.

Under energy power, Madhya Pradesh Electricity Board, Narmada Valley Development Authority and Urja Vikas Nigams, find place. Under industry and mining, handloom, khadi and gramodyog, handicrafts, leather development, sericulture, large and medium industries, mining and industrial cooperatives find place.

Transport sector includes aviation, roads and bridges, and Madhya Pradesh State Road Transport Corporation (MPSRTC).

In Science and technology not only scientific research but also Ecology and Environment are included.

Under the category, general economic services, State Planning Board, tourism, Computer centre, Statistics, District plan and untied funds, Weights and Measures find place.

All the educational programmes find place in category i.e. Social services. Thus, School, collegiate, adult and technical eduction, sports, youth welfare, art and culture are included under this category.

Public Health and Family Welfare and Employees' State Insurance Scheme are included in the tenth category i.e. Public Health, Family welfare and Employees State Insurance (ESI).

In the eleventh category i.e. water supply, sanitation & Housing Services viz. Drinking water, all categories of housing, Urban administration which include local self-government and Urban Welfare are included.

Information and Publicity also known as public relations is very important sector as it gives information relating to development schemes etc. to the public. It is included in the twelfth category.

Though, the entire tribal sub-plan is aimed at tribal development, separate funds are earmarked for the welfare of Scheduled Tribes. From this fund the Tribal Welfare Department runs educational activities, basically for the tribal people. Besides educational activities, legal aid to the poor, payments to the victims of atrocities, deprivation, physical injuries etc. are paid by way of relief measures.

In the year 1988-89 it was thought that the tribal sub-plan funds should be made available not as percentage of funds from each department but carved out as a "pool" from the total plan resources. Due to various reasons this could not be implemented during the year, although, a cabinet decision was taken in this regard. However, in the third year of the eighth Five Year Plan period i.e. 94-95, it was decided to keep 10 per cent funds of the total tribal sub-plan as a 'pool'. From this amount, schemes of immediate necessities for the tribals could be taken up in addition to the budget provisions. During the year 1995-96 the proportion of this "pool" was raised from 10 per cent to 15 per cent.

Under Labour and Employment, labour welfare activities, mainly in urban towns, craftsmen training, employment services and special employment schemes are taken.

In the fifteenth category of schemes, social welfare and nutrition, is mentioned. Under this, social welfare, women and child welfare, nutrition, legal aid to poor, codification of customary laws are included.

In the last category i.e. Sixteenth, general services under which jail, stationery and printing, Sanjay Gandhi Institute of Training for Youth and other administrative services find place.

With a view to examining the impact of these schemes the financial investments and physical achievements made will therefore have to be assessed. Financial investments are available from state plan, special central assistance as cent per cent grant from Government of India, central sector and centrally sponsored schemes and institutional financing.

The major share comes from state plan resources. During the plan period from the Fifth to Eighth the total investments made from state plan are as follows:

TABLE NO. 3

Provisions & Expenditure during different Plan Period and Annual Plans

(Rs. in crore)

S. No.	*Plan Period*	*Provision*	*Expenditure*	*Percentage of Expenditure to Provision*
1.	Fifth Plan	205.79	205.79	100
2.	Sixth plan	641.11	666.09	103.90
3.	Seventh plan	1379.76	1355.12	98.25
4.	Annual Plan 1990-91	463.39	391.03	84.39
5.	Annual plan 1991-92	520.06	442.00	84.99
6.	Eighth plan	2745.60	2039.15	74.27
	Total	5955.71	5099.18	85.62

Note : Slight difference in the figures as compared to the totals in Table No. 1 is due to converting and rounding up the figures into crores.

Agriculture and Allied Activities

Major sector wise performance during Sixth to Eighth Plan including Annual Plans 90-91 and 91-92 shows that under total provisions in TSP 14.15 per cent (Refer Table No. 1) was made for agriculture and allied Activities, under Agriculture and Allied activities, Agriculture production, horticulture, agriculture marketing, soil and water conservation including Agriculture and Forest department, animal husbandry, dairy, fisheries, Forest, co-operation, food and Civil Supplies—Public Distribution System are included. The plan period wise performance is shown below:

(Rs. in lakh)

Sl. No.	*Plan Period*	*Provision*	*Expenditure*	*Percentage of Expenditure to Provision*
1.	VIth plan	12009.81	8681.27	72.28
2.	VIIth plan	17610.80	13741.18	78.03
3.	Annual plan 90-91	9371.44	4296.03	45.84

Sl. No.	*Plan Period*	*Provision*	*Expenditure*	*Percentage of Expenditure to Provision*
4.	Annual plan 91-92	7073.64	5860.00	82.84
5.	VIIIth plan	35376.04	28635.44	80.94
	Total	81442.23	61213.92	75.16

Under this major head i.e. agriculture and allied activities, the figures show that substantial amount is provided under forests, Co-operation and agricultural production. It is quite natural because the tribal economy depends to a large extent on the forest and agriculture, co-operative structure too provides a system for better economic gains. The Public Distribution System (Food and Civil Supplies Department) was provided previously under non-plan sectors. During the Eighth Plan period, however, it has been provided under Plan, therefore, the provisions and expenditure under Public Distribution System is during the Eighth Plan period only.

Except for the year 1990-91, the level of expenditure as compared to the provision is in the range of 72.28 per cent to 82.84 per cent. During the year 1990-91, however, it is less than 50 per cent i.e. 45.84 per cent only.

Due to financial constraints, many a time, the finance department does not release the total amount provided in the budget and keeps some proportion of money under reserve.

Many a time the schemes provided in the budget are not sanctioned which results in utilization of a lesser amount provided in the budget. During the year 90-91 the expenditure is less than 50 per cent. During this year least expenditure has been incurred under cooperatives, Rs 46 crores was provided but only 2.80 crores (6.09 per cent) could be spent. The reason given for this state of affairs of cooperative department is that their schemes could not get sanctioned from the finance department.

Rural Development: This major head of development includes basically the poverty alleviation programmes—integrated rural Development, drought prone area programme, integrated rural employment programmes, and Jawahar Rozgar Yojana which help the people in rising above the poverty line. In addition, land reforms, community development programmes and Panchayats are also included. The plan-period-wise provision and expenditure under this head of development are as follow:-

(Rs. in lakh)

Sl. No.	*Plan Period*	*Provision*	*Expenditure*	*Percentage of Expenditure to Provision*
1.	VIth plan	8878.96	6513.75	73.36
2.	VIIth plan	11524.69	13639.87	118.62
3.	Annual plan 90-91	4106.92	3566.59	86.84
4.	Annual plan 91-92	42277.77	3608.77	85.36
5.	VIIIth plan	35851.67	29299.76	81.72
	Total	64590.01	56628.74	86.67

The schemes under this head of development, receive quite substantial amount from Government of India. At the district level, Rural Development Agencies have been set up under the supervision of a senior officer known as Executive Officer. The chairman of this agency used to be the Collector of the district, now under the Panchayati raj the chief executive officer is the chairman of this agency. The Government of India monitor this programme very well under a time frame, therefore the performance under this head of development is better as compared to the agriculture and allied activities. The expenditure under rural development is in the range of 73.36 per cent-118.62 per cent.

During the Seventh plan period the expenditure is more than the provision. It is because the Government of India has released more funds than the original budget provisions. As the Panchayati Raj system has been launched in the state from the year 1994, the Provision for the panchayats have increased substantially during the Eighth plan period. In the earlier plan periods, it was in the range of 6 to 7 crores but during the Eighth plan it increased to 13.16 crores. As the Panchayati Raj system is in the process of taking roots the position of expenditure is low for the present but will definitely increase in the coming plan periods.

Irrigation and Flood Control: This head of development includes major and medium, Narmada valley development, and minor irrigation of irrigation and agriculture departments. It also included micro-minor irrigation schemes and command area development programme. The programmes included under this sector are quite crucial for tribal development as they form the base line of agriculture and allied activities, the back bone of tribal economy. The provision and expenditure plan period-wise under this sector are as follow:

(Rs. in Lakh)

Sl. No.	*Plan Period*	*Provision*	*Expenditure*	*Percentage of Expenditure to Provision*
1.	VIth Plan	14788.00	16698.36	112.92
2.	VIIth Plan	32291.09	30058.96	93.09
3.	Annual Plan 1990-91	9945.37	8361.91	84.08
4.	Annual Plan 1991-92	12921.76	9584.76	74.18
5.	VIIIth Plan	50307.11	34639.40	68.86
	Total	120253.33	99343.39	82.61

The range of expenditure under this head of development is between 68.86 per cent -112.92 per cent. During the Eighth plan period, the expenditure was 68.86 per cent but during Sixth plan period the expenditure was more than the provisions i.e. 112.92 per cent. In this period more funds were provided as compared to budget provisions.

Industry and Mining: This head of development includes handloom, khadi Gramodyoga, handicrafts, leather Development, Sericulture, large and medium industries, village and small scale industries, mining and industrial cooperatives. Leather Development is in respect of Scheduled Caste Development, therefore, the provisions under this is nil under tribal sub-plan. Traditionally, the tribal people have a number of cottage industries which bring subsidiary income to them. Under this head of development those measures are included which help in developing the traditional cottage industries. The developmental measures include provision of raw material, improved tools and equipment, better technology and know–how for improving their traditional skill. The provisions and expenditure under this head of development are as follows:

(Rs. in Lakh)

Sl. No.	Plan Period	Provision	Expenditure	Percentage of Expenditure to Provision
1.	VIth plan	2102.44	1987.33	94.52
2.	VIIth plan	7526.01	6897.73	91.65
3.	Annual plan 90-91	1992.94	1068.22	53.60
4.	Annual plan 91-92	1823.42	1078.47	59.15
5.	VIIIth plan	5506.13	4207.96	76.42
	Total	18950.94	15239.71	80.42

Under Industry and Mining, Sericulture is an important activity. During VIth plan period, the level of expenditure was 89.75 per cent, in VIIth it was cent percent (100.20 per cent). But during Annual Plans 1990-91 and 1991-92 the deterioration in performance is notable as during 1990-91 the level of expenditure was 14.21 per cent and during 91-92, though no provision was made there was an expenditure of 303.69 lakh. In Eighth plan, the performance improved as against provision of Rs 1526.99. an expenditure was made of Rs. 1796.48 lakh which comes to 117.65 per cent of the provisions. The pattern of investment under village and small scale industries is same as that of seri-culture, as during the Sixth plan the percentage of expenditure was 33.76 per cent. During Seventh plan though provisions was Rs 2548.80 but no expenditure is reported. During the annual plans 90-91 and 91-92 the provision and expenditure were reported as nil. But during the Eighth plan provision of Rs. 1742.96 was made but the expenditure was only Rs. 111.36 i.e. 6.39 per cent of the total.

The mining activities include exploration and excavation of minerals found in tribal areas. As compared to other sub-sectors under industry and mining, in every plan period from the Sixth to the Eighth and Annual Plans 1990-91 and 91-92 the provisions were made regularly and against the provision expenditure has also been reported regularly. The provisions in different plan periods is given below:

(Rs. in Lakh)

Sl. No.	*Plan Period*	*Provision*	*Expenditure*	*Percentage of Expenditure to Provision*
1.	VIth plan	311.12	274.66	88.28
2.	VIIth plan	662.75	662.75	100
3.	Annual plan 90-91	198.76	169.23	85.14
4.	Annual plan 91-92	55.00	48.22	87.67
5.	VIIIth plan	290	292.81	100.97
	Total	1517.64	1447.67	95.39

It will be seen that during the Seventh plan maximum provisions were made which declined during the Eighth plan.

Transport and Communication

Under this sector, sub-sectors like aviation, roads and bridges and MPSRTC are included. Though there are airfields in the tribal sub-plan area but these are not relevant to the tribals, therefore, expenditure on this activity has not been reported under tribal sub–plan. The construction of roads and bridges is quite an important activity for the tribal sub-plan area, therefore the provisions and expenditure are reported under this sector. The MP State Road Transport Corporation (MPSRTC) which ply buses in tribal areas is also included this sector.

The provisions and expenditure under roads and bridges are as follows:

(Rs. in Lakh)

Sl. No.	*Plan Period*	*Provision*	*Expenditure*	*Percentage of Expenditure to Provision*
1.	VIth plan	4927.90	6118.24	124.16
2.	VIIth plan	11651.97	11840.66	101.62
3.	Annual plan 90-91	2575.00	2020.00	78.45
4.	Annual plan 91-92	00.00	2011.00	—
5.	VIIIth plan	14074.09	7770.18	55.21
	Total	33228.96	29760.08	89.56

It is evident from the table that provisions and expenditure under the sector, roads and bridges has been progressively increasing from the Sixth to Eighth plan including Annual Plans 1990-91 and 1991-92. The programme of roads and bridges are quite useful for the tribal areas as these provide network for transport which is quite essential for the development activities.

The MPSRTC has started showing their flow of funds to tribal sub-plan area from annual plan 1990-91, 1991-92 and Eighth plan. During annual plan 1990-91 Rs. 150 lakh was the provision and same was the expenditure. During 1991-92, Rs. 2721 lakh was the provision but no expenditure has been reported. During the Eighth plan Rs. 512 lakh was the provision and Rs. 510.66 lakh forming 99.74 per cent was the expenditure.

Science and Technology: Science and Technology, head of development provide those inputs to tribal areas which are quite helpful in raising the level of employment and thereby ensuring a better standard of life. This head of development includes Science and Technology, Ecology and Environment and Scientific Research, sub-sectors. However, provisions and expenditure under Science and technology was nil during Sixth and Seventh Plan periods. In the annual plan 90-91 Rs. 10 lakh were provided but there was no expenditure. During 91-92, there was a provision of Rs. 10 lakh again but the expenditure was only Rs. 8 lakh. During Eighth Plan Rs. 62.40 lakh was provided but the expenditure was only Rs. 16.20 lakh forming 25.96 per cent of the provisions.

Under Ecology and Environment, schemes relating to improvement of environment through cleaning of ponds, tanks, lakes and planting trees in urban surrounding are included. There was no provision during the Sixth plan but there was an expenditure of Rs. 1.01 lakh. During the Seventh Plan Rs. 228.50 lakh was provided but there was no expenditure.

During annual plan 90-91 Rs. 117.85 lakh was provided and expenditure was Rs. 111.97 lakh or 95.01 per cent of the total. Again during the year 91-92, Rs. 150 lakh was provided and the expenditure was Rs. 102 lakh i.e. 68 per cent of the total provision.

During Eighth plan, Rs. 453.81 lakh was provided and Rs. 440.00 lakh or 96.96 per cent was the expenditure. The third sub-sector under this head of development is scientific research pertaining to environment. But a provision of Rs. 13.41 lakh was made during the Eighth plan. In earlier plan periods and Annual Plan 1990-91 and 1991-92 the provision and expenditure was nil.

General Economic Services: Under this head of development, state Planning Board, special programmes, tourism computer centre, statistics, district plan, untied funds, weights and measures are included. As the tribal areas provided nature based tourist centres including old historical places for tourism, provisions during different plan periods and annual plans 90-91 and 91-92 were made. The provision made was in the range of Rs. 85.23 lakh during Sixth plan, Rs. 282.36 lakh under Seventh plan Rs. 81.90 lakh under Annual Plan 90-91, Rs. 83.00 lakh under annual plan 91-92 and Rs. 178.85 lakh during Eighth Plan period. The percentage of expenditure varied from 57.98 per cent to 100.77 per cent. The services under computer centre and statistics are not available for tribal sub-plan area. Under district plans and united funds, provisions were made during the Sixth plan and annual plan 90-91 and 91-92 and Eighth plan. But no expenditure has been reported during the Seventh plan, Annual Plan 90-91 and 91-92. However, during Eighth plan a provision was made of Rs. 5379.00 lakh and the expenditure was Rs. 4809.09 lakh. The weights and measures are quite an important sub-sector for the tribal areas. In tribal areas there are un-regulated weekly markets in which the transactions take place with the help of local weights and measures. The traders and businessmen exploit the tribals by faulty weights and measures. Measures to check exploitation by appointing inspectors who visit these weekly markets have been taken. These inspectors check the weights and measures in the weekly markets and impose fines on those found guilty. But the amount provided under weights and measures is meagre in the range of Rs. 1.06 lakh to Rs. 11.88 lakh only. The amount provided is also not spent fully.

Social services: The Social services sector is quite important for the Scheduled Tribes as they guarantee a better standard of living. Under this head of development, education, schools, colleges, adult and technical, Sports and Youth welfare, Art and culture, public health an family welfare, water supply, sanitations and housing are included. In addition information and publicity and welfare of SC/ST and the BC are also included.

Under Education the maximum investment is under school

education in the range of Rs. 1997.39 lakh to a maximum of Rs. 32372.19 lakh.

In the Annual Plans 90-91 and 91-92 Rs. 4112.66 lakh and Rs. 7421.60 lakh was provided respectively.

During the year, looking at the demand under education additional resources were provided. Therefore, the expenditure is invariably more than the provisions. It is evident from the figures of provision and expenditure given in the table below:

(Rs in Lakh)

Sl. No.	*Plan Period*	*Provision*	*Expenditure*	*Percentage of Expenditure to Provision*
1.	VIth Plan	1977.39	2768.92	140.03
2.	VIIth Plan	11494.12	11671.27	101.54
3.	Annual Plan 1990-91	4112.66	6772.71	164.68
4.	Annual Plan 1991-92	7421.60	9598.59	129.33
5.	VIIIth Plan	32372.19	16800.22	51.90
	Total	57377.96	47611.71	82.98

Though in other plan period and annual plans expenditure is more than the provision but during the Eighth plan the expenditure is only 51.90 per cent, therefore, the aggregate percentage of expenditure comes to 82.98 per cent only.

Adult education include the schemes for making the adults literate. This sector creates awareness among adult people specially women. However, the aggregate percentage of expenditure to provision from the Sixth to the Eighth plan including annual plans 90-91 and 91-92 is 61.12 per cent only. The technical education includes the Industrial Training Institute, polytechnics and engineering colleges. However, the aggregate level of expenditure is 36.10 per cent only from the Sixth to the Eighth plan period.

Health and Family Welfare: Measure include the primary health centres, sub-health centres and measures of family planning. The aggregate level of expenditure come to 71.38 per cent from the Sixth to the Eighth plan.

The Water Supply, Sanitation and Housing head of development includes schemes under drinking water, housing schemes, run by Housing Board, Rural Housing Rental, Police Housing, Urban Development, Town and Country Planning, Urban Administration and Urban Welfare. M.P. Housing Board provides housing facilities to the tribals in urban areas whereas under rural housing facilities of housing specially under the scheme of Indira Awas Yojana are provided. Rental housing provide facilities to government officers and sub-ordinate officials posted in tribal areas, while Police housing ensures housing facilities to Police department officials. Under urban administration the local self-government and under urban welfare, the schemes for tribals coming in urban areas are included. Out of all these sub-sectors the water supply and sanitation is very important. The level of expenditure of this sector is in the range of Rs. 4085.70 lakh to Rs. 9125.59 lakh from the Sixth to the Eighth plan. During the annual plan also an expenditure of Rs. 1371 lakh and Rs. 1213.01 lakh during 1990-91 and 1991-92 respectively is reported.

Another head of development is Information and Publicity. Under this head of development publicity of development schemes together with other information relevant to adding to the knowledge of the people are provided. During the Sixth plan as against a provision of Rs. 30.26 lakh expenditure of Rs. 27.68 lakh, i.e. 91.47 per cent of the total was made. But this declined during the seventh plan as provision was Rs. 188.14 lakh but the expenditure was only 97.24 lakh which is 51.68 per cent of the provisions. Decline in expenditure is also reflected during the annual plans 1990-91 and 1991-92, as the percentage of expenditure was 33.06 and 51.26 of the provisions respectively. During the Seventh plan and Eighth plan the expenditure is 51.68 per cent and 66.14 per cent respectively.

Welfare of Scheduled Tribes, Scheduled Castes and Backward Classes

Though all the expenditure under this head of development relate to the development of the STs, here the provision and expenditure made for the tribal welfare department only, is reflected. Besides, normal provisions made for the development of ST outlay for 'pool' for TSP programmes during the Seventh plan is also included. The provisions and expenditure under welfare of ST during different plan periods and Annual Plans 90-91 and 91-92 are as follow:

(Rs in Lakh)

Sl. No.	*Plan Period*	*Provision*	*Expenditure*	*Percentage of Expenditure to Provision*
1.	VIth Plan	3730.05	2654.03	71.15
2.	VIIth Plan	6625.02	6979.58	105.35
3.	Annual Plan 1990-91	2088.80	1962.88	93.97
4.	Annual Plan 1991-92	2288.67	2306.67	100.79
5.	VIIIth Plan	31474.09	28812.94	91.54
	Total	46207.39	42716.10	92.44

The schemes included are education, nutrition, legal aid to poor tribals, relief measures and administrative structure created under tribal welfare in tribal areas. Under education, the Primary, Middle and Higher Secondary schools, pre-matric and post-matric hostels, stipend and scholarship are included.

With the growing number of children, for educational institutions the ceiling provided under tribal welfare was found insufficient. Therefore a special pool of funds was earmarked from which the additional financial resources were provided to different schemes under tribal welfare.

Labour and Employment: Under this head, labour welfare, craftsmen training, employment services and special employment schemes are included. Total amount provided from Sixth, Seventh, both the annual plans i.e. 1990-91, 1991-92 and Eighth plan is Rs. 3288.08 lakh and expenditure incurred is 1234.59 lakh i.e. 37.55 per cent. The less percentage of expenditure is because the schemes included are located in urban areas where the tribals are less in number.

Social Welfare and Nutrition: Under this head of development social welfare, welfare of women and child, nutrition (other than mid-day meal programmes in school) legal aid to poor, including codification of customary laws are included. A sum of Rs. 12927 lakh was provided against which Rs. 9631.31 lakh i.e. 74.50 per cent was spent.

With a view to providing justice to tribal people, their customs and traditions were codified so that justice could be ensured as per their customs and traditions.

The law department with help of tribal welfare department codified the customs and traditions of the tribal people. After obtaining the approval of the Tribes Advisory Council it will be brought to force.

General Services: The last head of development is general service which include jail welfare of prisoners, stationery and printing, Sanjay Gandhi Institute, other administrative services and public works. The expenditure on jails include the facilities added to the jails in tribal sub-plan area for making shades to be used by relatives of tribal prisoners, adding barracks and the like. Though stationery and printing is mentioned no funds has either been provided or spent as there is no press located in tribal sub-plan area. Similarly under Sanjay Gandhi Institute, other administrative services, public works etc. the provision and expenditure are quite small. Thus, during the period between Sixth, Seventh plan, annual plans 1990-91, 1991-92 and Eighth plan total provisions made was 280.86 lakh but the expenditure was 59.11 lakh i.e. 21.05 per cent only.

In this manner all the schemes being implemented in tribal sub-plan area are divided into 16 heads of development. The tribal sub-plan strategy in the state has been evolved from fifth plan therefore the total provisions and expenditure from fifth plan to Eighth plan including two Annual Plans can be summed up as follows:

(Rs in Lakh)

Sl. No.	*Plan Period*	*Provision*	*Expenditure*	*Percentage of Expenditure to Provision*
1.	VIth Plan	20579.00	20579.00	100.00
2.	VI, VIIth Plan Annual Plans 1990-91, 1991-92 Eighth Plan	574991.78	489339.03	85.10
	Total	595570.78	509918.03	85.62

In addition to the State Plan Resources, Special Central Assistance has also been provided by the Government of India during different plan periods which is as follows:

(Rs in Lakh)

Sl. No.	Plan Period	Provision	Amount Released by Govt. of India	Expenditure
1.	Vth Plan	50.00	50.00	0.00
2.	VIth Plan	18835.18	13772.00	15048.85
3.	VIIth Plan	24232.13	23405.00	23013.07
4.	Annual Plan 1990-91	7559.19	6237.00	6603.43
5.	Annual Plan	8787.90	6830.00	7350.61
6.	VIIIth Plan	38763.97	39714.00	35358.05
	Total	98228.37	90008.00	87424.01

Thus, budget provisions were made to the tune of Rs. 98228.37 lakh, Government of India released Rs. 90008.00 lakh only. The expenditure incurred has been Rs. 87424.01 which is 89.00 per cent of the provision and 97.13 per cent of the released amount. During the Fifth Plan the amount provided in the budget has been spent but the expenditure has exceeded the amount released by Government of India in the annual plans 90-91 and 91-92.

In the Constitution under Article 275(i) grants under Special Central Assistance (SCA) is provided to certain states promoting the welfare of the ST or raising the level of administration in the scheduled area as compared to the rest of the area of that state.

The Government of India has made working arrangements for the release of Special Central assistance. In category 1-normal Special Central Assistance (SCA) is given on the basis of the population of the ST in a particular state. However, as per letter No. 110/14/1/85 - TD (R) dated 11.6.85 the Government of India felt a need to introduce an element of control/guidance to dissuade investment of this assistance in sectors where benefits are not directly and substantially co-relatable to tribal population. With this end in view it was suggested by Government of India that SCA may be divided into two components:[1]

A major portion of SCA representing 75 per cent of the total may be sanctioned as an additive and gap filler to state plan efforts as hitherto continuing the emphasis on schemes benefiting families.

Secondly, about 25 per cent of the total provision of the special central assistance should be utilised as incentives to be given to the states excelling in performances in the tribal development field. The factors include coverage of families, preparation of project report, number of families benefitted by schemes. In addition to these factors formulation of integrated tribal development project reports, project reports for tribal pockets, project reports for primitive tribal groups, quality of the tribal sub-plan of the state, performance during the preceding year relative to the targets fixed in the fields of production programmes, family oriented schemes, human resources development programmes and infrastructure etc. could be included.

The SCA wax meant primarily for family oriented income generating schemes, while giving adequate weightage to infrastructure incidental to such schemes.[2] Further SCA was intended as an additive to state plan effort and is not intended to be a substitute for existing plan schemes. The Government of India gave illustrative list of items under various development sectors which could be funded by SCA.[3]

Besides SCA funds are also made available to state through grants under Article 275 (i), first provision of the Constitution, for the following items[4] (i) resettlement of tribals, practising shifting cultivation, (ii) schemes for development of forest villages, (iii) development of tribal suffering from special disease (iv) reclamation of ravine areas intended to be specially alloted to the scheduled tribes. Detailed instructions were given for formulating the project proposals to be funded out of funds under Article 275 (i) of the Constitution. Under such project proposals the programme of family oriented schemes and infrastructure development were to be clearly demarcated.

Funds under SCA and Article 275(i) of the Constitution are quite substantial and important for the development of the tribals in a particular state. The Government of India has issued specific guidelines for the schemes to be funded out of SCA. The schemes funded out of SCA during the latest plan period i.e. Eighth plan is given in the annexure No. VII. While a number of schemes are for the family oriented incomes generating programmes, majority of the scheme are for construction of various types of buildings, plantation, irrigation works and building up of infrastructure.

Under family oriented schemes subsidies at different rates are provided to the families. No mechanism has been development to assess whether these subsidies have been able to help the tribal families in increasing their income. Similarly, the infrastructure development programme works under water resources and PWD should have been incidental to family oriented income generating scheme. But no such co-relation or association is reflected in the pattern of schemes funded out of SCA.

Government of India lays great emphasis on furnishing the accounts of funds under SCA from the state governments. In this regard a quarterly return has also been prescribed. But as shown in the table on budget provision, amount released by Government of India and expenditure, systematic maintenance of accounts and financial control over the utilisation of funds received does not seem to have been maintained.

In addition to state plans SCA funds are also received under central sector and centrally sponsored programmes. These schemes are oriented by Government of India. Under central sector schemes cent per cent funding is made by the Government of India. Under centrally sponsored scheme, if the state governments adopted these schemes the Government of India provide its share as per norms of the scheme, sometimes it is 40 per cent and sometimes it is 50 per cent. The list of schemes under centrally sponsored and central sector is given in the annexure No. V.

Non-government Organizations

Looking to the populations of the Scheduled Tribes and their level of development there is good scope for running the educational activities. Nearly 23026 institutions of different kinds including junior primary, middle and high and higher secondary schools are being run by the department. Even then it has been felt that more and more educational institutions should be opened. The role of Non-Governmental Organizations (NGOs) is quite important in this regard. It is the policy of both central and the state governments to encourage the NGO. Under the approved policy of the Government, Grant-in-Aid has been sanctioned to NGOs for running the Institutions in the farflung tribal areas. The NGOs receive Grant-in-Aid easily, therefore, the Grant-in-Aid rules have been simplified during the year 1995-96. Under the simplified rules the Collectors can sanction Grant-in-Aid upto two instalments i.e. up to 75 per cent in a year to old institutions. In addition, the Collectors have also been empowered to sanction Rs. 3.00 lakh in old cases and the Head of the Department Rs. 10 lakh.

With a view to ensuring the fullest utilization of Grant-in-Aid provided, a system has been evolved to inspect the activities run by the NGOs thrice a year. As and when required very senior officers can also inspect these institutions.

Cent per cent Grant-in-Aid is provided for running 363 activities to the NGOs. In addition, 90 per cent grant is provided for the construction of buildings. Only 10 per cent amount has to be managed by the NGO concerned.

Grant-in-Aid sanctioned to the NGOs during the last three years is as follows:

(Rs in Lakh)

Year	*Provisions*	*Grant-in-Aid Sanctioned*
94-95	881.00	858.11
95-96	928.35	795.59
96-97	1352.00	1289.00

Conclusions

With a view to assessing the impact of development schemes on the tribals, financial arrangements made have been discussed. The development programmes have been divided into 16 sub-heads of development. Budget provisions and expenditure have been shown as per this sub-head of development. However, there are certain discrepancies in the figures included under the financial management. During Sixth Plan, in provisions under agriculture production, provisions for soil and water conservation, minor irrigation and micro-minor irrigation have been put together but the expenditure has been shown separately under each sub-sector. Under rural development also, the provisions for DPAP, IREP, Jawahar Rojgar Yojana have not been shown separately but grouped under IRDP. However, the expenditure has been shown separately, therefore, it is not possible to assess the impact of expenditure as compared to the provisions. Similar situation is seen in respect of other sectors also.

Another discrepency is in respect of showing much more expenditure as compared to budget provisions. During Sixth plan under urban administration the expenditure is 181.85 per cent. Similarly, in the following sub-sector the percentage of expenditure is much more than budget provisions.

	Sector	*Percentage of Expenditure*
1.	Labour Welfare	169.79
2.	Craftsman training employment Services	186.68
3.	Legal aid to poor	155.40

These discrepancies have been pointed out because due to these it is difficult to assess the impact of the development programmes on the tribals.

However, with all due limitation of financial management of the figures shown by way of provisions and expenditure do show some impact on the tribals. Total provisions during different plan periods both under the state plan and Special Central Assistance have been shown above. If this figure is divided by the total scheduled tribe population of the state which is 153.99 lakh then atleast per capita provisions and expenditure could be known. The per capita provisions and expenditure from different sources are as under:

	State Plan	*Amount in Rs.*
1.	Per capita provisions from Fifth to Eighth Plan	3867.59
2.	Per capita expenditure from Fifth to Eighth Plan	3311.37

Special Central Assistance

	State Plan	*Amount in Rs.*
1.	Per capita provisions from Fifth to Eighth Plan	637.89
2.	Per capita expenditure from Fifth to Eighth Plan	567.73

Impact of this investment can be seen in reference to certain sector e.g. education. The increase in literacy percentage as shown in decadal census operations has been discussed in Chapter - II.

The amount spent under economic development schemes has its impact on the economic development of families. Similarly, the amount spent on infrastructure development have shown their results in the increase of facilities and institutions in tribal sub-plan area.

These aspects have been discussed in Chapter Seventh plan period wise Coverage of families have also been discussed under 20-point programme and other sectors plan period wise in Chapter 7.

REFERENCES

1. Compendium of circulars/guidelines on Tribal Development Government of India, Ministry of Welfare, Tribal Development Division, (Research Unit, New Delhi-1990) p. 115.
2. *Op. cit.*, p. 116.
3. *Op. cit.*, pp. 117-19.
4. *Op. cit.*, p. 128.
5. *Ibid.*

7

Impact of Developmental Programmes: Physical

As against the financial investments made, physical achievements can be assessed in different plan periods. Though financial provisions and expenditures made during Fifth Plan period is available physical achievements during Fifth Plan is not. During the Sixth Plan period, however, physical achievements in respect of certain important sectors are as follows:

Physical Achievements During the Sixth Plan

Sector	*Target*	*Achievement*
Irrigation	8 per cent of the cropped areas	8.62 per cent of the cropped area
Rural electrification	267 villages to be electrified.	6,300 villages electrified
Road and bridges	9.5 km/100 sq. km	11.30 km/100 sq. km.
Education	70 per cent enrolment of school going children in 6-11 age group	53.69 per cent
Drinking water	Provision of drinking water in 12,057 villages.	11,826 villages.

Except in irrigation and roads and bridges, the achievements in other sectors i.e. rural electrification, education and drinking water has been less than the target. The reasons may be many but the most important is less provision of money and bad implementation of schemes.

With a view to assessing the impact of various schemes on

tribals, it would be proper to get details of each scheme financed under the tribal sub-plan while at the planning stage the financial and physical target under each scheme excluding of course those under establishment and administration are given. But the physical achievements under only selected schemes are available and that too not on uniform basis under different plan periods. Therefore, a comparative assessment from different plan periods is not possible. Under the Fifth Plan period physical achievements are not available. The achievements on selected items during the Sixth plan have been attempted as above. During the Seventh and the Eighth Plans the sector–wise achievements can be given as follows:–

Physical Achievements During the Seventh Plan Under Selected Sectors

Agriculture:

As mentioned in the previous chapter agriculture and its allied sector is one of the important heads of development under the tribal sub-plan. Physical achievements sector-wise are given as follows:

Sl. N.	*Scheme*	*Unit*	*Target*	*Achievement*
1.	Agricultural production subsidy on distribution of wheat and paddy	No. of beneficiaries.	14,000	10,780
2.	National project for bio-gas development	-do-	5,500	4,260
3.	National oil seed development	-do-	27,500	21,130
4.	Training and refresher programme for cultivators	-do-	65,000	51,140
5.	Siesal development	-do-	650	501
6.	Sugar–cane development	-do-	250	171
7.	Mini kit distribution	-do-	2,00,000	1,60,200
8.	Subsidy to cultivators	-do-	2,500	1,912
9.	Intensive cotton development programme	-do-	5,750	4,202

It will be seen that the achievements are always less than the target. As mentioned in reference to the Sixth Plan, here also the less release of funds as compared to budgetary provisions and bad administration of schemes may be responsible for less achievement as compared to the target.

Soil and water conservation

Scheme	Unit	Target	Achievement
(a) Agriculture department	No. of beneficiaries		
(i) assistance to small and marginal farmers for development of agriculture	-do-	25,000	19,651
(ii) development of water shed in dry farming areas.	-do-	200	161
(b) forest department			
(i) soil conservation	hect.	1,300	1,763

It may be seen that under soil and water conservation in Forest department the achievement has been more than the target.

Dairy

Scheme	Unit	Target	Achievement
(a) Average milk production per day	Lt. per day	23,300	5,778

It may be seen that the achievement is much less than the target. Traditionally the tribals do not milk their cattle. The cattle is kept for agricultural and consumption purpose. The dairy units were given cattle belonging to the sophisticated breed about which the tribals were not very well trained for their upkeeping. These are the reasons which resulted in very low achievements.

Fisheries

Scheme	Unit	Target	Achievement
(i) Fisheries extension			
(a) storage of seedlings in village tanks including forest villages	Million	10.00	33.21
(b) assistance to fish farmers.	Number	400	3152
(ii) production of seedlings			
(a) production of dry fish	Million	30.68	85.48

Scheme	Unit	Target	Achievement
(b) assistance to fish farmers	Number	6	6
(iii) Development of tanks	Number	18	30
(iv) Study tours of tribal fish farmers	Number	150	58
(v) Fish farmers development agcncies.	Number	905	1,816

Under this sector though achievements are more than the targets the schemes do not seem to have large coverage of the tribals. Needless to mention the tribals are good fish farmers. Traditionally, they are used to consume fish available from any source, therefore, the fisheries sector has very good scope of development among the tribals.

Forest

S. No.	Scheme	Unit	Target	Achievement
(i)	economic plantation	hect.	5,500	10,640
(ii)	plantation of fuel wood	hect.	15,500	12,724
(iii)	reformation of degraded forest and socio-economic development	hect.	15,000	85,047
(iv)	social forestry	hect.	18,500	85,047

Tribals and forests are inter-dependent. The tribals depend on the forest for various things quite important for making their living, for collection of leaves, fruits, roots for consumption, minor forest produces for income, fuel and timber root. It may be seen that except in the plantation of fuel woods, the achievements are much more than the target. The reasons for this state of affairs has not been clarified. It may be that the forest department might have received additional funds during the year or may have used funds not utilized during previous years.

Rural Development

Under this head, integrated rural development programmes are included. As against a target of 6.88 lakh beneficiaries, 5.54 lakhs beneficiaries were covered. The achievements under this head shouid have been much more as the programmes included under this head guarantee raising tribals above the poverty line.

It may be interesting to note that 17.92 lakh i.e. 66.44 per cent tribal families in rural areas and 0.41 lakh or 25.94 per cent in urban areas of the total Scheduled Tribes population (1991-92 survey) are living below the poverty line but the achievements and targets are not commensurate with that.

Water resources under this head

Under this head though major, medium and minor irrigation schemes are included, in tribal areas only medium and minor schemes are implemented. The target under medium irrigation scheme was to irrigate 3.2 thousand hectares and the achievements were 36.0 thousands hectares. More than the medium irrigation schemes, under minor irrigation 87.5 thousand hectares was the target but achievement was only 80.4 thousand hectares. It may be mentioned that the benefits under medium irrigation schemes take longer time to reach the people. The schemes under minor irrigation are completed in lesser time than the medium irrigation but as has been shown the achievements are less than the target. It may be due to bad administration of the schemes.

Ayacut

Under this head the command areas of various major and medium irrigation projects are developed. The tribals are exposed to new crops and the methods through which high yield can be ensured. Therefore, demonstration of crops especially with a view to getting higher yields are organized on the fields of the tribals. As against a target of 5,000 demonstrations only 1,110 could be organized i.e. much below the target. It may be because the tribals may not be interested in demonstration and as such their plots may not be available for this scheme.

M.P. Electricity Board (MPEB)

Reaching Electricity is in itself a very good indicator of development. The MPEB takes up the programme of rural electrification, energization of pumps and providing single point connections to tribal families. The achievements under these schemes are much more than the target as will be reflected in the table given below:

Sl. No.	*Scheme*	*Unit*	*Target*	*Achievement*
I.	Electrification of villages	Number	5,000	7,949
II.	Energization of pumps	Number	18,000	39,355
III.	Single bulb connection	Number	1,50,000	6,27,876

Industries

Every tribal household is quite adept in making goods for their day to day use. The tribal women are expert in making different kinds of articles as part of their household activities. In this manner household industries and crafts are quite popular in tribal areas. The targets and achievements are given as follows:

Dairy

S. No.	*Scheme*	*Unit*	*Target*	*Achievement*
(a)	Establishment of small industries			
(i).	Unit	Number	13400	17016
(ii)	Investment	in lakh	429	501
(iii)	Employment	Number	15763	24669
(b)	Entrepreneur development programme	Number of bene.	1500	921
	Financial assistance for establishing small industries by M.P. finance corporation.	Number of bene.	4080	762
II	(a) Handloom	Rs. in lakh	15100	11016
	(b) Employment	Number of families	18000	5041
III	(a) Industrial cooperatives	Persons	300	1187
IV	Sericulture. (cumulative) families	Number of	97140	37074

It may be seen that the establishment of industries have achieved the targets desired. In fact it is much more than the targets fixed. But in respect to other items except employment and industrial co-operatives, the achievements are much below the target. It may be because the tribals are used to cottage industries and crafts but may not find themselves suitable for entrepreneur development, handlooms, industrial cooperatives and sericulture industries. However, the collection of Kosa cocoons is quite popular among the tribals under sericulture.

School education

The Tribal welfare department runs educational activities. Its impact is quite good as can be assessed by a single indicator i.e. enrolment of school going children in the age group 6-11 years in class I to V i.e. primary school. The target fixed during the Seventh Plan for the enrolment of boys was 13.44 lakh and the achievement was 27.51. In respect to girls it was 4.71 lakh and the achievements were almost three times i.e. 11.11 lakh. The same tendency is reflected in middle schools i.e. class VI to VII age group 11 to 13 years. The target fixed in respect to boys was 3.37 lakh and the achievement against this was 6.178 lakhs. In respect to girls the target was 1.98 lakh and the achievement was 3.06 lakh.

Public Health and Family Welfare

The schemes under Public health and family welfare are quite important in respect of tribals as they help in human resource development. The following schemes are included under the minimum needs programme, the progress under each in respect of targets and achievements are shown below:–

	Scheme	*Unit*	*Target*	*Achievement*
I	Establishment of subsidiary health centres	Number	2,000	2,148
II	Establishment of Primary health centres	Number	280	283
III	Establishment of community health centres	Number	40	49

The achievements are not much more than the targets but it can be said that the targets fixed have been achieved.

Drinking Water

It is an important programme for the tribal areas. The problem villages are identified at the district level with the help of Public health & engineering department and sources of drinking water are provided there. During the Seventh Plan 6,173 problem villages were targeted to be provided with drinking water source and 6,587 villages were provided with source of drinking water. Thus, the achievement is more than the target which may be due to getting additional funds.

Women & Child Development

This deptt runs 'Balvadis' for children and tailoring centres for women. The targets and achievement under these schemes are given below:

Scheme	Unit	Target	Achievement
Child Development			
(i) Distribution of article	Number of Balvadis	150	115
(ii) Gram Sevika (village level worker) run Balvadi	Number of Beneficiaries	5000	2650
(iii) Women development	Tailoring	Centre-10 Ladies-300	27 645

M.P. Housing Board

The M.P. Housing Board provides housing facilities in urban areas. It builds LIG houses for the economically weaker section and also distributes plots. The progress under housing and plots are as follows:

	Scheme	Unit	Target	Achievement
(I)	Houses	Number	3267	2067
(II)	Plots	Number	996	4786

It may be mentioned that the tribals in urban areas are less in number, those who come at all, come in search of employment and that too for a short period. They keep contact with their villages for agricultural and other purposes. The houses built by the Housing board is costlier and unsuitable because the tribals are not traditionally used to live in such houses. Therefore housing schemes are not popular among them. The achievement under this scheme also shows this tendency. In respect of plots however the achievements are much more than the target because once the tribals get the plots they develop it as per their convenience and liking.

While discussing the financial investments during different periods Annual Plan 1990-91 and 1991-92 have been discussed but the physical targets and achievements during these two Annual Plans are not available.

Physical Achievements during the Eighth Plan

During the Eighth plan, i.e., 92-93 to 96-97 the physical targets and achievements under different sectors are available and discussed as follows:

Agriculture

Sl.No.	*Scheme*	*Unit*	*Target*	*Achievement*
I.	Agriculture production			
(i)	Integrated rice development programme.	beneficiaries	3,50,000	1,64,083
(ii)	National pulse development programme.	beneficiaries	1,00,000	1,37,368
(iii)	Intensive crop insurance scheme.	beneficiaries	1,95,000	49,115
(iv)	Intensive cotton development programme.	beneficiaries	20,000	13,861
(v)	Surajdhara yojana.	beneficiaries	Nil	23,750
(vi)	Assistance to small marginal farmers for increasing the production-mini kits.	beneficiaries	50,000	22,067

Though tribal areas are mostly rice producing, the achievements under the Integrated Rice Development Programme is much below the target. But in National Pulses Development Programme the achievements are more than the target. Similar is the case in respect of Intensive Crop Insurance Scheme, the achievements are 2.5 times more than the target.

In respect of Intensive Cotton Development Programme and assistance to small farmers for increasing the production the achievements are much below the target. In respect of Suraj Dhara Yojana though no targets were fixed but the achievements are 23,750. In the schemes where achievements are more than the target it seems that the extension officers have worked efficiently and received more fund for implementation of the schemes. But in schemes where the achievements are less the extension officers seem to have not worked well and may have received less funds than the budget provisions.

Soil and water conservation

Sl. No.	Scheme	Unit	Target	Achievement
(a)	Agriculture department			
	(i) National water shed programme	beneficiaries	15000	12689
	(ii) Development of water shed in dry farming areas.	beneficiaries	30000	5367
	(b) Forest	hect.	2390	1400

As in case of agricultural production, in respect of soil and water conservation also the achievements are much below the target.

Dairy Development

Sl. No.	Scheme	Unit	Target	Achievement
(I)	Assistance to tribal farmers for fodder development	beneficiaries	10,000	28,688

Fisheries

Sl No	Scheme	Unit	Target	Achievement
(I)	Fisheries extension			
	(a) Storage of fry in rural tanks	(a)	200 lakh	175.77 lakh
	(b) Fishermen	(b)	1,500	3,523
(II)	Development of fisheries	fingerling seeds	230 lakh	261.23 lakh
(III)	Education and training	Number	2,500	1,988

As fisheries programme are quite popular among the tribals, better performance of schemes is visible under fisheries in comparison to other sector.

Forest

Sl. No.	Scheme	Unit	Target	Achievement
(I)	Improvement of degraded forests.	hect.	98,950	1,04,761
(II)	Fuel fodder project under rural development.	hect.	26,642	24,750

The targets and achievements show that it is much better in comparison to other sectors.

Rural Development

Sl. No.	*Scheme*	*Unit*	*Target*	*Achievement*
(I)	IRDP	Number of beneficiaries in lakh	3.54	3.41

As compared to the Seventh Plan the target is ½ and so also the achievement. Although the budget provisions were Rs. 12,124.69 lakh, and the expenditure was Rs. 13,639.87 lakh i.e. 112.50, per cent of the provisions. During the Eighth Plan the budget provision was Rs. 35,851.67 lakh and the expenditure was Rs. 29,299.76 lakh i.e. 81.72 per cent. Due to rise in prices, it seems that the coverage of beneficiaries was less during the Eighth Plan than the Sixth Plan.

Water resources

Sl.No.	*Scheme*	*Unit*	*Target*	*Achievement*
(I)	Major and medium irrigation	hect.	58.00	18.00
(II)	Minor irrigation	hect.	125.00	50.00

The achievements are much less than the target. It is because the funds were not spent to the tune of budget provisions. Under the major and medium irrigation scheme the budget provision during the Eighth Plan was Rs. 19,186.41 lakh, but expenditure was Rs. 8,841.49 lakh i.e. 46.08 per cent only of the provisions. Similar is the case with minor irrigation. Though the budget provisions was Rs. 1,371.66 lakh the expenditure was Rs. 9,53.75 lakh i.e. 69.53 per cent only.

Ayacut

Under ayacut four schemes are included as follows:

Sl.No.	*Scheme*	*Unit*	*Target*	*Achievement*
(I)	Challenge crop demonstration	Number	5,000	2,597
(II)	Subsidy on improved agriculture implement	Number	16,700	10.040
(III)	Field channel	hect.	6,570	1,691
(IV)	Development of water shed	hect.	6,570	1,257

As is evident the achievements are below the target. Here also the expenditure is not commensurate to the budget provisions. Therefore the achievements are less than the target.

MPEB

As usual, the following three schemes are taken up by the MPEB in tribal areas:

Sl.No.	*Scheme*	*Unit*	*Target*	*Achievement*
(I)	Electrification of villages	Number	3,506	1,396
(II)	Energization of pumps	Number	11,000	19,510
(III)	Single point connection	Number	—	22,951

Industries

The industries sector has four components namely handloom, industrial Cooperatives, khadi and handicraft Industries development (hastshilp) and Sericulture. The progress of schemes under each are as follows:

(a) Handlooms

Sl.No.	*Scheme*	*Unit*	*Target*	*Achievement*
(I)	Increase in number of handlooms	Number	4975	12058
(II)	Functioning handlooms	Number	3375	9131
(III)	Training	Number	5000	1235
(IV)	Modernisation of handlooms	Number	5000	1959
(V)	Employment	Number	10125	27384

As will be seen from the above figures there is definite progress in the spread of handlooms, at least 2.5 times the target, which was 4,975 and the achievement 12,050. Similarly in the case of working handlooms also there is increase but in training and modernization of handlooms the achievements are less than the target. In employment also the achievements show a good progress as compared to the target.

(b) Industrial cooperative

There are three schemes under industrial co-operatives and the assessment of achievement in reference to the target show a good progress:

Sl.No.	*Scheme*	*Unit*	*Target*	*Achievement*
(I)	Socieities	Number	90	323
(II)	Working societies	Number	90	212
(III)	Employment	Number	5,000	17,028

(c) Khadi and Village Industries

There are two schemes under Khadi and Village Industries which are as follows:

Sl. No.	*Scheme*	*Unit*	*Target*	*Achievement*
(I)	Training		4,800	965
(II)	Subsidy for security of family oriented schemes		8,000	2,678

The achievements in reference to the targets do not show a good progress. It is because the expenditure is less than the budget provision as shown in the financial assessment section.

(d) Handicrafts

There are four schemes under handicrafts development as follows:

Sl. No.	*Scheme*	*Unit*	*Target*	*Achievement*
(I)	Training craftsmen	Number	2,700	2,910
(II)	Tools/workshed	-do-	1,634	1,440
(III)	Job work	-do-	600	1,755
(IV)	Procurement	-do-	400	1,211

Thus, in respect of training, job work and procurement the achievement is good as compared to the target. But in respect of tools/work sheds the achievement is less than the target.

(e) Sericulture

Instead of physical achievements financial achievements are given. As against a target of Rs. 0.27 lakh the achievement is 65 lakh.

School education

Progress under the following three schemes as follows:

Sl. No.	Scheme	Unit	Target	Achievement
(I)	Free distribution of text books	Lakh	30.00	28.30
(II)	Free distribution of uniforms to girls	Lakh	30.00	8.50
(III)	Book bank schemes in higher secondary school	Lakh	2.50	5.82

While free distribution of text books can be said to be satisfactory the distribution of uniform to girls is not at all satisfactory. As against a target of 30 lakh uniforms, 8.50 lakh uniforms only, were distributed. In respect of book bank schemes in higher secondary school the achievements are more than double.

Public health and family welfare

Progress under six schemes are as follows. As will be seen the achievements are much below the target.

Sl. No.	Scheme	Unit	Target	Achievement
(I)	Subsidiary health centre	Number	635	Nil
(II)	Conversion of mini health centres into primary health centres	Number	280	136
(III)	Purchase of X-ray machine	Number	100	80
(IV)	Purchase of ambulance	Number	100	09
(V)	Increase in head of district hospitals.	Number	800	50
(VI)	Jeevan Jyoti Mobile Health Units	Number	95	37

Public health and family welfare sector is quite important for the tribals but the achievements are much below the target.

Drinking water

Progress under the two schemes are as follows:

Sl. No.	Scheme	Unit	Target	Achievement
(I)	Drinking water in problem villages	Number of village	2,600	6,384
(II)	Supply of drinking water in hamlets	Number of village	8,000	9,139

As is evident the progress under the above two schemes can be said to be quite satisfactory. Under the first scheme the achievement is nearly 2.5 times.

MP Housing Board

The progress under two scheme is as follows:

Sl. No.	*Scheme*	*Unit*	*Target*	*Achievement*
(I)	Housing	Number	4,419	1,957
(II)	Plots	Number	23,572	4,743

It is clear that the achievements are much below the target. In chapter VI, the financial section, it has been noted that funds to the tune of budget provisions made have not been released to the housing board, therefore, the progress is not upto the targets fixed.

Women and child development

The target fixed and achievements against that under the following schemes are:

Sl. No.	*Scheme*	*Unit*	*Target*	*Achievement*
(A)	Child development			
	(i) balvadi	Number	200	482
	(ii) beneficiaries	Number	2,000	6,000
(B)	Women development			
	(i) centres	Number	10	40
	(ii) tailoring centre	Number	1,500	1,208
	(iii) awareness camp.	Number	750	1,048
	(iv) inspection tours of women			
	(a) inspection tours	Number	40	32
	(b) beneficiaries	Number	1,000	880
	(c) grant-in-Aid			
	(i) child development organization	Number	170	410
	(ii) assistance to voluntary organization	Number	173	516

The achievements under child development and in some of the schemes under women development is quite satisfactory. Under grant-in-aid, the achievement again is quite high as compared to the targets fixed.

In this manner the target and achievement (physical) under 15 heads of development during the Eighth Plan period has been analyzed as above. By and large it can be said that the achievement are not commensurate to the targets fixed.

20-point programme

Late Smt. Indira Gandhi, the Prime Minister of India, inaugurated the 20 point programme during the year 1980-81. This programme focused attention on economic development, self employment, infrastructural development, training for employment etc. for the weaker sections. The speciality of the programme was to identify the schemes outlined above and report monthly progress to be monitored by the office of the Prime Minister.

Point number 7(A) and 7(B) which related to the SC and ST respectively was identified separately and its monitoring was entrusted to Tribal and Scheduled Caste Welfare Department from the year 1994-95.

Late Shri Rajiv Gandhi, the then Prime Minister of India gave a new orientation to this programme from the year 1986. This programme was renamed, as 'Twenty point programme, in 1986, point number 11(A) and 11(B) related to SC and ST respectively. Both these points have been renamed as 'Ensuring social justice to the SC/ST.

The Five Year Plan period–wise target and achievements under point 11 (B) relating to ST is shown in the table below:-

Plan Period Programme Under Pt. 11 (B), ST

Figures in lakh

Plan period Programme under pt. 11 (B), ST.

	Target	*Achieve-ment*	*Cummula-tive*	*Total achievement*
1980-85 (VI)	7.76	7.64	7.76	7.64
1985-90 (VII)	10 lakh	12.40 lakh	17.76 lakh	20.04 lakh
1990-91	2.05	2.23	19.81	22.27
1991-92	2.15	2.24	21.96	24.51
1992-97 (VIII)	12.10	13.25	34.06	37.76
Total	34.06	37.76		

The target and achievements show the number of ST families covered.

The analysis of the targets and achievements show that except during the Sixth Plan period the achievements have always been more than the target. It may be due to getting more funds during the year ensuring more coverage of the families than the targets fixed.

8

Conclusions-Highlights of the Study

The objective of the study is to present a vivid historical account of the development of the tribal people in M.P. from 1947-1990. This period is full of making a number of policy framework which involved structural changes in the implementation of the schemes, the broad principles of the schemes to be taken, their priorities and the manner in which they have to be implemented.

Before independence, the British policy of isolating the tribals in excluded and partially excluded areas, from the mainstream of the march of progress of the country was in vogue. The traditional leadership of the tribals, their social structure, ethos and eiods were weakened.

Their self-sufficient economy was put to a number of exploitation by outsiders including missionaries, contractors, especially forest contractors, businessmen and the public at large. This resulted in discontentment among the tribals which was reflected in a number of revolts against the establishment, may it be the Britishers or the Princely States.

In this background the constitutional provisions were made after the country got Independence. Through various constitutional provisions the development of the tribal people specially bringing them on par with the general population, helping them against exploitation of all sorts, doing away with the historical injustice done to them i.e. restoring their place in the society at large, through reservation in services was made. In addition to these reservations, seats in proportion to their population was reserved both in the Parliament and the State Legislatures. The responsibility of development was bestowed upon the members from among the tribals by making them, Minister of Tribal Welfare.

A 'protective', developmental and paternalistic approach was enshrined in the Constitution for the development of the tribals. As such a number of rules, regulations, Acts have been passed. H.E. the President of India and H.E. the Governor of the State have been vested with the various responsibilities in respect of the Scheduled Tribes. As per provisions, in Schedule Five of the Constitution, the Tribes Advisory Council has to review the policies of tribal development and give recommendations pertaining to various issues of tribal development. It is mandatory on the part of the state governments to follow these recommendations. The government of the state has to submit, Annual Reports on the administration, peace and good governance in the scheduled area to the President of India.

Article 338 of the Constitution provides for the appointment of special officers to investigate all matters, relating to the safeguards, provided for the STs under the Constitution and report to the President upon the working of those safeguards at such intervals as the President may direct and the President shall cause all such reports to be laid before each House of Parliament. After suitable revision of this article, the post of the commissioner ST\SC has been merged with a permanent commission. Now, instead of one officer, Seven persons, have been kept in the commission to watch the process of tribal development throughout the whole country.

Article 339 provides for the appointment of a commission to investigate the conditions of STs and assess the level of their development. No commission, however, has been appointed after 1960 under the chairmanship of Shri U.N. Dhebar. Constitutional provisions have also been made for providing sufficient funds for the tribal development.

Upto the Fourth Plan period, sporadic efforts were made both by central and state governments for the development of tribal people. Education was given top most priority with little success due to various reasons. One was the formal educational institution not fiting into the traditional educational institutions of the tribals.

The experiment of Special Multipurpose Tribal Development Blocks (SMPT) and thereafter Tribal Development Blocks was further intensified by adopting, 'The Tribal sub–plan approach'. Under the tribal sub–plan approach, the predominant tribal areas of each state were delineated into Integrated Tribal Development projects, MADA pockets and clusters. The special primitive tribal groups have also been identified.

A project officer with exclusive responsibility of development of the tribals in the project area has been appointed. For his assistance in implementing the schemes, Project Implementation Committee, including officers of various departments with the Collector as Chairman, has been constituted. With a view to providing advice for various developmental, protective and legislative measures, Project Advisory Boards known as 'Pariyojana Salahkar Mandal' has been constituted with representative of the people as its Chairman and as its member also.

Separate agencies at the district level known as 'Abhikarans' where the primitive tribal group population is 20,000 or more, has been constituted with members of this group as its Chairman. Thus, the powers and responsibilities have been decentralised and transferred to the community concerned to take decisions, choose measures and the ways and means for development.

The 'Pariyojana Salahkar Mandals' have been vested with the powers of sanctioning Rs. 10 lakh for various schemes.

Under the tribal sub-plan strategy, protective, regulatory and developmental measures have been adopted. The developmental measures can be divided broadly in three categories namely, economic, Infrastructural, and human Resources. As the tribal areas lack in basic minimum services i.e. education, specially, primary education, drinking water, health facilities, nutrition and housing in urban areas, these measures have been taken on a priority basic for their development.

The tribal people live side by side with the non-tribal people, therefore, such a financial mechanism has been evolved so that the money allotted for the welfare and development of the tribal people is not diverted for the development of non-tribal area and people. Demand numbers 41, 42—roads and bridges in tribal areas, 68—buildings in tribal areas have been created, in addition to the old demand number 33. Besides, these demands, demand number 75 has been created for keeping a small 'pool' of funds for those schemes not provided in the budget but are of immediate importance. Funds kept in these demand are voted and passed in the legislature for tribal development and is non-divertable for other purposes. Senior officers have been kept incharge to see that the financial management laid down for the tribal funds are strictly adhered to. In addition to planning, implementation, arrangements for monitoring and evaluation of the schemes have also been made. As mentioned the Pariyojana Salahkar Mandals at the project level are responsible not only for planning but for monitoring too. At the district level Collector and the representative of the people monitor the schemes. At the divisional level, the Scheduled Caste and Scheduled Tribes Development Pradhikarans were constituted to plan and monitor the tribal development schemes but these have been done away with from 30.10.96.

At the state level the cabinet sub-committee monitors the tribal development scheme. One Commission under the Chairmanship of one very experienced statesman Late Shri Vasat Rao Uike has been set up to work as a 'watch-dog' for tribal development. The Directorate, Tribal Area Development Planning (DTADP) do quarterly review and monitoring with various heads of the departments. The Tribal Research Institute does the evaluation of the schemes.

In this manner separate planning, implementation, monitoring and evaluation of tribal development schemes have been made. Late Pt. Jawaharlal Nehru while laying the Panchsheel for tribal development mentioned that 'we should judge result not by statistics but by the quality of human character that is evolved.' It was with this end in view, the financial and physical progress of schemes were analysed. It was observed that maximum utilisation of funds is to the tune of 132.22 per cent and minimum is 21.05 per cent, the aggregate percentage of utilisation is 84.89 per cent. Both the situations are present in financial terms. One, in which the budget provisions have not been made but the expenditure has been shown and, secondly, the budget provisions are there but there is no expenditure. It is not the purpose of the present study to find out the drawbacks in the administration of tribal development activities and suggest measures to improve it. That may be the job of a sociologist and not that of a historian. But the facts as emerge from the historical analysis of the pattern of budget provisions and expenditure has been pointed out. The future studies done in this regard may take into account this factor and gather more facts to understand the situation.

It has been found to be quite difficult to assess the physical achievements. Physical achievements, leaving of course the educational institutions, statistics pertaining to other institutions opened in terms of economic, infrastructural and human resource development are not available.

During the Sixth Plan in respect of some sectors and during the Seventh and the Eighth plan in respect of some selected sectors, the targets fixed and achievements there on have been given. Both the situations emerge from the physical achievements. In some schemes though the targets have not been fixed but the achievements are there. The achievements are much behind the targets; sometimes, the achievements are more than the targets.

Besides financial and physical targets and achievements, no mechanism has been evolved to judge the quality of human life 'human character evolved,' as was envisaged by Pt. Jawaharlal Nehru. A number of acts, regulations even Atrocities Act has been passed but there is no mechanism available to monitor them.

As per the 73rd Constitutional Amendment, the M.P. Panchayati Raj Adhiniyam, 1993 has been passed. Under this Adhiniyam three tier Panchayati Raj System i.e. at the village, block-Janpad and Jila-district levels has been constituted. Since Part 9 and Part 9-A Amendment of the Constitution have not been extended to the scheduled areas the repeal clauses therein namely Article 243-N and 243-ZF also do not extend to the scheduled areas. However the Parliament has passed the Act (December, 1996) pertaining to the extension of Panchayati Raj to the scheduled areas also. In accordance with the provisions of this Act various rules, regulations and Acts either have to be made afresh or amended in so far as they apply to the scheduled areas. The 'gram sabhas' have to be given wide powers in respect of self-governance and be custodian of their natural resources and development. This is under active consideration. The Ninth Plan has started in the state with the Annual Plan 1997-98. During the Ninth Plan some of the special features of the tribal sub-plan are (i) implementation of the 'pool' concept, (ii) three tier Panchayati Raj system and its extension to the scheduled areas, (iii) framing new Acts or modifying old Acts as a result of extension of Panchayati Raj to the scheduled tribal areas, restructuring the financial mechanism, implementation of the schemes and revamping the monitoring and evaluation system and (iv) dovetailing the Panchayati Raj system with the continuing tribal sub-plan structure.

Discontented with the present system of planning, implementation and monitoring of the tribal development schemes, there was demand from All-India Tribal Forum, Adivasi Vikas Parishad, to implement the Sixth Schedule in the tribal sub-plan area of the state as it is in vogue in the North-Eastern tribal states i.e. Assam, Meghalaya, Tripura and Mizoram. Implementation of the Sixth Schedule envisage formation of autonomous district and regional councils and making them all-powerful in so far as the running of the government is concerned, in other words empowerment of the people.

A committee under the chairmanship of Shri Dilip Singh Bhuria, honourable MP examined this issue and found that some of the elements of the Sixth Schedule i.e. district and regional councils should be included in the new Panchayati Raj system for the scheduled areas.

As the formulation of autonomous and regional councils have been included in the Act pertaining to the extension of Panchayati Raj system to the scheduled areas, the demand for implementation of the Sixth schedule in the state of M.P. to some extent has now subsided.

In the approach paper prepared by the state government for the tribal sub-plan during the Ninth Plan it has been mentioned that it was only at the inception of the Fifth Plan period, Government of India realised that not enough has been done in the field of tribal development and a more pro-active approach was required. The total investment in the field of tribal development was less than 1 per cent of the plan outlay during the first three plans. Even in the Fourth Plan there was no increase in real terms in direct investment in tribal development. It was against this backdrop that the tribal sub-plan was inaugurated at the beginning of the Fifth Plan period.

Now after a lapse of more than 20 years it may be pertinent to ask how far has the tribal sub-plan succeeded as an instrument of affirmative action? The consensus is that the results have not been commensurate with the investments made. There is also a general agreement that while the objectives of the tribal sub-plan have been laudable and its strategy well conceived, implementation has been less than satisfactory. Indeed the general feeling is that corruption and inefficiency have been rampant and the quality of output is low. In the approach paper for the Ninth Plan[1] in tribal sub-plan it has again been mentioned that the problem of corruption, lack of transparency and inefficient implementation are not unique to the tribal sub-plan. They bedevil the planning process in general; the only difference is that they have been more virulent in tribal area, therefore, more harmful in effect.

As a suggestive measure to do away with this shortcoming the obvious remedy has been suggested to pass on Plan funds directly to the cutting edge level. In the context of the tribal sub-plan this would mean transmitting plan allocation directly to the Integrated Tribal Development Project (ITDP) and bypassing the heads of department at the zonal and divisional level. Red tape can be cut short by delegating adequate administrative and financial powers to the ITDP level so that frequent reference to higher level is not required.

Furthermore, transparency can be improved if people's representative, members of the local tribal communities and stake-holders are involved in the management of project affairs.

However, the concept of efficiency does not stop short at this stage. Another aspect needs to be examined. This is the question of high administrative costs and overheads involved in most government operations.

This is specially true of the tribal sub-plan where large establishments are deployed to do relatively small volumes of work.

This inefficiency can be overcome if we use the Self-Help groups of the tribals as the executing agency and confine the role of the Government to that of a 'watch dog' and technical adviser. The concept of stake-holder, as the parties affected by a given project or scheme is less nebulous than the concept of "community" and there would be obvious gains in efficiency of the commitment of the stake–holders to any scheme could be secured by involving them in its execution. This could be done by organizing them into co-operative societies or by informal associations and placing the funds at their disposal.

These Self-Help Groups could also be entrusted the maintenance of development schemes. It is reasonable to suppose that people who stand to benefit from any given service or facility would be more committed to its maintenance than its salaried functionary whose interests are not really with the well-being of the project. The government employs a vast standing army of low paid and poorly motivated functionaries to do an indifferent job of maintenance and the gains in efficiency that will accrue if the job of maintenance is given to the stake–holders can be easily imagined. (However the question of technical feasibility and optimization of resources will have to be kept in mind here.) This system, not only eliminates the large and overt establishment costs that are a part of the tribal sub-plan but also weed out the hidden costs that lurk behind such innocuous budgetary heads as 'other charges and grant-in-aid'. The break-up of tribal sub-plan by object of expenditure looks something like this:

Object-wise Budget Estimate for 1996-97 (Rs. in thousands)

Sl. No.	*Object*	*Provision under plan*
1.	Salaries	9,66,686
2.	Wages	1,66,041
3.	Travel allowance	1,00,093
4.	Office expenses	74,579
5.	Petrol and oil charges	6,925
6.	Rent, Rates and Taxes	29,493
7.	Advertisement and publicity	2,585
8.	Payment of professional and special salary	391
9.	Stipend & scholarship	5,30,089
10.	Grant-in-Aid	20,22,744

Sl. No.	Object	Provision under plan
11.	Payment of decretal amount (charges	7,000
12.	Conference	1,059
13.	Rewards	121
14.	Other charges	9,24,164
15.	Maintenance work	7,671
16.	Material and supplies	1,42,804
17.	Major works	7,08,592
18.	Minor works	3,32,034
19.	Machinery and equipments	31,244
20.	Contributions	1,354
21.	Compensation	83
22.	Investment	35,002
23.	Tools and plants	1,125
24.	Purchase of vehicles	2,968
25.	Loans and advances	3,91,263
26.	Suspense	10,500
27.	Add T and P charges on percentage	2,24,966
	Total	67,21,574

The table given above shows that apart from salary and wages which constitute about 15 per cent of the tribal sub-plan, element of hidden establishment costs (Grant-in-Aid) and Major works as well as minor works could total as much as 40 per cent of the whole.

This large establishment is a drag on the plan and a major cause of inefficiency. As a matter of principle, all overt and hidden establishment cost must be taken out of tribal sub-plan and put into the non-plan. Not only this, we must go a step further and scrutinize all establishment costs in the non-plan which is nearly three times as large as the plan.

No less important than the question of efficiency is the question of quality. The poor quality of work done in the tribal areas is well established yet the reason for this is seldom analyzed.

Quality is a concept that is not easy to define though we can all recognize quality when we come across it. It may be said in general that quality is a compound of technical skill and commitment. It is in the last analysis and ethical concept because the commitment required to do quality work has to be sustained over a long period and without some strong inner urge this is seldom possible.

However, while the moral aspects of quality are fundamental to the concept on a more mundane level it would be true to say that material rewards to affect motivation in a system that rewards good performance and punishes indifferent work is more likely to lead to quality work than a system which does not. Like-wise organizational structures that permits upward motibility to the talented worker on the basis of performance rather than traditional structure that follow only the criterion of seniority are more likely to be conducive to high quality work.

Finally we come to the issue of sectoral priorities in the tribal sub-plan. Even a casual scrutiny of plan and budget document pertaining to any given year of the Eighth Plan or indeed any from the Fifth Plan onwards will make one thing clear that the Plan lacks a sense of direction. Virtually all the 54 departments, of the state government have received a slice of the cake. Dispersal of resources and dissipation of effort has led to loss of impact. In future allocations must be confined to Education, Health, Agriculture, local development work and beneficiary oriented, income generating schemes.[2]

The process of quantifying funds under tribal sub-plan has to be given a fresh look. The tribal sub-plan is an area plan. The original intention of the policy makers was that the tribal sub-plan would be an additive to the general plan in tribal areas. However, this was not explicitly stated anywhere. As a result, the tribal sub-plan has become a substitute for the general plan in tribal areas. This being the case the formula for quantifying funds under the sub-plan which is based on population becomes inherently unfair. The following statistics will clarify this further:

(i) Total population of the state—661 lakh.

(ii) Total tribal population of the state—154 lakh (23.27 per cent of the states population.)

(iii) Tribal sub–plan area—180 sq. km. (40. 63 per cent of the state area.)

(iv) Total tribal population of the sub–plan area—111.30 lakh.

(v) Total population of sub-plan area—180 lakh. 27 percent of the states population.

(vi) Total tribal population outside sub-plan area—42.69 lakh (6 per cent of the state population).

It can be seen from this chart that 27 per cent of the states population reside in the tribal sub-plan area which come as 40 per cent of the state. The funds available for tribal sub-plan are only 23 per cent of the state plan and these funds have also to cater to the 6 per cent of the tribal population residing outside the tribal sub-plan area. Need more be said about the inherent unfairness of the population formula.[3]

A better way to quantify funds would be on the basis of certain selected indicators of development covering both infrastructure and human resources development. These could then be developed into a composite indicator of backwardness which can then be used as a multiplier to determine districtwise allocations.

The ideas outlined as above in the approach paper for the Ninth Plan has to be put into action during the Annual Plans of the Ninth Plan. It would be a further object of study in so far as these laudable ideas have been put into action and to what extent the tribals have benefited out of it.

REFERENCES

1. An appraisal of the tribal sub-plan in the context of the forthcoming Ninth Plan-unpublished approach paper of the state Government, p. 1.
2. *Op. cit.*, p. 7.
3. *Ibid.*

Annexure–I

Basic Information about Tribal Sub-Plan Provided as a Benchmark for further Studies

(Source: Census 1991)

Total geographical area of the state (in lakh per sq. km.)	4.43
Total geographical area of the tribal sub-plan (in lakh per sq. km.)	1.80
Total scheduled area of the State (in lakh per sq. km.)	1.49
Percentage of TSP area of the total area of the State	40.63
Population	
Total population of India (lakh)	8,385.84
Total ST population of India (lakh)	677.58
Percentage of ST population in India	8.08
Total population of state (lakh)	661.81
Total ST population in the state (lakh)	153.99
Percentage of ST population in M.P. to total ST population in India	22.73
Ranking of state in India according to the ST population	1
Percentage of ST population in M.P.	23.27
Total population of sub-plan area (lakh)	182.71
Percentage of the total population of TSP area to the total population of the State	27.61
Total ST population of sub-plan area (lakh)	111.08
Percentage of ST population of TSP area (lakh) to the total population in TSP area	60.80
Percentage of ST population in TSP area to ST population of the state	72.13
ST population outside the TSP area (lakh)	42.91
Percentage of ST population outside the TSP area	27.86

Population growth (1981 to 1991)

	Total	Rural	Urban
Persons	26.84	22.24	44.89
STs	28.46	26.93	71.90

Density of population

(i) State 149.00 per sq. km.

(ii) TSP area 99.85 per sq. km.

ST literacy Percentage

Total	Male	Female
21.54	32.16	10.73

(a) Total no. of scheduled tribes 46

(b) Sub-groups 161

No. of Villages having 80 per cent and above ST population in M.P. 14199

No. of villages having 100 per cent ST population in M.P. 4145

Primitive tribes and their population (Source: Survey 92-93)

Sl. No.	*Name of the Group*	*Population*	*Villages*	*Dev. Block*	*District*	*Area of Habitation*
1.	Abujhmaria	17,016	235	1	1	Abujhmar of Bastar district
2.	Baiga	1,34,357	1197	30	5	Mandla, Shahdol, Balaghat, Rajnandgaon and Bilaspur district
3.	Saharia	4,17,171	1159	26	6	Gwalior and Chambal division
4.	Bharia	2,012	12	1	1	Patalkot (Chhindwara district)
5.	Pahari Korwa	27,109	320	16	3	Raigarh and Surguja district
6.	Kamar	13,110	249	4	1	Raipur district
7.	Birhor	935	26	7	1	Jashpurnagar Teshil (Raigarh district)
	Total	6,11,710	3198	88	16	

15. Coverage of the sub-plan in administration units

Units	*Total No. in the State*	*Under Total*	*Tribal Fully*	*Sub-Plan Partly*
District	45	35	4	31
Tehsil	317	111	45	66
Blocks	459	299	177	118
(Village including forest villages)	76,468	30,042	30,042	

(a) Integrated Tribal Development Project	Major	44
	Medium	5
	Total	49
(b) MADA Pockets		39
(c) Clusters		8

Occupational Distribution: Scheduled Tribes

Category	*Total*	*Per cent*	*Male*	*Per cent*	*Female*	*Per cent*
I. Total Main workers	68,32,274	44.37	43,36,773	55.90	24,95,951	32.67
1. Cultivators	43,19,064	63.21	2,19,880	67.33	13,99,184	55.06
2. Agricultural Labourer	20,14,142	29.49	10,24,887	23.63	9,89,255	39.63
3. House Hold Industries	3,40,877	4.99	2,66,831	6.15	74,046	2.97
4. Other than H.H.	1,58,641	2.32	1,25,175	2.89	33,466	1.34
II. Marginal Workers	12,77,360	8.30	81,607	1.05	11,95,753	15.65
III. Non-Workers	72,88,950	47.33	33,39,794	43.05	39,49,156	51.68
Total (I+II+III)	1,53,99,034	—	77,58,174	—	76,40,860	—

Scheduled Tribes Land Holding (1990-91)

(*fig. in lakh*)

Category	*No. of ST Holding*	*Per cent to total*	*Area (in hect.)*	*Per cent to total*
Marginal (0 to 1 hect.)	6.98	33.61	3.21	5.77
Small (1 to 2 hect.)	4.71	22.68	6.86	12.33

Category	*No. of ST Holding*	*Per cent to total*	*Area (in hect.)*	*Per cent to total*
Semi-medium (2 to 4 hect)	4.88	23.49	13.46	24.19
Medium (4 to 10 hect)	3..48	16.75	20.79	37.36
Large (10 and above)	0.72	3.47	11.32	20.35
Total	20.77	100.00	55.64	100.00

Average land holding among ST families — 2.68 hect.

Annexure–II

The Scheduled Areas of the State

Published in Gazette of India Extraordinary Part II, Section 3, Section (i), dated the 31st December, 1977 as Constitution Order No. 109.

The Scheduled Areas (States of Bihar, Gujarat, Madhya Pradesh and Orissa) Order, 1977

In exercise of the powers conferred by sub-paragraph (2) of paragraph 6 of the Fifth Schedule to the Constitution of India, the President hereby rescinds the Scheduled Areas Part A State Order, 1950. In so far as it relates to the areas now comprised in the states of Bihar, Gujarat, Madhya Pradesh and Orissa and the Scheduled Areas (Part B States) Order, 1950, in so far as it relates to the areas now comprised in the state of Madhya Pradesh, and in consultation with the Governors of the state conferred is pleased to make the following order, namely:—

1. (1) This order may be called the Scheduled Area (States of Bihar, Gujarat, Madhya Pradesh and Orissa) Order, 1977.

   (2) It shall come into force at once.

2. The areas specified below are hereby redefined to be the Scheduled Areas within the states of Bihar, Gujarat, Madhya Pradesh and Orissa.

Madhya Pradesh

(1) Jhabua district.

(2) Mandla district.

(3) Sarguja district.

(4) Bastar district.

(5) Sardarpur, Dhar, Kukshi and Manawar tehsils in Dhar district.

(6) Barwani, Rajpur, Sendhwa, Bhikangaon, Khargone and Maheshwar tehsils in Khargone (West Nimar) district.

(7) Khalwa Tribal Development Block of Harsud tehsil, and Khaknar Tribal Development Block of Burhanpur tehsil, in Khandwa (East Nimar) district.

(8) Sailana tehsil in Ratlam district.

(9) Betul tehsil (excluding Betul Community Development Block) and Bhainsdehi Tehsil in Betul district.

(10) Lakhnadon tehsil and Kurai Tribal Development Block of Seoni tehsil in Seoni district.

(11) Baihar tehsil in Balaghat district.

(12) Kesla Tribal Development Block of Hoshangabad tehsil in Hoshangabad district.

(13) Pushparajgarh and Sohagpur tehsil, and Jaisinghnagar Community Development Block of Beohari tehsil in Shahdol district.

(14) Kusmi Tribal Development Block of Gopadbans tehsil in Sidhi district.

(15) Jashpurnagar, Udaipur and Gharghoda tehsils, and Kharsia Tribal Development Block of Raigarh tehsil in Raigarh district.

(16) Katghora tehsil and Marwahi Tribal Development Block, Gorella Tribal Development Block and Gorella Community Development Block and Kota Revenue Inspector Circle of Bilaspur tehsil in Bilaspur district.

(17) Dondi Tribal Development Block of Balod tehsil in Durg district.

(18) Manpur and Mohla Tribal Development Blocks and Chowki Community Development Block of Rajnandgaon tehsil in Rajnandgaon district.

(19) Gariaband, Mainpur and Chhura Tribal Development Blocks of Bindranawagarh tehsil and Sihawa Community Development Block of Dhamtari tehsil, in Raipur district.

(20) Kararhal Tribal Development Block of Sheopur tehsil in Morena district.

(21) Tamia and Jamai Tribal Development Blocks, Patwari Circle nos. 63 to 68 and nos. 72 and 73 villages Seargaon Khurd and Kirwari of Patwari Circle no. 62 villages Mairawari and Gaulie Parasia of Patwari Circle no. 69 and village Bamhari of Patwari Circle No. 97 of Chhindwara tehsil.

Harriai Tribal Development Block and Patwari Circle nos. 26, 27, 30, 31, 32, 41 to 44, 48, 49, 50-B and 60 of Amarwara tehsil.

Bichhua Tribal Development Block and Patwari Circle Nos. 1 to 19, 25 to 30, 32 to 37, village Nandapur of Patwari Circle No. 20, villages Nilkanthi and Dhandi-Khapa of Patwari Circle No. 34, villages Ramudhana, Silora and Jobni of Patwari Circle No. 31 and villages excluding village Muli of Patwari Circle No. 39 of Saunsar tehsil in Chhindwara district.

3. Any reference in preceding paragraph to a territorial division by whatever name indicated shall be construed as a reference to the territorial division of that name as existing at the commencement of this order.

Annexure–III

The Scheduled Castes and Scheduled Tribes Order (Amendment) Act, 1976 dated 18th September, 1976

Scheduled Tribes

1. Agaria.
2. Andh.
3. Baiga.
4. Bhaina.
5. Bharia, Bhumia, Bhuinhar Bhumia, Bhumiya, Bharia, Paliha, Pando.
6. Bhattra.
7. Bhil, Bhilal, Barela, Patelia.
8. Bhil Mina.
9. Bhunjia.
10. Biar, Biyar.
11. Binjhwar.
12. Birhul, Birhor.
13. Damor, Damaria.
14. Dhanwar.
15. Gadaba, Gadba.
16. Gond: Arakh, Arrakh, Agaria, Asur, Badi Maria, Bada Maria, Bhatola, Bhimma, Bhutta, Koilabhuta, Koliabhuti, Bhar, Bisonhorn Maria, Chota Maria, Dandami Maria, Dhuru, Dhurwa Dhoba, Dhulia, Dorla, Gaiki, Gatta, Gatti, Gatia, Gond, Gowari, Hill Maria, Kandra, Kalanga, Khatola, Koitar, Koya, Khirwar, Khirwara, Kuccha Maria,

Kuchaki Maria, Madia, Maria, Maas, Mannewar, Moghya, Mogia, Monghya, Muds, Muria, Nagarchi, Nagwanshi, Ojha, Raj, Sonjhari Jhareka, Thatia, Thotya, Wade Maria, Vade Maria, Daroi.

17. Halba, Halbi.
18. Kamar.
19. Karku.
20. Kawar, Kanwar, Kaur, Cherwa, Rathia, Tanwar, Chattri.
21. Keer (in Bhopal, Raisen and Sehore districts).
22. Khairwar, Kondar.
23. Kharia.
24. Kondh, Khond, Kandh.
25. Kol.
26. Kolam.
27. Korku, Bopchi, Mouasi, Nahul, Najul, Bondhi, Bondeya.
28. Korwa, Kodaku.
29. Majhi.
30. Majhwar.
31. Mawasi.
32. Mina (in Sironj sub-division of Vidisha district).
33. Munda.
34. Nagesia, Nagasia.
35. Oraon, Dhanka, Dhangad.
36. Panika (in Chhatarpur, Datia, Panna, Rewa, Satna, Shahdol, Sidhi and Tikamgarh districts).
37. Pao.
38. Pardhan, Pathari, Saroti.
39. Pardhi (in Bhopal, Raisen and Sehore districts).
40. Pardhi, Bahelia, Bahellia, Chita Pardhi, Langoli Pardhi, Phanse Pardhi, Shikari, Takankar Takia [in (1) Bastar, Chhindwara, Mandla, Raigarh, Seoni and Sarguja districts, (2) Baihar tehsil of Balaghat district, (3) Betul and Bainsdehi tehsils of Betul district, (4) Bilaspur and

Katghora tehsils of Bilaspur district, (5) Durg and Balod tehsil of Durg district, (6) Chowki, Manpur and Mohala Revenue Inspector's Circles of Rajnandgaon district, (7) Murwara, Patan and Sihora tehsils of Jabalpur district, (8) Hoshangabad and Sohagpur tehsils of Hoshangabad district and Narsimhapur district, (9) Harsud tehsil of Khandwa district, (10) Bindra-Nawagarh, Dhamtari and Mahasamund tehsils of Raipur district.]

41. Parja.
42. Sahariya, Saharia, Seharia, Sosia, Sor.
43. Sonta, Saunta.
44. Saur.
45. Sawar, Sawara.
46. Sonr.

Annexure–IV

Integrated Tribal Development Projects: Pockets under the Modified Area Development Approach and Clusters according to 61 Districts

Census–1991

Names of district I.T.D.P., M.A.D.A., Clusters	*Total population*	*Scheduled tribe population*	*Percentage of tribal population to total population*	*Percentage of tribal population in the total population of scheduled tribes in the state*	*Percentage of Scheduled Tribe population (Col. 3) to the total Scheduled Tribe population in the sub-plan area*
1	*2*	*3*	*4*	*5*	*6*
A. Western Zone					
1. District Dhar					
I.T.D.P.					
(a) Dhar	4,21,215	1,97,317	46.84	1.28	1.77
(b) Kukshi	6,41,720	4,60,751	71.80	2.99	4.14
M.A.D.A.					
(a) Badnawar	47,379	29,489	62.24	0.19	0.26
2. District Jhabua					
I.T.D.P.					
(a) Jhabua	5,86,843	5,30,573	90.41	3.45	4.77
(b) Alirajpur	4,46,023	4,10,456	92.02	2.66	3.69

1	2	3	4	5	6
3. District Khargone					
I.T.D.P.					
(a) Khargone	5,41,194	2,81,752	52.06	1.83	2.53
(b) Maheshwar	1,49,068	34,607	23.22	0.22	0.31
4. District Badwani					
I.T.D.P.					
(a) Badwani	3,60,137	2,37,347	65.90	1.54	2.13
(b) Sendhwa	2,86,664	2,35,898	82.29	1.53	2.12
5. District Khandwa					
I.T.D.P.					
(a) Khandwa	3,17,292	1,67,618	52.83	1.09	1.51
M.A.D.A.					
(a) Andhawadi	17,278	12,828	74.24	0.08	0.12
(b) Pipalkota	20,584	15,028	73.01	0.10	0.14
Cluster					
(a) Pamakhedi	11,207	5,618	50.13	0.04	0.05
6. District Ratlam					
I.T.D.P.					
(a) Sailana	2,11,110	1,73,165	82.03	1.12	1.56
7. District Dewas					
I.T.D.P.					
(a) Bagli	1,31,378	86,974	66.20	0.56	0.78

1	2	3	4	5	6
8. District Indore					
M.A.D.A.					
(a) Mhow	32,744	23,716	72.43	0.15	0.21
Total : Western Zone	**42,21,836**	**29,03,137**	**68.76**	**18.85**	**26.09**
B. Central Zone					
1. District Dhar					
I.T.D.P.					
(a) Betul	3,81,864	1,99,272	52.18	1.29	1.79
(b) Bhainsdehi	2,53,264	1,57,574	62.21	1.02	1.42
M.A.D.A.					
(a) Prabhatpatam	38681	23874	61.72	0.15	0.21
2. District Chhindwara					
I.T.D.P.					
(a) Tamia	5,05,371	3,08,649	61.07	2.00	2.77
(b) Saunsar	1,89,653	97,971	51.66	0.64	0.88
M.A.D.A.					
(a) Lahgudwa	22,727	11,961	52.63	0.08	0.11
3. District Seoni					
I.T.D.P.					
(a) Lakhnadone	3,80,050	2,00,648	52.80	1.30	1.80

1	2	3	4	5	6
(b) Kurai	85,992	41,245	47.96	0.27	0.37
M.A.D.A.					
(a) Seoni	1,05,856	57,466	54.29	0.37	0.52
4. District Mandla					
I.T.D.P.					
(a) Mandla	5,17,775	3,02,697	58.46	1.97	2.72
(b) Niwas	1,65,664	1,18,915	71.78	0.77	1.07
5. District Dindori					
I.T.D.P.					
(a) Dindori	2,87,971	1,89,848	65.92	1.23	1.71
(b) Bajag	1,66,509	1,10,914	66.61	0.72	0.99
6. District Balaghat					
I.T.D.P.					
(a) Baihar	2,74,797	1,46,404	53.28	0.95	1.31
7. District jabalpur					
I.T.D.P.					
(a) Kundam	92,438	65,610	70.98	0.43	0.59
M.A.D.A.					
(a) Bargipatan	25,392	16,855	66.38	0.11	0.15
Cluster					

1	2	3	4	5	6
(a) Hinotia	8,785	4,180	47.58	0.03	0.04
(b) Pratappur	9,181	5,460	59.47	0.03	0.05
(c) Majholi	5,240	2,199	41.96	0.01	0.02
8. District Katni					
I.T.D.P.					
(a) Katni	85,436	49,909	58.41	0.32	0.45
M.A.D.A.					
(a) Murwara - II	14,841	7,581	51.08	0.05	0.07
Cluster					
(a) Mohari	7,355	3,713	50.48	0.02	0.03
9. District Hoshangabad					
I.T.D.P.					
(a) Kesla	1,57,637	70,178	44.52	0.45	0.64
10. District Harda					
I.T.D.P.					
(a) Harda	63,570	47,100	74.09	0.30	0.42
11. District Sehore					
M.A.D.A.					
(a) Ichhawar, Nasrullaganj and Budni	64,289	40,683	63.28	0.26	0.37

1	2	3	4	5	6
12. District Raisen					
M.A.D.A.					
(a) Silwani Bareli	43,123	29,292	67.93	0.19	0.26
(b) Goharganj	31,889	21,634	67.84	0.14	0.19
13. District Narsinghpur					
M.A.D.A.					
(a) Narsinghpur	58,474	36,802	62.94	0.24	0.34
14. District Damoh					
(a) Jabera	29,962	12,612	42.09	0.08	0.12
(b) Tendukheda	20,130	9,502	47.20	0.06	0.08
(c) Hata	18,998	9,748	51.31	0.06	0.09
Total Central Zone	**41,12,914**	**24,00,496**	**58.36**	**15.59**	**21.57**
C. North-Eastern Zone					
1. District Shahdol					
I.T.D.P.					
(a) Shadol	6,65,224	3,24,191	48.73	2.10	2.91
(b) Pushparajgarh	1,68,039	1,31,607	78.32	0.85	1.18
(c) Jaisinghnagar	1,26,292	66,740	52.85	0.43	0.59
M.A.D.A.					
(a) Beohari	45,255	27,648	61.09	0.18	0.25

1	2	3	4	5	6
2. District Umaria					
I.T.D.P.					
(a) Bandhogarh	2,10,799	1,40,549	66.67	0.91	1.26
3. District Sidhi					
I.T.D.P.					
(a) Kusmi	2,03,364	1,24,380	61.16	0.81	1.12
(a) Deosar	3,68,559	1,61,261	43.75	1.05	1.45
4. District Rewa					
M.A.D.A.					
(a) Mauganj	20,893	13,604	65.11	0.09	0.12
5. District Sagar					
M.A.D.A.					
(a) Deorikala	55,910	26,547	47.48	0.17	0.24
6. District Satna					
M.A.D.A.					
(a) Ragurajnagar	43,229	22,964	53.12	0.15	0.21
(b) Nagod	20,181	12,982	64.33	0.08	0.12
(c) Maihar	24,499	12,745	52.02	0.08	0.11
(d) Amarpatan	16,698	9,814	58.77	0.06	0.09
7. District Panna					
M.A.D.A.					
(a) Pawai	31,589	20.643	65.35	0.13	0.18

1	2	3	4	5	6
8. District Sheopur					
I.T.D.P.					
(a) Karahal	93,396	55,655	59.59	0.36	0.51
9. District Shivpuri					
M.A.D.A.					
(a) Shivpuri	14,357	7,015	48.86	0.04	0.06
(b) Pohri	17,147	10,613	61.89	0.07	0.09
Cluster					
(a) Kotla	9,530	6,261	65.70	0.04	0.06
10. District Chhatarpur					
Cluster					
(a) Kishangarh	14,386	7,566	52.59	0.05	0.07
11. District Guna					
M.A.D.A.					
(a) Guna	30,385	21,801	71.75	0.14	0.20
(b) Chachoda	18,774	12,671	67.19	0.08	0.11
(c) Parsolia	13,706	11,051	80.63	0.07	0.10
Total: North-Eastern Zone	**22,12,212**	**1228308**	**55.52**	**7.98**	**11.04**
D. Eastern Zone					
1. District Sarguja					
I.T.D.P.					
(a) Ambikapur	5,93,432	3,85,326	64.93	2.50	3.46

1	2	3	4	5	6
(b) Surajpur	5,12,948	2,41,331	47.05	1.57	2.17
(d) Pal	3,99,689	2,59,276	64.87	1.68	2.33
2. District Koria					
I.T.D.P.					
(a) Baikuntpur	4,48,840	2,12,203	47.28	1.38	1.91
3. District Raigarh					
I.T.D.P.					
(a) Dharamjaigarh	4,54,896	2,65,704	58.41	1.72	2.39
M.A.D.A.					
(a) Sarangarh	22,873	11,930	52.16	0.08	0.11
(b) Gopalpur	13,786	7,889	57.22	0.05	0.07
4. District Jashpur					
I.T.D.P.					
(a) Jashpurnagar	6,28,224	4,18,312	66.58	2.72	3.76
5. District Bilaspur					
I.T.D.P.					
(a) Gorella	3,52,235	2,11,091	59.92	1.37	1.89
M.A.D.A.					
(a) Bilha-Masturi	21,219	13,049	61.49	0.08	0.12
6. District Korba					
I.T.D.P.					
(a) Korba	8,10,862	3,54,043	43.66	2.30	3.18

1	2	3	4	5	6
7. District Janjgir Champa					
M.A.D.A.					
(a) Rukja	19,886	10,337	51.98	0.07	0.09
Total: Eastern zone	**42,78,890**	**23,90,491**	**55.87**	**15.52**	**21.48**
E. Southern Zone					
1. District Bastar					
I.T.D.P.					
(a) Jagadalpur	5,34,150	3,63,719	68.09	2.36	3.27
(b) Kondagaon	4,59,933	3,39,070	73.72	2.20	3.05
2. District Kanker					
I.T.D.P.					
(a) Bhanupratappur	5,24,686	3,02,802	57.71	1.97	2.73
3. District Dantewara					
I.T.D.P.					
(a) Dantewara	2,14,321	1,48,899	69.47	0.97	1.34
(b) Konta	1,76,592	1,46,821	82.14	0.95	1.32
(c) Bijapur	1,91,268	1,55,976	81.55	1.01	1.40
4. District Raipur					
I.T.D.P.					
(a) Gariaband	2,42,075	1,25,325	51.77	0.81	1.13

1	2	3	4	5	6
M.A.D.A.					
(a) Baloda bazar	61,586	33,559	54.49	0.22	0.30
Cluster					
(a) Dhuribandha	14,214	7,464	53.51	0.05	0.07
5. District Dhamtari					
I.T.D.P.					
(a) Sihawa	1,14,787	63,892	55.66	0.41	0.57
M.A.D.A.					
(a) Gangrel	11,254	5,910	52.51	0.04	0.05
6. District Mahasamund					
M.A.D.A.					
(a) Mahasamund-I	111552	58440	52.39	0.38	0.52
(b) Mahasamund-II	70369	37203	52.86	0.24	0.33
7. District Durg					
I.T.D.P.					
(a) Dondi lohara	3,05,880	1,53,742	50.26	0.99	1.39
8. District Rajnandgaon					
I.T.D.P.					
(a) Rajnandgaon	2,94,107	1,80,883	61.50	1.17	1.63
M.A.D.A.					
(a) Nachania	14.728	9.455	64.20	0.06	0.08

1	2	3	4	5	6
Cluster					
(a) Bachherabhata	11,521	9,702	68.59	0.06	0.09
9. District Kawardha					
M.A.D.A.					
(a) Kawardha	53,869	38,454	71.38	0.25	0.35
(b) Pandaria	29,013	22,698	78.23	0.15	0.20
Total: southern zone	**34,35,905**	**22,04,014**	**64.14**	**14.31**	**19.82**
Grand total	**1,82,61,757**	**1,11,26,446**	**60.92**	**72.25**	**100.00**

Zone wise Number of Integrated Tribal Development Project/Modified Area Development Approach/ Cluster (Proposal)

Zone	I.T.D.P.	M.A.D.A.	Cluster
A. Western Zone	11	4	1
B. Central Zone	15	12	4
C. North–Eastern Zone	7	13	2
D. Eastern Zone	8	4	-
E. Southern Zone	10	7	2
Total	**51**	**40**	**9**

Annexure–V

Centrally Sponsored and Central Sector Schemes Under Tribal Sub-Plan

Demand No. 41, 1997-98. (The schemes included under centrally sponsored and sector schemes are only illustrative. The amount shown is to give an idea of funds allotted from State and Central Governments).

A. Centrally Sponsored Schemes.

Department	Name of Schemes	*Budget provision*		
		Total Provision	*Share of Central Govt.*	*Share of State Govt.*
1. Forest department	(i) Project schemes fuel fodder/development	288.00	144.00	144.00
	(ii) Development of forest sanctuaries—Bandhogarh, Kanha National Park and Tiger Project	249.20	124.60	124.60
	Total	537.20	268.60	268.60
2. Agriculture	(i) Pulse production programme	140.00	105.00	35.00
	(ii) Special programme of Paddy development on the field of the farmers.	140.00	105.00	35.00
	(iii) Intensive cotton development.	40.00	30.00	10.00
	(iv) Sugarcane development programme.	32.00	24.00	8.00
	(v) Oilseed development programme	760.00	570.00	190.00
	Total	1112.00	834.00	278.00

3. Public Health and Family Welfare	(i) Malaria Eradication	1183.90	591.95	59.95
4. School Education	(i) Non-formal education centres (40:60)	572.62	343.57	229.05
	(ii) Non-formal education centre (90:10)	100.00	90.00	10.00
	Total	672.62	433.57	239.05
5. Panchayat and Rural Development	(i) Construction of cottage	100.00	50.00	50.00
	(ii) Training for self-employment of Rural unemployeds.	1000.00	500.00	500.00
	(iii) Training	—	—	—
	(iv) Water shed treatment/development works/activities	—	—	—
	(v) Watershed community organisation.			
	(vi) Administrative expenditure	—	—	—
	(vii) Indira Housing Scheme	6555.00	5244.00	1311.00
	(viii) Jeevan Dhara Yojana	2622.00	2098.00	524.00
	(ix) Employment Guarantee Programme	—	—	—
	(x) Jawahar Rozgar Yojana	10925.00	8740.00	2185.00
	Total	21202.00	16632.00	4570.00
6. Scheduled Tribe Development Dept	(i) Book bank	90.00	45.00	45.00
	(ii) Relief work (Rahat Yojana)	200.00	100.00	100.00
	(iii) Ashram and schools	200.00	100.00	100.00
	Total	490.00	245.00	245.00
7. Fisheries	Fisheries extension and subsidy to fishery development authorities (Abhikaran)	80.00	30.00	50.00
	(ii) Accident insurance to members of tribal fishermen cooperative society	1.80	.90	.90
	Total	81.80	30.90	50.90
8. Manpower planning	Purchase of machines in industrial training institutes	100.00	50.00	50.00
9. Rural industries/handloom / industrial co-	(i) Project package (handloom)	5.00	2.50	2.50
	(ii) Welfare scheme package	.90	.45	.45

operative societies	(iii) Development of marketing (rebate assistance)	0.50	0.25	0.25
	(iv) Project package (handloom)	5.00	2.50	2.50
	(v) Project package (handloom)	5.00	2.50	2.50
	Total	16.40	8.20	8.20
10. Law department	(i) Legal administration (construction works)	250.00	125.00	125.00
	(ii) Legal administration (construction works)	250.00	125.00	125.00
	Total	500.00	250.00	250.00
11. School education	(i) Non-formal education centre (40:60)	665.15	399.09	266.06
	(ii) Non-formal education centre (40:60)	408.90	368.01	40.89
	Total	1074.05	767.10	306.95
12. Public Health engineering	(i) Maintenance of rural water supply	200.00	100.00	100.00
	(ii) Rural sanitary schemes	300.00	150.00	150.00
	Total	500.00	250.00	250.00

B. Central Sector Schemes

Department	Scheme	Budget Provision Unit
1. Forest department	Plantation of medicinal plant	200.00
	Total	200.00
2. Agriculture department	(i) Development of maize crop	11.00
	(ii) Cashewnut development	110.40
	(iii) Integrated soil conservation scheme in river valley project	1555.00
	(iv) National watershed development programme.	3550.00
	Total	5226.40
3. Public health and Family Welfare	(i) Integrated child development scheme	111.25
	(ii) Establishment of sub health centres	224.85
	(iii) Establishment of sub health centres	110.80
	Total	446.90

4. Food and Civil Supplies	(i) Mobile shops management	80.00
	(ii) Construction of godown grid	172.50
	(iii) Running of mobile shops (loan+advance)	80 lakh
	(iv) Construction of godown gird (load+advance)	172.50
	Total	6378

Annexure–VI

Budget Provision and Expenditure from Sixth Plan (80-85) to Eighth Plan (92-97) State Plan

Rs. in Lakh

Sl. No.	Head of Development	Sixth Plan			Seventh Plan			Anual Plan (1990-91)		
		Provision during Sixth Plan towards flow to TSP	Expenditure during Sixth Plan period	Percentage Col. No. 4 to 3	Provision during Eighth Plan towards flow to TSP	Expenditure during Eightth Plan period	Percentage Col. No. 7 to 8	Provision during Annual Plan towards flow to TSP	Expenditure during Annual Plan period	Percentage Col. No. 10 to 9
1	2	3	4	5	6	7	8	9	10	11
1.	**Agriculture and Allied Activities**									
	Agriculture production	0.00	1676.88	0.00	5282.97	4699.28	88.95	1721.00	1619.25	94.09
	Horticulture	7568.30	753.57	9.96	1188.26	1198.41	100.85	335.00	229.91	68.63
	Agriculture marketing	0.00	0.00	0.00	36.42	33.00	90.61	8.46	6.60	78.01
	Soil and Water Conservation									
	(a) Agriculture department	0.00	1461.71	0.00	1121.24	1048.06	93.47	434.00	355.34	81.88
	(b) Forest department	0.00	0.00	0.00	50.00	0.00	0.00	18.57	13.35	71.89
	Animal Husbandry	629.64	673.61	106.98	1049.53	1012.00	96.42	280.00	207.47	74.10
	Dairy development	98.44	64.79	65.81	322.89	208.30	64.51	99.38	70.60	71.04
	Fisheries	255.72	201.85	78.93	481.91	377.00	78.23	120.00	99.62	83.02

Forest	1734.29	2042.94	117.79	6102.34	3635.00	59.57	1755.03	1413.71	80.55
Cooperation	1723.42	1805.92	104.78	1975.24	1530.13	77.47	4600.00	280.18	6.09
Food and Civil Supply (Public Distribution System)	0.00	0.00	0.00	0.00	0.00	0.00	0.00	0.00	0.00
Sub Total	12009.81	8681.27	72.88	17610.80	13741.18	78.03	9371.44	4296.03	45.84
2. **Rural Development**									
I.R.D.P.	7049.94	2477.18	35.14	4585.49	4177.95	91.11	1503.41	1503.41	100.00
D.P.A.P.	0.00	951.31	0.00	1399.35	2378.01	169.94	290.71	269.10	92.57
I.R.E.P.	0.00	2463.82	0.00	0.00	0.00	0.00	0.00	0.00	0.00
Jawahar Rojgar Yojana	0.00	0.00	0.00	3338.24	4936.00	147.86	1946.77	0.00	0.00
Land reforms	1091.39	574.80	52.67	1222.72	1263.14	103.31	116.00	1460.63	1259.16
Community development	0.00	27.00	0.00	243.92	488.00	200.07	56.03	107.74	192.29
Panchayats	737.63	19.64	2.66	734.97	396.77	53.98	194.00	225.71	116.35
Sub Total	8878.96	6513.75	73.36	11524.69	13639.87	118.62	4106.92	3566.59	86.84
3. **Irrigation and Flood Control**									
Major and Medium	6203.00	5563.00	89.68	11265.21	10906.00	96.81	2538.00	2356.93	92.87
N.V.D. irrigation	0.00	0.00	0.00	1821.00	1856.41	101.94	795.05	1201.46	151.12
Minor irrigation	0.00	0.00	0.00	0.00	0.00	0.00	0.00	0.00	0.00
(a) Irrigation department	8585.00	9071.00	105.66	16879.00	15968.00	94.60	5137.00	4434.98	86.33
(b) Agriculture department	0.00	1938.04	0.00	1770.03	998.27	56.40	1128.00	170.58	15.12
(C) Micro Minor	0.00	126.32	0.00	270.42	224.39	82.98	300.00	187.21	62.40

Command Area Development	0.00	0.00	0.00	285.33	105.89	37.11	47.32	10.75	22.72
Sub Total	14788.00	16698.36	112.92	32290.99	30058.96	93.09	9945.37	8361.91	84.08
4. Energy									
Power (M.P.E.B.)	7373.00	10918.00	148.08	13090.70	21132.00	161.43	3181.26	4591.68	144.34
N.V.D.A.	0.00	0.00	0.00	0.00	0.00	0.00	0.00	0.00	0.00
Urja Vikas Nigam	0.00	0.00	0.00	373.02	145.00	38.87	0.00	49.57	0.00
Sub Total	7373.00	10918.00	148.08	13463.72	21277.00	158.03	3181.26	4641.25	145.89
5. Industry and Mining									
Handloom	0.00	35.01	0.00	—	3453.04	—	0.00	34.05	0.00
Khadi gramodyog	13.72	5.13	37.39	—	—	—	0.00	66.40	0.00
Handicraft	0.00	0.00	0.00	—	—	—	0.00	0.00	0.00
Leather development	0.00	0.00	0.00	0.00	0.00	0.00	0.00	0.00	0.00
Sericulture	479.93	430.76	89.75	1492.32	1495.31	100.20	1794.18	254.87	14.21
Large and medium industries	0.00	816.55	0.00	2822.14	1286.63	45.59	0.00	543.67	0.00
Village and small scale industry	1243.21	419.74	33.76	2548.80	0.00	0.00	0.00	0.00	0.00
Mining	311.12	274.66	88.28	662.75	662.75	100.00	198.76	169.23	85.14
Industrial Cooperatives	54.46	5.48	10.06	0.00	0.00	0.00	0.00	0.00	0.00
Sub Total	2102.44	1987.33	94.52	7526.01	6897.73	91.65	1992.94	1068.22	53.60

6. Transport									
Aviation	0.00	0.00	0.00	0.00	0.00	0.00	0.00	0.00	0.00
Roads and Bridges	4927.90	6118.24	124.16	11651.97	11840.66	101.62	2575.00	2020.00	78.45
M.P.S.R.T.C.	0.00	0.00	0.00	0.00	0.00	0.00	150.00	150.00	100.00
Sub Total	4927.90	6118.24	124.16	11651.97	11840.66	101.62	2725.00	2170.00	79.63
7. Science and Technology									
Science and Technology	0.00	0.00	0.00	0.00	0.00	0.00	10.00	0.00	0.00
Ecology and Environment	0.00	1.01	0.00	228.50	0.00	0.00	117.85	111.97	95.01
Scientific research	0.00	0.00	0.00	0.00	0.00	0.00	0.00	0.00	0.00
Sub Total	0.00	1.01	0.00	228.50	0.00	0.00	127.85	111.97	87.58
8. General Economic Services									
State Planning Board	0.00	0.00	0.00	0.00	0.00	0.00	0.00	1121.59	0.00
Special programmes	0.00	0.00	0.00	0.00	0.00	0.00	0.00	0.00	0.00
Tourism	85.23	83.00	97.38	282.36	284.53	100.77	81.90	61.12	74.63
Computer centre	0.00	0.00	0.00	0.00	0.00	0.00	0.00	0.00	0.00
Statistics	0.00	0.00	0.00	0.00	0.00	0.00	0.00	0.00	0.00
District plan and untied fund	0.00	0.00	0.00	1455.00	0.00	0.00	1500.00	0.00	0.00
Weights and measures	3.50	1.66	47.43	2.82	2.82	100.00	1.06	0.00	0.00
Sub Total	88.73	84.66	95.41	1740.18	287.35	16.51	1582.96	1182.71	74.72

9. Social Sevices									
School education	1977.39	2768.92	140.03	11494.12	11671.27	101.54	4112.66	6772.71	164.68
College education	374.28	335.83	89.73	1345.25	1353.80	100.64	541.52	401.38	74.12
Adult education	285.60	228.07	79.86	617.59	480.40	77.79	182.89	0.00	0.00
Technical Education	248.15	198.88	80.15	1260.56	629.51	49.94	402.22	371.94	92.47
Sports and Youth Welfare	56.24	45.66	81.19	95.32	75.97	79.70	27.49	11.25	40.92
Art and Culture	79.06	89.61	113.34	147.18	45.02	38.59	41.10	25.89	62.99
Sub Total	3020.72	3666.97	121.39	14960.02	14255.97	95.29	5307.88	7583.17	142.87
10. **Public Health and Family Welfare**	2262.31	2612.25	115.47	8491.49	5699.59	67.12	2535.00	1483.43	58.52
E.S.I.	0.00	0.00	0.00	0.00	0.00	0.00	0.00	0.00	0.00
Sub Total	2262.31	2612.25	115.47	8491.49	5699.59	67.12	2535.00	1483.43	58.52
11. **Water Supply Sanitation and Housing**									
Water Supply and Sanitation	2600.14	4085.70	157.13	5520.30	4756.00	86.15	1646.38	1371.00	83.27
Housing	**0.00**	**0.00**	**0.00**	**0.00**	**0.00**	**0.00**	**0.00**	**0.00**	**0.00**
M.P. housing	463.66	363.66	78.43	699.11	1195.50	171.00	160.00	152.00	95.00
Rural housing	1115.08	576.01	51.66	1165.68	1165.69	100.00	133.21	0.00	0.00
Rental housing	166.42	33.95	20.40	434.90	265.50	61.05	16.00	0.00	0.00
Police housing	42.40	6.90	16.27	181.10	119.24	65.84	80.35	0.00	0.00
Urban development	0.00	0.00	0.00	0.00	0.00	0.00	0.00	0.00	0.00

Urban development (town and Country Planning)	0.00	0.00	0.00	0.00	0.00	0.00	184.00	174.80	95.00
Urban administration	86.12	156.61	181.85	440.93	379.49	86.87	87.75	87.64	99.87
Urban welfare	92.11	73.88	80.21	275.80	148.84	53.97	70.83	55.00	77.65
Sub Total	4565.93	5296.71	116.01	8717.82	8030.26	92.11	2378.52	1840.44	77.38
12. **Information and publicity**	30.26	27.68	91.47	188.14	97.24	51.68	47.58	15.73	33.06
Sub Total	30.26	27.68	91.47	188.14	97.24	51.68	47.58	15.73	33.06
13. Welfare of SC.ST. & Backward Classes									
Welfare of Scheduled Tribes	3730.05	2654.03	71.15	6625.02	6979.58	105.35	2088.80	1962.88	93.97
Outlay in pool for T.S.P./S.C.P. Programme	0.00	0.00	0.00	0.00	0.00	0.00	0.00	0.00	0.00
Sub Total	3730.05	2654.03	71.15	6625.02	6979.58	105.35	2088.80	1962.88	93.97
14. **Labour and Employment**									
Labour Welfare	37.74	64.08	169.79	114.78	75.00	65.34	233.07	0.00	0.00
Craftsman training	—	—	—	189.91	189.91	100.00	0.00	137.04	0.00
Employment services	26.51	49.49	186.68	10.56	11.14	105.49	5.00	4.03	80.60
Special employment schemes	71.74	27.64	38.53	30.11	42.79	142.11	8.74	2.86	32.72
Sub Total	135.99	141.21	103.84	345.36	318.84	92.32	246.81	143.93	58.32

15. Social Welfare and Nutrition									
Social Welfare	145.91	94.05	64.46	173.94	178.00	102.33	60.00	109.49	182.48
Women and Child Welfare	0.00	0.00	0.00	291.92	292.10	100.06	165.99	544.88	328.26
Nutrition	0.00	0.00	0.00	2036.30	1830.00	89.87	448.00	0.00	0.00
Legal aid to poor	31.86	49.51	155.40	52.40	71.42	136.30	20.33	4.74	23.32
Codification of customary laws	0.00	0.00	0.00	20.24	0.00	0.00	0.00	9.93	0.00
M.P. Instt. of Train. for Y.L.* and	0.00	0.00	0.00	0.00	0.00	0.00	0.00	0.00	0.00
Infrastructure development	0.00	0.00	0.00	0.00	0.00	0.00	0.00	0.00	0.00
Tribal Welfare Department	0.00	1040.08	0.00	0.00	0.00	0.00	0.00	0.00	0.00
Sub Total	177.77	1183.64	665.83	2574.80	2371.52	92.83	694.32	669.04	96.36
16. General Services									
Jail (Welfare of prisoners)	19.38	23.71	122.34	36.62	16.69	45.58	6.30	5.40	85.71
Stationary and printing	0.00	0.00	0.00	0.00	0.00	0.00	0.00	0.00	0.00
Sanjay Gandhi Institute	0.00	0.00	0.00	0.00	0.00	0.00	0.00	0.00	0.00
Other administrative services	0.00	0.00	0.00	0.00	0.00	0.00	0.00	0.00	0.00
Public Works	0.00	0.00	0.00	0.00	0.00	0.00	0.00	0.00	0.00
Sub Total	19.38	23.71	122.34	36.62	16.69	45.58	6.30	5.40	85.71
TOTAL	64111.25	66608.82	103.90	137976.13	135512.44	98.21	46338.95	39102.70	84.38

* Madhya Pradesh Institute of Training for Youth Leadership.

Annexure VI (Contd.)

Budget Provision and Expenditure from Sixth Plan (80-85) to Eighth Plan (92-97) State Plan

Rs. in Lakhs

Sl. No.	Head of Development	Annual Plan (1991-92)			VIIIth Plan			Total VIth Plan to VIIIth Plan		
		Provision during Annual towards flow to TSP	Expenditure during Annual Plan period	Percentatge Col. No. 13 to 12	Provision during Eighth Plan towards flow to TSP	Expenditure during Eighth Plan period	Percentage Col. No. 16 to 15	Provision upto Eighth Plan towards flow to TSP	Expenditure upto Eighth Plan period	Percentage Col. No. 19 to 18
1	2	12	13	14	15	16	17	18	19	20
1.	**Agriculture and Allied Activities**									
	Agriculture production	2201.45	1831.41	83.19	9835.26	8978.87	91.29	19040.68	18805.69	98.77
	Horticulture	465.85	454.85	97.64	2385.34	2875.61	120.55	11942.75	5512.35	46.16
	Agriculture marketing	7.02	0.00	0.00	11.84	0.75	6.33	63.74	40.35	63.30
	Soil and Water Conservation	—	—	—	409.00	0.00	0.00	409.00	0.00	0.00
	(a) Agriculture department	573.28	153.74	26.82	1231.72	2579.39	209.41	3360.24	5598.24	166.60
	(b) Forest department	25.45	15.65	61.49	77.60	72.41	93.31	171.62	101.41	59.09
	Animal Husbandary	336.00	263.88	78.54	1923.[illegible]	1652.75	85.94	4218.35	3809.71	90.31
	Dairy Development	109.32	87.46	80.00	980.63	820.81	83.70	1610.66	1251.96	77.73
	Fisheries	136.00	117.98	86.75	707.24	625.29	88.41	1700.87	1421.74	83.59

	Forest	2577.17	2609.57	101.26	14330.20	9410.65	65.67	26499.03	19111.87	72.12
	Cooperation	642.10	325.46	50.69	2815.01	995.89	35.38	11755.77	4937.58	42.00
	Food and Civil Supply (Public Distribution System)	0.00	0.00	0.00	669.52	623.02	93.05	669.52	623.02	93.05
	Sub Total	7073.64	5860.00	82.84	35376.54	28635.44	80.94	81442.23	61213.92	75.16
2.	**Rural Development**									
	I.R.D.P.	1406.00	1373.87	97.71	8492.55	7537.44	88.75	23037.39	17069.85	74.10
	D.P.A.P.	267.00	279.95	104.85	2182.85	2819.65	129.17	4139.91	6698.02	161.79
	I.R.E.P.	0.00	0.00	0.00	0.00	179.64	0.00	0.00	2643.46	0.00
	Jawahar Rojgar Yojana	2058.00	0.00	0.00	22603.74	16656.88	73.69	29946.75	21592.88	72.10
	Land Reforms	160.43	1595.28	994.38	680.45	547.84	80.51	3270.99	5441.69	166.36
	Community development	18.00	129.54	719.67	575.41	318.98	55.44	893.36	1071.26	119.91
	Panchayats	318.34	230.13	72.29	1316.67	1239.33	94.13	3301.61	2111.58	63.96
	Sub Total	4227.77	3608.77	85.36	35851.67	29299.76	81.72	64590.01	56628.74	86.87
3.	**Irrigation and Flood Control**									
	Major and Medium	3074.69	2395.80	77.92	19186.41	8841.49	46.08	42267.31	30063.22	71.13
	N.V.D. irrigation	1740.39	1856.89	106.69	2984.03	5739.31	192.33	7340.47	10654.07	145.14
	Minor irrigation	0.00	0.00	0.00	5275.00	0.00	0.00	5275.00	0.00	0.00
	(a) Irrigation department	5894.96	4865.10	82.53	17262.97	16839.22	97.55	53758.93	51178.30	95.20
	(b) Agriculture department	1874.98	231.23	12.33	4063.59	2178.28	53.60	8836.60	5516.40	62.43

	(C) Micro Minor	275.90	226.25	82.00	1371.66	953.75	69.53	2217.98	1717.92	77.45
	Command Area Development	60.84	9.49	15.60	163.45	87.35	53.44	556.94	213.48	38.33
	Sub Total	12921.76	9584.76	74.18	50307.11	34639.40	68.86	120253.33	99343.39	82.61
4.	**Energy**									
	Power (M.P.E.B.)	4591.68	4597.32	100.12	11857.28	12872.62	108.56	40093.92	54111.62	134.96
	N.V.D.A.	0.00	0.00	0.00	1802.04	1380.72	76.62	1802.04	1380.72	76.62
	Urja Vikas Nigam	0.00	0.00	0.00	152.92	404.98	264.83	525.94	599.55	114.00
	Sub Total	4591.68	4597.32	100.12	13812.24	14658.32	106.13	42421.90	56091.89	132.22
5.	**Industry and Mining**									
	Handloom	1745.06	60.70	3.48	162.62	147.33	90.60	1907.68	3730.13	195.53
	Khadi gramodyog	0.00	57.00	0.00	391.39	330.57	84.46	405.11	459.10	113.33
	Handicraft	23.36	24.20	103.60	178.77	253.76	141.95	202.13	277.96	137.52
	Leather development	0.00	0.00	0.00	0.00	0.00	0.00	0.00	0.00	0.00
	Sericulture	0.00	330.69	0.00	1526.99	1796.48	117.65	5293.42	4308.11	81.39
	Large and medium Industries	0.00	557.66	0.00	1213.39	1275.65	105.13	4035.53	4480.16	111.02
	Village and small scale industries	0.00	0.00	0.00	1742.96	111.36	6.39	5534.97	531.10	9.60
	Mining	55.00	48.22	87.67	290.01	292.81	100.97	1517.64	1447.67	95.39
	Industrial cooperatives	0.00	0.00	0.00	0.00	0.00	0.00	54.46	5.48	10.06
	Sub Total	1823.42	1078.47	59.15	5506.13	4207.96	76.42	18950.94	15239.71	80.42

6. Transport									
Aviation	0.00	0.00	0.00	0.0C	0.00	0.00	0.00	0.00	0.00
Roads and Bridges	0.00	2011.00	0.00	14074.09	7770.18	55.21	33228.96	29760.08	89.56
M.P.S.R.T.C.	2721.00	0.00	0.00	512.00	510.66	99.74	3383.00	660.66	19.53
Sub Total	2721.00	2011.00	73.91	14586.09	8280.84	56.77	36611.96	30420.74	83.09
7. Science and Technology									
Science and Technology	10.00	8.00	80.00	62.40	16.20	25.96	82.40	24.20	29.37
Ecology and Environment	150.00	102.00	68.00	453.81	440.00	96.96	950.16	654.98	68.93
Scientific Research	0.00	0.00	0.00	13.41	3.35	24.98	13.41	3.35	24.98
Sub Total	160.00	110.00	68.75	529.62	459.55	86.77	1045.97	682.53	65.25
8. General Economic Services									
State Planning Board	0.00	1696.76	0.00	3000.00	1925.84	64.19	3000.00	4744.19	158.14
Special programmes	0.00	0.00	0.00	0.00	0.00	0.00	0.00	0.00	0.00
Tourism	83.00	65.55	78.98	178.85	103.69	57.98	711.34	597.89	84.05
Computer centre	0.00	0.00	0.00	0.00	0.00	0.00	0.00	0.00	0.00
Statistics	0.00	0.00	0.00	0.00	0.00	0.00	0.00	0.00	0.00
District plan and untied fund	1556.45	0.00	0.00	5379.00	4806.09	89.35	9890.45	4806.09	48.59
Weights and Measures	1.25	0.08	6.40	11.88	12.44	104.71	20.51	17.00	82.89
Sub Total	1640.70	1762.39	107.42	8569.73	6848.06	79.91	13622.30	10165.17	74.62

9. Social Sevices									
School education	7421.60	9598.59	129.33	32372.19	16800.22	51.90	57377.96	47611.71	82.98
College education	0.00	400.31	0.00	2597.81	1686.37	64.92	4858.86	4177.69	85.98
Adult education	0.00	0.00	0.00	780.52	432.48	55.41	1866.60	1140.95	61.12
Technical education	591.70	119.30	20.16	6073.60	1776.35	29.25	8576.23	3095.98	36.10
Sports and youth welfare	0.00	38.38	0.00	512.85	450.47	87.84	691.90	621.73	89.86
Art and Culture	1.50	37.62	2508.00	342.14	245.67	71.80	610.98	443.81	72.64
Sub Total	8014.80	10194.20	127.19	42679.11	21391.56	50.12	73982.53	57091.87	77.17
10. Public Health and Family Welfare	2367.54	1139.46	48.13	12052.98	8844.39	73.38	27709.32	19779.12	71.38
E.S.I.	0.00	0.00	0.00	155.00	0.00	0.00	155.00	0.00	0.00
Sub Total	2367.54	1139.46	48.13	12207.98	8844.39	72.45	27864.32	19779.12	70.98
11. Water Supply Sanitation and Housing									
Water supply and sanitation	1650.00	1213.01	73.52	7840.00	9125.59	116.40	19256.82	20551.30	106.72
Housing	**0.00**	**0.00**	**0.00**	**0.00**	**0.00**	**0.00**	**0.00**	**0.00**	**0.00**
M.P. housing	720.00	268.40	37.28	1300.53	994.56	76.47	3343.30	2974.12	88.96
Rural housing	0.00	0.00	0.00	768.22	684.84	89.15	3182.19	2426.54	76.25
Rental housing	0.00	0.00	0.00	40.00	1.00	2.50	657.32	300.45	45.71
Police housing	0.00	0.00	0.00	950.00	289.60	30.48	1253.85	415.74	33.16
Urban development	0.00	0.00	0.00	0.00	0.00	0.00	0.00	0.00	0.00

Urban Development (Town	0.00	8.00	0.00	854.65	0.00	0.00	1038.65	182.80	17.60
and Country Planning)	—	—	—	0.00	116.00	0.00	0.00	116.00	0.00
Urban Administration	348.45	78.76	22.60	303.05	388.31	128.13	1266.30	1090.81	86.14
Urban Welfare	0.00	38.20	0.00	375.46	253.83	67.61	814.20	569.75	69.98
Sub Total	2718.45	1606.37	59.09	12431.91	11853.73	95.35	30812.63	28627.51	92.91
12. **Information and Publicity**	52.40	26.86	51.26	371.68	245.82	66.14	690.06	413.33	59.90
Sub Total	52.40	26.86	51.26	371.68	245.82	66.14	690.06	413.33	59.90
13. **Welfare of SC./ST. & Backward Classes**									
Welfare of Scheduled Tribes	2288.67	2306.67	100.79	14699.65	24832.74	168.93	29432.19	38735.90	131.61
Outlay in pool for T.S.P./S.C.P. Programme	0.00	0.00	0.00	16775.20	3980.20	23.73	16775.20	3980.20	23.73
Sub Total	2288.67	2306.67	100.79	31474.85	28812.94	91.54	46207.39	42716.10	92.44
14. **Labour and employment**									
Labour welfare	335.42	0.00	0.00	755.39	20.39	2.70	1476.40	159.47	10.80
Craftsman training	0.00	33.49	0.00	697.56	466.94	66.94	887.47	827.38	93.23
Employment services	0.00	4.38	0.00	749.66	93.73	12.50	791.73	162.77	20.56
Special employment schemes	0.00	1.28	0.00	21.89	10.40	47.51	132.48	84.97	64.14
Sub Total	335.42	39.15	11.67	2224.50	591.46	26.59	3288.08	1234.59	37.55

15. Social Welfare and Nutrition									
Social Welfare	0.00	197.68	0.00	1267.13	0.00	0.00	1646.98	579.22	35.17
Women and Child Welfare	565.74	50.77	8.97	658.31	346.62	52.65	1681.96	1234.37	73.39
Nutrition	500.00	0.00	0.00	6203.74	1474.97	23.78	9188.04	3304.97	35.97
Legal aid to poor	0.00	11.22	0.00	39.82	3249.90	8161.48	144.41	3386.79	2345.26
Codification of customary laws	0.00	11.93	0.00	10.40	46.25	444.71	30.64	68.11	222.29
M.P. Instt. of Train for Y.L. and R	0.00	0.00	0.00	5.48	12.43	226.82	5.48	12.43	226.82
Infrastructure Development for	0.00	0.00	0.00	250.00	5.34	2.14	250.00	5.34	2.14
tribal welfare department	0.00	0.00	0.00	0.00	0.00	0.00	0.00	1040.08	0.00
Sub Total	1065.74	271.60	25.48	8434.88	5135.51	60.88	12927.27	9631.31	74.50
16. General Services									
Jail (Welfare of prisioners)	2.67	2.56	95.88	24.76	8.51	34.37	89.73	56.87	63.38
Stationary and printing	0.00	0.00	0.00	0.00	0.00	0.00	0.00	0.00	0.00
Sanjay Gandhi Institute	0.00	0.00	0.00	0.00	0.00	0.00	0.00	0.80	0.00
Other administrative services	0.00	0.00	0.00	52.44	1.44	2.75	52.44	1.44	2.75
Public works	0.00	0.00	0.00	118.45	0.00	0.00	118.45	0.00	0.00
Sub Total	2.67	2.56	95.88	195.65	10.75	5.49	280.86	59.11	21.05
TOTAL	52005.66	44199.58	84.99	274559.69	203915.49	74.27	574991.78	489339.03	85.10

Annexure–VII

Statement Showing Sector–wise Budget Provision and Expenditure Incurred Under Special Central Assistance for Tribal Sub-plan During VIth, VIIth Plan, Annual Plans 90-91 and 91-92 and VIIIth Plan

Rs. in Lakh

		VI PLAN			*VII PLAN*			*Anual Plan (1990-91)*		
S. No.	*Name of Sector*	*PROV.*	*EXP.*	*%*	*PROV.*	*EXP.*	*%*	*PROV.*	*EXP.*	*%*
1	*2*	*3*	*4*	*5*	*6*	*7*	*8*	*9*	*10*	*11*
1.	Agriculture production	1706.22	1076.99	63.12	891.12	507.62	56.96	180.00	134.90	74.94
2.	Horticulture department		86.13		1306.25	1272.24	97.40	231.00	272.88	118.13
3.	Agriculture marketing	Nil	Nil		Nil	Nil		Nil	Nil	
4.	Soil conservation									
	(a) Agriculture department				330.60	120.20	36.36			
	(b) Forest department									
5.	Animal husbandry	481.59	367.66	76.34	586.04	477.84	81.54	150.00	Nil	
6.	Dairy development	20.00	10.44	52.20	338.00	376.97	111.53	100.00	100.00	100.00
7.	Fisheries	135.34	47.95	35.43	185.50	131.09	70.67	25.00	24.98	99.92
8.	Forest department	1942.51	1358.56	69.94	3130.56	2631.47	84.06	471.17	200.84	42.62
9.	Cooperation	1033.42	972.22	94.08	950.00	892.62	93.96			
10.	Food and Civil Supply							168.00		

Note: Prov.—Provision Exp.—Expenditure

11. I.R.D.P.									
12. D.P.A.P.									
13. Jawahar Rojgar Yojana									
14. Land reforms	280.12	190.20	67.90	200.00	200.00	100.00	200.00	181.17	90.59
15. Community development	409.28	5.44	1.33						
16. Panchayat									
17. Major and Medium Irrigation									
18. N.V.D. irrigation									
19. Minor irrigation									
(a) Irrigation department	1612.10	1612.10	100.00	1200.00	1200.00	100.00	928.00	928.00	100.00
(b) Agriculture department	874.15	32.83	3.76	477.00	345.11	72.35			
20 Micro Minor									
21 Command Area Development	50.00		0.00						
22. Power (M.P.E.B.)							200.00	200.00	100.00
23. Urja Vikas Nigam							50.00	50.00	100.00
24. Handloom							50.00	50.00	100.00
25. Khadi gramodyog	610.88	564.14	92.35						
26. Sericulture				686.00	359.03	52.34	25.00	20.84	83.36
27. Large and medium industries									
28. Village and small scale industries				655.00	612.71	93.54			
29. Hastshilpa Vikas							50.00	38.97	77.94

30. Mining	43.98								
31. Roads and Bridges	180.00	179.00	99.44	330.00	283.98	86.05	1704.23	1611.01	94.53
32. Ecology and Environment									
33. Tourism							4.86		
34. District Plan and Untied Fund									
35. Weights and Measures									
36. School Education							1579.95	1363.29	86.29
37. College Education	60.00						293.95	98.54	33.52
38. Adult Education				145.00	70.55	48.66	151.76	70.55	46.49
39. Technical Education	35.45	12.04	33.96	120.00	32.84	27.37	548.25	196.61	35.86
40. Sports and Youth Welfare				5.00	5.00	100.00	6.95	6.95	100.00
41 Art and Culture								0.75	
42. Health and Family Welfare	100.00	36.65	36.65	777.00	455.95	58.68	2030.44	1366.67	67.31
43. Water Supply and Sanitation	200.00	126.15	63.08				1761.94	2124.63	120.58
44. M.P. Housing				2150.00	1627.98	75.72	2283.16	1627.98	71.30
45. Rural Housing									
46. Rental Housing									
47. Police Housing									
48. Urban Administration	21.25						92.50	37.18	40.19
49. Urban Welfare							90.00		
50. Information and Publicity							9.91	8.62	86.98
51. Welfare of Scheduled Tribes	5196.29	4293.71	121.02	23039.03	21476.19	93.22	49293.43	46617.14	94.57

52. Labour Welfare							20.75		
53. Craftsmen Training									
54. Employment Services									
55. Special Employment Schemes									
56. Social Welfare	21.43								
57. Women and Child Welfare				210.00	179.02	85.25	210.00	179.02	85.25
58. Nutrition							102.00	463.50	454.41
59. Legal Aid to Poor				2.79	2.79	100.00	11.70	9.92	84.79
60. Codification of Custmry Laws	3.00	1.34	44.67				20.27	12.04	59.40
61. Jail (Welfare of Prisoners)									
Grand Total	8787.90	7350.61	83.64	38763.97	35358.05	91.21	98178.37	87374.01	89.00

Annexure–VII (Contd.)

Statement Showing Sector–wise Budget Provision and Expenditure Incurred Under Special Central Assistance for Tribal Sub-plan During VIth, VIIth Plan, Annual Plans 90-91 and 91-92 and VIIIth Plan

Rs. in Lakh

		Annual Plan 91-92			*VIII Plan*			*Grand Total VI to VIII Plan Including Annual Plans 1990-91, 91-92*		
S. No.	*Name of Sector*	*PROV.*	*EXP.*	*%*	*PROV.*	*EXP.*	*%*	*PROV.*	*EXP.*	*%*
1	*2*	*12*	*13*	*14*	*15*	*16*	*17*	*18*	*19*	*20*
1.	Agriculture Production				220.00	140.76	63.98	2997.34	1860.27	62.06
2.	Horticulture Department	436.56	432.17	98.99	1056.19	910.21	86.18	3030.00	2973.63	98.14
3.	Agriculture Marketing									
4.	Soil and Water Conservation									
	(a) Agriculture Department							330.60	120.20	36.36
	(b) Forest Department									
5.	Animal Husbandry	215.00	215.00	100.00	677.27	627.27	92.62	2109.90	1687.77	79.99
6.	Dairy Development	379.35	366.09	96.50	970.00	960.00	98.97	1807.35	1813.50	100.34
7.	Fisheries	25.00	24.44	97.76	339.44	332.60	97.98	710.28	561.06	78.99
8.	Forest Department	700.00	436.90	62.41	1077.00	961.56	89.28	7321.24	5589.33	76.34
9.	Cooperation							1983.42	1864.84	94.02
10.	Food and Civil Supply	180.00	174.98	97.16	368.00	230.00	62.50	716.00	404.98	56.56

11.	I.R.D.P.								
12.	D.P.A.P.								
13.	Jawahar Rojgar Yojna								
14.	Land Reform	300.00	296.15	98.72	200.00	140.82	70.41	1180.12	1008.34	85.44
15.	Community Development							409.28	5.44	1.33
16.	Panchayats									
17.	Major and Medium Irrigation									
18.	N.V.D. Irrigation									
19.	Minor Irrigation									
	(a) Irrigation Department	566.00	566.00	100.00	2777.08	2423.30	87.26	7083.18	6729.40	95.01
	(b) Agriculture Department							1351.15	377.94	27.97
20.	Micro Minor									
21	Command Area Development							50.00		
22.	Power (M.P.E.B.)				1950.00	2742.99	140.67	2150.00	2942.99	136.88
23.	Urja Vikas Nigam									
24.	Handloom	50.00	50.00	100.00	168.90	81.60	48.31	268.90	181.60	67.53
25.	Khadi Gramodyog	50.00	50.00	100.00	174.00	59.00	33.91	884.88	723.14	81.72
26.	Secriculture	40.00	39.99	99.98	1187.55	807.92	68.03	1938.55	1227.78	63.33
27.	Large and Medium Industries									
28.	Village and Small Scale Industries							655.00	612.71	93.54
29.	Hastshilpa Vikas	50.00	50.00	100.00	819.72	805.72	98.29	919.72	894.69	97.28

30. Mining							43.98		
31. Roads and Bridges	699.23	699.23	100.00	200.00	160.80	80.40	295.00	288.00	97.63
32. Ecology and Environment									
33. Tourism	4.86								
34. District plan and untied fund									
35. Weights and Measures									
36. School education	1579.95	1363.29	86.29						
37. College education	98.95	25.97	26.25	60.00	35.36	58.93	75.00	37.21	49.61
38. Adult education	6.76								
39. Technical education	190.51	78.65	41.28	100.21	69.41	69.26	102.08	3.67	3.60
40. Sports and Youth Welfare	1.95	1.95	100.00						
41 Art and Culture					0.75				
42. Health and Family Welfare	573.44	412.64	71.96	380.00	461.43	121.43	200.00	0.00	
43. Water Supply and Sanitation	861.94	861.94	100.00	650.00	1072.85	165.05	50.00	63.69	127.38
44. M.P. housing	133.16								
45. Rural housing									
46. Rental housing									
47. Police housing									
48. Urban Administration	71.25	37.18	52.18						
49. Urban Welfare				90.00					
50. Information and Publicity	9.91	8.62	86.98						
51. Welfare of Scheduled Tribes	5352.59	5227.59	97.66	11699.58	11613.71	99.27	4005.94	4005.94	25.11

52. Labour Welfare	20.75								
53. Craftsman Training									
54. Employment service									
55. Special Employment Schemes									
56. Social Welfare	21.43								
57. Women and Child Welfare									
58. Nutrition				102.00	463.50	454.41			
59. Legal aid to poor	8.91	7.13	80.02						
60. Codification of customary laws				14.27	8.36	58.58	3.00	2.34	78.00
61. Jail (Welfare of prisioners)									
Grand Total	18835.18	15048.85	79.90	24232.13	23013.07	94.97	7559.19	6603.43	87.36

Bibliography

Bajpai, S.R. Dr., 'Methods of Social Survey and Research', Kitab Ghar, 1982.

Barraclough, G., 'An Introduction to Contemporary History'.

Basham, A.L., 'The Wonder that was India', Rupa & Co., 1988.

Basu, D.D., 'Introduction to the Constitution of India' Prentice Hall International, 1989.

Brett, E.A., 'Chhatisgarh Feudatory States,' Vanya Prakashan, Bhopal, 1988.

Dube, B.K. and Bahadur, F., 'A Study of the Tribal People and the Tribal Areas of M.P. Tribal Research and Development Institute, 1967.

Elwin, Verrier, 'The Aboriginals', Oxford University Press, 1944.

Elwin, Verrier, 'Philosophy for NEFA', NEFA administration, 1958.

Grigson, W.V., 'The Aboriginal Problem in the Central Provinces and Berar' Oxford University Press, 1944.

Grigson, W.V., 'The Maria Gonds of Bastar,' special reprint for Vanya Prakashan, 1991.

Majumdar, R.C., 'An Advanced History of India,' Macmillan & Co. Ltd., 1967.

Panikkar, K.M. 'A Survey of Indian History', 1962.

Raizada, Ajit, 'Tribal Development in Madhya Pradesh', Inter India Publication, 1984.

Russell, R.V. and Raibahadur, Hiralal, 'Tribes and Castes of the Central Provinces of India', Cosmos Publications.

Sarkar, Sumit, 'Modern India (1885-1947)' Macmillan India Ltd., 1983.

Sen, S.N., 'Ancient Indian History and Civilization', Wiley Eastern Ltd., 1988.

Sharma, B.D. 'Tribal Development: The Concept and the Frame' 1978.

Sharma, B.D., 'Legislative Powers about Tribal Affairs', 1968.

Sharma, B.D., 'Adivasi Vikas Ke Liye Prashashan, Bharat Sarkar Grih Mantralaya, New Delhi.

Sheel, Yogendra Nath, 'Madhya Pradesh Aur Berar Ka Itihas,' Indian Press Ltd., Prayag, 1922.

Singh, K.S., 'Colonial Transformation of the Tribal Society in Middle India,' 1978.

Singh, K.S., 'State Formation in Tribal Society: Some Preliminary Discussion,' *Journal of the Indian Anthropological Society*, Vol. VI.

Thakkar, A.V. (ed.) 'Tribes of India,' Bharatiya Adimjati Sevak Sangh, Kingsway, Delhi, 1950.

Verghese, K.E., 'General Sociology' Macmillan India Ltd., 1992.

Young, P.V., 'Scientific Social Survey and Research,' Prentice Hall India, 1968.

Government Publications

Centre for Panchayati Raj, National Institute of Rural Development Hyderabad, 'Seminar on Panchayati Raj and Social Justice.'

Committee on Plan Projects, Planning Commission, 'Report of the Study Team on Tribal Development Programme,' 1969.

Department of Planning and Development, 'Madhya Pradesh, Fourth Five Year Plan of Madhya Pradesh 1969-74'.

Department of Planning, Economics and Statistics, Madhya Pradesh, 'Draft Five Year Plan (1974-79)'.

Dhebar, U.N., 'Report of the Scheduled Areas and Scheduled Tribes Commission,' 1961.

Directorate of Economics and Statistics, Madhya Pradesh. 'Third Five Year Plan of Madhya Pradesh, Progress Report 1961-66'.

Directorate of Tribal Area Planning, Bhopal, 'Draft Medium Term Plan, 1978-88 and Annual Plan 1979-80'.

Directorate, Tribal Area Development Planning 'Adivasi Upyojana Avam Vishes Ghatak Yojana Antargat Bharat Sarkar Se Prapt Vishesh Kendriya Shayata. Margdarshika,' 1994.'

Directorate of Tribal Area Development Planning, Bhopal, 'Draft Tribal Sub-Plan, Eighth Plan 1990-95 and Annual Plan 1991-92'.

Directorate of Tribal Area Development Planning, Bhopal, 'Draft Tribal sub-Plan and Annual Plan 1995-96'.

Government of India, Ministry of Home Affairs, New Delhi, 'Annual Report of the Commissioner for Scheduled Castes and Scheduled Tribes'.

Government of India, Ministry of Home Affairs, New Delhi, Approach to Tribal Development in the Sixth Plan., A Preliminary of Perspective, 1997.'

Government of Madhya Pradesh, 'Madhya Bharat Land Revenue Code.' 1959.

Government of India, Ministry of Home Affairs, New Delhi, 'Tribal Development in the Fifth Plan (some basic policy papers) Vols. 1 and 2 1975'.

Government of India, Ministry of Home Affairs, New Delhi, 'Report of the Study Team on Tribal Development Programme, 1969'.

Government of India, Ministry of Home Affairs, New Delhi, 'Preparation of Sub–Plan for Tribal Regions,' 1975.

Government of India, Ministry of Home Affairs, New Delhi, 'Report of the working group on Tribal Development during Medium Term Plan 1978–83', July, 1978.

Government of Madhya Pradesh Tribal and Scheduled Caste Welfare Department, 'Draft Tribal Sub-Plan Ninth Plan 1997-2002 and Annual Plan 1997-98'.

Government of India, Ministry of Home Affairs, Tribal Development Division, 'Compendium of Circulars/Guidelines of Tribal Development.'

'Integrated Tribal Development Planning' (ed. V.R.K. Paramahamsa), NICD Hyderabad, 1975.

Madhya Pradehs Government Jansampark Vibhag, 'Madhya Pradesh Main Jan-Kalyan Aur Vikas Pramukh Yojnain.'

Madhya Pradesh Government Tribal and Scheduled Caste Welfare Department 'Utpiran Mukt Anusunchit Jati Avam Anusuchit Janjati Samaj Ke Hitarth Parit Vividh Adhiniyamon, Niyamon Avam, Adeshon Ka Adhatan Sankalan'.

Madhya Pradesh Shasan, Admjati Avam Anusuchit Jati Kalayan Vibhag, 'Anusuchit Jati Avam Anusuchit Janjati Kalyan Sambandhi Jankari' September, 1996.

National Commission for Scheduled Castes, and Scheduled Tribes, 'Historical background, Functions, General information'.

'Perspective on Tribal Development and Administration', NICD, Hyderabad, 1975.

Singh, K.S. (ed), 'Our Tribal Heritage,' Regional Development Commissioner, Ranchi, in collaboration with the Anthropological Survey of India.

Tiwari, D.N., 'Primitive Tribes of Madhya Pradesh Government of India, Ministry of Home Affairs, Tribal Development Division, New Delhi, 1985.

Unpublished Papers.

'An Appraisal of 'Tribal Sub-Plan,' In Context of the Forthcoming Ninth Plan.

'Perspective on Tribal Development', Government of India, Ministry of Home Affairs, New Delhi.

'Role of Voluntary Organizations in Tribal Development,' 'Government of India, Ministry of Home Affairs, New Delhi.

'Tribal Development, The New Strategy,' Government of India, Ministry of Home Affairs, New Delhi.

Index

EMPHASIS ON EDUCATION-MAINWAY TO DEVELOPMENT

MID- DAY MEALS PROGRAMME-INCENTIVE FOR EDUCATION

TUBEWELL-SOURCE OF HYGIENIC DRINKING WATER